Organizational Behaviour in Healthcare



**Series Editors**

Jean-Louis Denis
School of Public Health
University of Montreal
Montréal, QC, Canada

Justin Waring
University of Birmingham
Birmingham, UK

Paula Hyde
Birmingham Business School
University of Birmingham
Birmingham, UK

Published in co-operation with the Society for Studies in Organizing Healthcare (SHOC), this series has two strands, the first of which consists of specially selected papers taken from the biennial conferences held by SHOC that present a cohesive and focused insight into issues within the field of organizational behaviour in healthcare.

The series also encourages proposals for monographs and edited collections to address the additional and emergent topics in the field of health policy, organization and management. Books within the series aim to advance scholarship on the application of social science theories, methods and concepts to the study of organizing and managing healthcare services and systems.

Providing a new platform for advanced and engaged scholarship, books in the series will advance the academic community by fostering a deep analysis on the challenges for healthcare organizations and management with an explicitly international and comparative focus.

All book proposals and manuscript submissions are single blind peer reviewed. All chapters in contributed volumes are double blind peer reviewed. For more information on Palgrave Macmillan's peer review policy please visit our website: https://www.palgrave.com/gp/book-authors/your-career/early-career-researcher-hub/peer-review-process.

To submit a book proposal for inclusion in this series please contact Liz Barlow for further information: liz.barlow@palgrave.com. For information on the book proposal process please visit this website: https://www.palgrave.com/gp/book-authors/publishing-guidelines/submit-a-proposal.

More information about this series at
http://www.palgrave.com/gp/series/14724

Mark Bevir · Justin Waring
Editors

# Decentring Health and Care Networks

## Reshaping the Organization and Delivery of Healthcare

palgrave
macmillan

*Editors*
Mark Bevir
Department of Political Science
Berkeley, CA, USA

Justin Waring
Health Services Management Centre
University of Birmingham
Birmingham, UK

ISSN 2662-1045 ISSN 2662-1053 (electronic)
Organizational Behaviour in Healthcare
ISBN 978-3-030-40891-6 ISBN 978-3-030-40889-3 (eBook)
https://doi.org/10.1007/978-3-030-40889-3



This Palgrave Macmillan imprint is published by the registered company Springer Nature Switzerland AG
The registered company address is: Gewerbestrasse 11, 6330 Cham, Switzerland

# Contents

# Notes on Contributors

**Juan I. Baeza** is senior lecturer in Health Policy at King's Business School. His research focuses on analysing health policy and health sector reform in the UK and internationally. Juan has worked on a number of research projects in both primary and secondary health care in the UK and internationally. These include a study that evaluated the implementation of sustainable TB services in Russia, an SDO research project studying the roles and relationships in various NHS settings, a large research programme into Aboriginal health in Australia and a study into the implementation of research into practice in stroke services across the EU.

**Simon Bailey** is Research Associate at the Centre for Health Services Studies, University of Kent. His research interests are in the adoption of new knowledge, practices, technologies and roles and the manner in which these become embedded and institutionalised within healthcare organisations. My research expertise is in qualitative, ethnographic and arts-based methods. My research is strongly inter-disciplinary, spanning medical and organisational sociology, work and employment studies, education, and knowledge mobilisation and implementation. My work is theoretically informed by critical, post-structural and post-humanist theories, particularly inspired by the work of Michel Foucault, Bruno Latour and Annmarie Mol.

**Mark Bevir** a Professor in the Department of Political Science, and Director of the Center for British Studies, at the University of California, Berkeley. He is also a Professor in the Graduate School of Governance, United Nations University–MERIT, Maastricht, Netherlands, and a Distinguished Research Professor in the College of Arts and Humanities, Swansea University, UK. Currently he serves as President of the Society for the Philosophy of History (USA), a member of the Scientific Committee of the International Conference on Public Policy, a member of the Executive Council of the Western Political Science Association (USA), and Co-chair of the Interpretive Approaches group of the British International Studies Association. He is the author or editor of 23 books. Since 2010, he has authored *The State as Cultural Practice* (with R.A.W. Rhodes, Oxford University Press, 2010), *Democratic Governance* (Princeton University Press, 2010), *The Making of British Socialism* (Princeton University Press, 2011), *Governance: A Very Short Introduction* (Oxford University Press, 2012), and *A Theory of Governance* (University of California Press, 2013), and as editor: *Interpretive Political Science* (SAGE, 2010), *The SAGE Handbook of Governance* (SAGE, 2011), *Modern Pluralism: Anglo-American Debates since 1880* (Cambridge University Press, 2012), and *Interpreting Global Security* (with Oliver Daddow and Ian Hall, Routledge, 2014). He has also published over 150 academic articles.

**Simon Bishop** is Associate Professor in Organisational Behaviour at Nottingham University Business School. His research is primarily focused on issues of public policy organisational change in healthcare and other public service organisations. Simon's Ph.D. focused on organisational change during periods of public service outsourcing and partnership with the private sector. He has conducted several studies on new types of healthcare organisations and services, including Independent Sector Treatment Centres, integrated care providers and knowledge translations organisations. Simon's research seeks to examine the changing relationships between organisations following changes in public policy–for example those which encourage new forms of partnerships, supply and commissioning arrangements–and how this affects organisational management, work and employment.

**Annette Boaz** is Professor of Health Care Research at the Faculty of Health, Social Care and Education at Kingston University and St George's, University of London. She has spent more than 20 years exploring the relationship between research, policy and practice in the UK and internationally. She is a Founding Editor of the international journal Evidence & Policy and Vice-Chair of the UK Implementation Society.

**Mehdi Boussebaa** is Professor of International Business at the Adam Smith Business School. Previously, he worked at the universities of Bath and Oxford. He has also held visiting positions in Canada, China, France, and Sweden. He holds a Ph.D. and an M.A. (with Distinction) from the University of Warwick. Mehdi's research examines the impact of globalisation on organisational behaviour and the role of multinationals as agents of globalisation. Empirically, he focuses primarily on multinationals in knowledge-intensive and professional services sectors. In recent years, he has also extended his analysis to business schools and the geopolitics of management knowledge production. His work is informed by, and contributes to, theories of the multinational enterprise, institutional theory, discourse/identity theory, international political economy, postcolonial studies, and research on the professions and professional service firms.

**Mike Bresnen** is Professor and Head of Department at Manchester Metropolitan Business School. Mike's research is primarily concerned with understanding innovation, knowledge, networking and learning processes within and between organizations. He has been principal investigator on a number of large recent ESRC and EPSRC research projects investigating innovation processes, knowledge management, inter-organizational relations, project management and project-based learning across a range of sectors, including manufacturing, construction, biomedical and healthcare. His research interests also include leadership, managers and professionals and this is reflected in his involvement in recent NIHR-funded research on understanding knowledge mobilization and utilization by healthcare managers.

**Mike English** is Professor of Global Health in the Nuffield Department of Medicine, University of Oxford. He is a UK trained paediatrician who has worked in Kenya for over 20 years supported by a series of Wellcome Trust fellowships. His work often takes Child and Newborn Health as a focus but increasingly tackles health services or wider health systems issues. He works as part of the KEMRI-Wellcome Trust Research Programme (KWTRP) in collaboration in Kenya with the Ministry of Health, the University of Nairobi, and with a wide set of international collaborators. The work of his team has included: developing national, evidence-based guidelines for care of severely ill children and newborns, clinical trials and epidemiological studies, cluster randomised implementation trials, and qualitative studies of health worker and managers' behaviour as part of mixed-methods health systems research. He co-leads Health Systems Research in KWTRP, established the Oxford Health Systems Research Collaboration (OHSCAR) that supports Kenyan work and has helped launch the Oxford Global Health and Care Systems site (www.oghcs.ox.ac.uk) site to help link researchers across Oxford.

**Alec Fraser** is a Lecturer in Government & Business at King's Business School. His research centres on the use of evidence in policy making and practice across the public sector with a particular focus on health and social care. He previously spent five years at the Policy Innovation Research Unit at the London School of Hygiene and Tropical Medicine. Prior to entering academia he worked in NHS administration and management.

**Esmée Hanna** is VC2020 Lecturer at De Montfort University. She is a sociologist by background, and her work focuses on the intersections of health and gender. Her main areas of interest are male infertility, young age fatherhood and I am currently developing work around limb disposal after amputation. My work has a strong applied focus and I work closely with third sector organisations and healthcare professionals.

**John Hassard** is Professor of Organisational Analysis at Alliance Manchester Business School. His main research interests lie in the areas of organisational analysis and corporate change. For the former, he is interested in historical, philosophical and sociological approaches to organisation studies, notably contributing to debates on paradigms, labour processes, time, actor networks, historiography and post-modernism. For the latter, his work relates to corporate strategy, change management and organizational development. This work often takes an international dimension, as with studies of organizational restructuring in Chinese state-owned enterprises and corporate reform in American, British and Japanese multinationals.

**Damian Hodgson** is Professor of Organisation Studies. He joined the Management School in March 2020 from the Alliance Manchester Business School, University of Manchester where he was Director of the Institute for Health Policy and Organisation. He was awarded a Ph.D. from the University of Leeds in 1999, and has spent time as visiting faculty at the University of Sydney, the Royal Melbourne Institute of Technology and the Royal Institute of Technology, Sweden. He was visiting research fellow at CRISES Research Centre in Quebec, Canada, in 2009. Damian's research focuses on issues of power, knowledge, identity and control in complex organisations and on the management of experts/professionals in these settings. He has developed these interests through research in a range of industries including financial services, creative industries, R&D and engineering. However, his primary research interest is on the transformation of health and care, with a particular focus on the organisational and policy dimensions of this transformation.

**Paula Hyde** is Professor of Organisation Studies at Birmingham Business School, University of Birmingham and holds a visiting position at Macquarie University, New South Wales, Australia. She is a Fellow of the Academy of Social Sciences. Paula is one of the leading figures in the field of organisation studies in health and social care both nationally and internationally. Her standing in the field is well established and widely acknowledged both through extensive engagement with public and policy audiences and through regular engagement with the academic community worldwide.

**Jean Ledger** is a social scientist and researcher based at the Department of Applied Health Research, University College London. Her research interests are focused on health policy, public management, and the uptake of research, evidence and innovation in health care to improve quality and service delivery. She specialises in qualitative research methods and has undertaken a number of large-scale projects and evaluations funded by the UK's National Institute for Health Research.

**Russell Mannion** holds a Chair in Health Systems at the University of Birmingham with more than 30 years of experience of health services research. His areas of interest include evaluation of health systems reform, patient safety, quality improvement, and performance measurement and management. Russell has published extensively and has led and co-led a variety of funded projects, including 23 NIHR grants.

**Graham P. Martin** is Director of Research at THIS Institute, University of Cambridge. Graham's research interests are in the organisation and delivery of healthcare, and particularly the role of professionals, managers and patients and the public in efforts at organisational change. Primarily a qualitative researcher, he has long experience of undertaking research and evaluation in relation to healthcare improvement, from major policy-driven programmes to locally led initiatives.

**Gerry McGivern** is Professor of Organisational Analysis and Head of the Organisation and Human Resource Management at Warwick Business School, UK. His research focuses on organisation, management, leadership, regulation, professionals, knowledge and practice in health care. He has led large funded research projects, published in leading international social science and management journals, and co-authored 'Making Wicked Problems Governable: The Case of Managed Networks in Health Care' (Oxford University Press, 2013) and 'The Politics of Management Knowledge in Times of Austerity' (Oxford University Press, 2018).

**Ross Millar** is a Senior Lecturer in Health Care Policy and Management. He has extensive experience of healthcare organisational and policy research into quality improvement, governance, and organisational change. Ross has published across a range of journals and has led and co-led funded projects from the National Institute for Health Research, Department of Health, and the Health Foundation in the UK.

**Robin Miller** is a Professor and Head of the Department of Social Work and Social Care, University of Birmingham. He leads on a variety of applied research projects within health and care, with a particular focus on evaluating and learning from change initiatives. Current projects include local evaluations of new models of care programme. Robin is a Senior Associate of the International Federation of Integrated Care, an advisory group member of the European Primary Care Network, and a Fellow of the School for Social Care Research.

**Jacinta Nzinga** is health system researcher with a focus on social science research working with the Health Services Research Group, Kemri-Wellcome Trust Research Programme. She holds a masters degree in Global Health from University of Oxford and a Ph.D. in Health and Social Sciences from University of Warwick, UK. Her research work and interests are mainly in the areas of management of human resources for health, health policy analysis and the interpretive analysis of their implementation, organizational change and implementation of innovation, organizational behavior and clinical leadership in health care. Jacinta has several publications exploring engagement and development of health workers' leadership capacities in improving health service delivery in Kenyan public hospitals. She's also adjunct faculty at Strathmore University, teaches while doing collaborative research with county health managers and has been part of human resources for health technical working groups in Kenya.

**Jane O'Hara** is an Associate Professor in Patient Safety and Improvement Science, and Deputy Director of the YQSR Group. Jane has a broad range of research interests, which centre on the use of theory and robust methods to understand and improve the safety of healthcare. Principal interests include the involvement of patients in patient safety, how we measure quality and patient safety and use this information to improve care, the use of behaviour change approaches to support safety improvement, and the role of individual differences in influencing quality and safety outcomes.

**Charlotte Overton** is Researcher in Residence in the East Midlands Patient Safety Collaborative and Research Associate in the Centre for Health Innovation Leadership and Learning, Nottingham University Business School. Her previous role was working on the Implementation of Evidence and Improvement theme within the Collaboration for Leadership in Applied Health Research and Care East Midlands Charlotte's Ph.D. was a qualitative multi-site case study exploring the implementation of the sepsis care bundle, drawing on theory from Science and Technology Studies to inform Implementation Science. Charlotte's research interests are in the use of social science in patient safety and quality improvement, evaluation, implementation science and ethnography. Charlotte is also a practicing acute care nurse.

**Catherine Pope** is Professor of Medical Sociology in the Nuffield Department of Primary Care Health Sciences. She is also a senior research fellow at Green Templeton College, and was made Fellow of the Academy of Social Sciences in 2016. An internationally recognised researcher and teacher, Catherine spent thirty years working in Higher Education in London, Leicester, Bristol and Southampton, before moving to Oxford in July 2019. Catherine is an expert in qualitative and mixed methods for applied health research, and a key contributor to developing methods for evidence synthesis. She has published empirical, theoretical, and methodological work, including over 160 peer reviewed journal and conference papers for clinical, sociological, policy and practitioner audiences.

**Glenn Robert** is Professor at King's College, London. His research draws on the fields of organisational studies and organisational sociology, and incorporates the study of innovations in the organisation and delivery of health care services as well as quality improvement interventions. He has overarching interest in organisation development and change management that spans all three domains of health care research, policy and practice.

**Bridget Roe** is Research Fellow at the Health Services Management Centre, University of Birmingham. Her doctoral research examined the processes of professional identity formation amongst newly qualified nurses. She has particular expertise in supporting the implementation of complex interventions in health and care service, especially through team work development methodologies.

**Simon Turner** is Assistant Professor in the School of Management, University of Los Andes, Colombia. Prior to joining Los Andes, Simon was Senior Lecturer in Health Policy and Organisation at the University of Manchester. He previously held research positions at University College London, King's College London, the London School of Hygiene & Tropical Medicine, and the University of Cambridge. His research interests lie in the application of social science theory and methods (particularly ethnography) to the study of the organisation and improvement of public services, particularly health care.

**Robert Vickers** is a Research Fellow in the National Institute for Health Research Applied Research Collaborative, East Midlands, at the University of Nottingham. He completed a doctorate in Politics (2011) on 'high cost political participation' and held post-doctoral research posts at the International Centre for Guidance Studies, University of Derby (2014) and Nottingham Trent University, the University of Lincoln (2017) and with the Centre for Health Innovation, Leadership and Learning (CHILL), Nottingham University Business School (2018–2019).

**Justin Waring** is Professor of Medical Sociology and Healthcare Organisation at the Health Services Management Centre, University of Birmingham. His research examines the changing organisation and management of health and care systems, with a particular focus on the implementation of innovations aimed at improving the quality and safety of care. His work draws on diverse traditions and perspectives within sociological theory to interpret changing patterns of social organisation and power.

**Oli Williams** holds a THIS Institute Postdoctoral Fellowship and is based at King's College London. Oli completed his Ph.D. in the Department of Sociology at the University of Leicester. His research focuses on health inequalities, the promotion of healthy lifestyles, obesity, weight stigma, equitable intervention and co-production. He co-founded the art collective Act With Love (AWL) to promote social change. *The Weight of Expectation* comic is one example of their work, view others at: www.actwithlove.co.uk. In recognition of his work on weight stigma the British Science Association invited Oli to deliver the Margaret Mead Award Lecture for Social Sciences at the British Science Festival 2018.

**John S. F. Wright** is Associate Professor, Institute for Public Policy and Governance, University of Technology Sydney. John has held post-doctoral appointments at the University of Birmingham in the Department of Public Health and Epidemiology working on area-based regeneration schemes, with a focus on participation, decentralisation and methods and processes for health and environmental impact assessments. He also completed post-doctoral work at the Regulatory Institutions Network in the Research School Social Sciences, Australian National University, on regulation and governance theory. John was a lecturer at the London School of Hygiene and Tropical Medicine in the Department of Public Health and Policy working on the regulation and new governance arrangements of acute English hospitals.

# List of Figures

## Buddies and Mergers: Decentring the Performance of Healthcare Provider Partnerships



## Is Co-production Just Really Good PPI? Making Sense of Patient and Public Involvement and Co-production Networks

# List of Tables

# Decentring Networks and Networking in Health and Care Services

Mark Bevir and Justin Waring

## The Network Narrative

It is widely proclaimed we now live in a networked society, in which the proliferation of information communication technologies has made possible new and diverse forms of inter-connected social, cultural and economic activity (Castells 2011). Although the network concept is often invoked with reference to new social media and rapidly changing modes of social organisation, it also stems from a long-standing stream of sociological and anthropological thinking about

M. Bevir
Department of Political Science,
University of California, Berkeley, CA, USA
e-mail: mbevir@berkeley.edu

J. Waring (✉)
Health Services Management Centre,
University of Birmingham, Birmingham, UK
e-mail: J.Waring@bham.ac.uk





M. Bevir and J. Waring (eds.), *Decentring Health and Care Networks*, Organizational Behaviour in Healthcare,
https://doi.org/10.1007/978-3-030-40889-3_1

the inter-connected and patterned features of everyday social life, such as kinship, occupational or community networks (Scott 2002). And yet, the network concept simultaneously encourages a distinct level of social science enquiry that attends, less to people or places as categorical units of social organisation, and more to the relationships between them as mediated by different interactions and technologies (Scott 2002).

The network narrative has become a ubiquitous feature of contemporary public policy (Hajer et al. 2003; Kickert et al. 1997). In broad terms, it is widely believed that the social, economic and political challenges facing society today require the diverse resources and capabilities of different specialists and stakeholders to participate in more inclusive policy making and to implement more coordinated solutions. The network narrative tends to follow a familiar logic (Bevir 2013). That is, traditional modes of public administration were dominated by the centralised, top-down authority of the State, with policy decisions implemented through bureaucratic planning and delegation. This supposedly stifled innovation and reinforced siloed working to the detriment of responsive and efficient public services. The neoliberal reforms of the 1980s and beyond saw the introduction of more business-like New Public Management (NPM) whereby a multitude of decentred policy actors became responsible for making and implementing policy decisions, typically on the basis of individual self-interest with market-like relations. This was seen as fragmenting public services to the extent that public service organisations could not collaborate around the complex problems facing society. The network narrative emerged as a response to the limits of both bureaucracy and markets by advocating for a model a public governance in which multiple policy actors share resources, make more joined-up decisions, and provide more coordinated services. For many advocates, New Public Governance (NPG) represents a more progressive, inclusive and democratic approach that is associated with qualities such as trust, mutuality and commitment, collaboration and co-design; rather than contractual obligation or delegated rule.

Within the public policy and management literature, the term 'policy networks' has been defined as '*(more or less) stable patterns of relations between independent actors, which take shape around policy problems and/ or policy programmes*' (Kickert et al. 1997). Advocates put forward a number of potential benefits. First, networks offer more inclusive and democratic decision-making through enabling multiple stakeholders to shape policies and services (Ansell and Gash 2008). Second, networks provide flexibility to help local actors work together to address 'wicked' policy problems whose solution is beyond the scope of a single organisation (Ferlie et al. 2013). Third networks bring together the skills and resources of divergent actors thereby enabling more dynamic and innovative responses to policy problems (Klijn and Koppenjan 2000). Fourth, networks promote open, trusting, reciprocal and cooperative relationships between organisations and individuals (Kickert et al. 1997), leading to more efficient ways of working and promoting knowledge sharing and innovation.

Arguably, the network narrative illustrates the influence of particular social science ideas on public policy and management. Klijn and Koppenjan (2012) describe how three distinct underpinning perspectives inform contemporary thinking on 'network governance'. The first draws from political science, where policy networks are associated with more inclusive and deliberative decision-making (Ansell and Gash 2008). The second stems from the field of economic sociology and later organisational studies where it is shown that inter-organisational networks promote innovation through facilitating resource sharing (Burt 2009; Granovetter 1973). The third, and most relevant here, is found within the field of public policy and management where networks are seen as an alternative model of service organisation and delivery that offers more coordinated and integrated responses to cotemporary policy problems (Ferlie et al. 2013). Through the convergence of these different traditions a, seemingly, dominant policy narrative has emerged.

And yet, in some ways the network narrative is in arguably idealised. It might be suggested, for example, that the idea of epoch-like shifts between bureaucratic public administration, NPM and NPG are over-stated with public governance characterised by more complex, layered or hybrid governance arrangements (Pollitt 2009). Although some have talked of a 'Hollow State' or 'polycentric' public services, we also know that centralised state regulations continue to influence how local policy actors operate both within markets and networks (Lowndes and Skelcher 1998). It also the case that policy actors are expected to simultaneously compete on some issues, whilst collaborating on others (Bevir and Waring 2017). Further still, changing professional institutions, boundaries and status hierarchies continue to complicate all varieties of public policy and management (Waring and Currie 2009).

In other ways, the network narrative adopted by policy makers has the potential to reify social relationships rendering them as concrete and amenable to planning and management. By this we mean, that networks are often presented as tangible or discrete entities based upon the formation of new working relationships between disconnected groups (Waring et al. 2017). As such, if the network is appropriately designed with the necessary agents, and appropriate directives and incentives are provided, it will result in the sharing of resources and service improvement. This can be seen, for example, with the extensive literature on 'mandated' or 'managed networks' and the corresponding upsurge of interests in 'network management' and 'network orchestration' which speak to the idea that managers need identify and recruit specific network actors, build network relationships and leveraging collective benefits (Klijn et al. 2010; McGuire 2006). And yet, the realities of 'network management' is far from straight forward because of the narrow ways network relations, much like cultures, are seen as amenable to management intervention (McGuire and Agranoff 2011; Waring and Crompton 2019).

Turning to the wider social science literature, 'social networks' might be understood, more broadly, as the relatively stable patterns of interaction common to practically all aspects of social life, which become institutionalised around certain activities or tasks in the form of a community or network (Crossley 2010). Early anthropological interest in social networks is often credited to Barnes (1954) who claimed that "the whole of social life" could be seen as a "set of points some of which are joined by lines" to form a total network of relations (1954: 43). Based on the conception of society as formed through an interconnecting web of relations, social scientist began systematically to denote patterns of existing relationships seeing social structure as a collection of points (representing individuals, groups or organisations) and various types and strengths of links between them. These networks are not designed, manufactured or created, but emerge overtime through social interaction, and become institutionalised through social conventions and customs, and eventually social rules (Owen-Smith and Powell 2008). These networks provide the social infrastructure through which meanings, values and identities are shared and reinforced; through which actors social position and influence can be understood; and through which social activities are organised. In this sense, networks are not, and cannot easily, be created or managed. (Crossley 2010).

## Networks and Networking in Healthcare

It is probably fair to say that the English health and care system has often been at the very forefront of broader transitions and trends in public policy and governance (Ferlie et al. 2013). Its creation in the immediate post-war period, and subsequent reforms in the 1960s and 1970s, very much illustrate the ideals of a centralised state-run public service bureaucracy. Management reforms of the 1980s and market reforms of the 1990s exemplified the rise and maturation of NPM as a template for more responsive, efficient and competitive public service delivery (Strong and Robinson 1990). Similarly, from the late 1990s onwards, the mantra of collaboration, partnerships and networks has come to redefine health policies and service organisation (Ferlie et al. 2013). The network narrative has re-shaped almost all aspects of the health care system from high-level policy decision-making where government departments coordinate activities around policy problems, to regional care planning through networks of health and social care agencies, through to inter-professional networking in frontline service delivery (Waring et al. 2017).

In their review of inter-organisational networks in healthcare, Sheaff and Schofield (2016) distinguish between six different types of networks, including (i) 'care networks' involved in the coordination of care services; (ii) 'professional networks' for the coordination and representation of occupational interests; (iii) 'project networks' that form around a specific initiative; (iv) 'programme networks' designed to implement a given policy or reform programme; (v) 'experience networks' that bring together patients or publics with shared experiences and interests; and (vi) 'interest networks' that mobilise around particular agendas. This typology reveals how networks in health care can vary according to purpose and intent, form and structure, and interest and ideology. Moreover, it shows how some are seemingly the object of policy or management, in so much that they are a tool or technique of governance; whereas other are more emergent and potential in opposition to policy, in so much that they advance divergent interests.

In the contemporary context, three prominent initiatives give a clear sense of the way the network narrative continues to guide health and care reforms; each of which is the subject of research presented in this collection. The first can be seen with the renewed emphasis on regional strategic networks as a platform for prioritising, planning and delivering a more coordinated care services, as set out in the NHS *Five Year Forward View* (NHS England 2015). The broad goal of policy is to change way multiple health and care agencies work together within a regional footprint in order to optimise the allocation of scarce resources, deliver more integrated services and improve population health. Prominent examples of this can be seen with the introduction of, what have been variously termed, Sustainability and Transformation Plans (later Partnerships), Accountable Care Organisations, and Integrated Care Systems. Other attempts to change 'system architecture' including the recent introduction of Primary Care Networks. In many ways, this particular policy agenda is shaped by the longstanding view that complex care needs require the involvement of multiple specialists working across the health and social care boundaries. At the same time, the promotion of regional networks stems from the necessity of dealing with resource constraints created by austerity measures and the removal of more formal administrative or bureaucratic strata within the NHS following the Health and Social Care Act of 2010, specifically Strategic Health Authorities.

The second example can be seen in the continued re-organisation of services through regional or locality service delivery networks (Fulop et al. 2015). Traditionally, acute and specialist NHS services have been organised and delivered through local or 'district' hospitals, but typically with limited horizontal integration with other care providers. The shift towards a network model is guided, in part, by mounting research evidence that suggests the distribution of specialist services across multiple care providers often results in sub-standard and variable outcomes, especially where smaller district hospitals have limited expertise in complex cases. It follows, therefore, that concentrating the provision of specialist services within fewer regional centres, and encouraging these services to work in more coordinated or networked ways will result in benefits for workforce development from greater exposure to complex case, increased resource optimisation from reducing unnecessary duplication, and improved patient outcomes from better specialised care. In other ways, this includes creating better links between specialist centres to promote care standards, share 'best practice' and reduce variations. Prominent examples include the introduction regional networks for cancer, stroke, and major trauma care.

The third example addresses the well-document 'translation gap' between the production of evidence-based innovations, on the one hand, and the implementation and adoption of these breakthroughs in everyday care delivery, on the other. It is said, for example, that it can take as much as 15 years for new therapies or technologies to make a routine impact on patient care, and whilst some time is needed to ensure safety and effectiveness, excessive delay represents potentially wasted resources and unnecessary human suffering (Cooksey 2006). For over a decade, policies have sought to address this problem through supporting more collaborative partnerships and networks between research 'producers' and 'users'. This often centres on encouraging NHS care providers to work more collaboratively with university-based researchers and industry in the form of research networks (Kislov et al. 2018). Prominent examples include Academic Health Science Networks (AHNS), Collaborations for Leadership in Applied Health Research and Care (CLARHCs), Applied Research Collaborations (ARCs), and other disease-specific research networks. Of relevance to the decentred approached developed in this collection, the formation of these networks is often shaped by the local traditions of university-healthcare collaboration (Rycroft-Malone et al. 2013), as well as the dilemmas of regional geo-politics between competing university and NHS partners (Waring et al. 2020).

These three prominent examples show how networks, or more precisely the network narrative, continues to shape the modernisation and transformation of health and care services. The chapters in this collection examine directly the manifestation of networks and networking in these and other areas of health and care reform. Unlike the much of the existing research on networks, this collection seeks to a develop a more enquiring, critical and decentred understanding of networks as an idealised or prescriptive model of health care governance.

## Decentred Theory

Modernist social science typically seeks mid-level or general theories by which to explain the particulars of social life, including the adoption, operation, and effects of a policy. They prefer formal and abstract explanations, as opposed to historical or context-specific, precisely because they conceive that explanations must be synchronic accounts that persist across multiple cases from which to build a mid-level or general theory (Brady and David 2004; King et al. 1994). Decentred theory contrasts sharply with this modernist approach. Decentred theory is overtly historicist in its emphasis on agency, contingency, and context (Bevir 2003a; Bevir 2013). It rejects the hubris of mid-level or comprehensive explanations that claim to unpack the essential properties and underlying logics of social and political life. So, for example, it suggests that neither the intrinsic rationality of markets, nor the path dependency of institutions, properly determines whether policies are adopted, how they coalesce into patterns of governance, or what effects they have. Rather, decentred theory conceives of public policies as contingent constructions of actors, inspired by competing beliefs that are rooted in different traditions and which evolve in the face of changing situations or dilemmas. That is, decentred theory examines the ways in which patterns of rule, including both institutions and policies, are created, sustained, and modified by individuals through their meaningful social practices that arise from the beliefs individuals adopt against the background of traditions and in response to dilemmas. It suggests that policies arise as conflicting beliefs, competing traditions, and varied dilemmas generate, sustain, and transform diverse practices. It focuses attention on the diverse ways in which situated agents make and remake policies as contested practices. Decentred theory therefore suggests that social scientists focus on a particular set of empirical topics, in this case health care networks as an example of contemporary governance.

Too many social scientists adopt forms of explanation that reduce actors' beliefs to formal axioms of rationality or to synchronic patterns associated with institutions, systems, or other social facts. Decentred theory begins instead with the idea that actions should be explained with reference to the reasons and meanings that actors have for those actions. Crucially, decentred theory suggests, first, that social scientists explain these reasons by locating them in the agents' *webs of belief*, and second, that social scientists explain these webs of belief by locating them in a historical context of traditions and dilemmas. If we reject positivism, and the idea of understanding human behaviour by reference to objective social facts, we must explore the beliefs and meanings through which actors themselves construct their world, including the ways they understand all their position, the norms affecting them, and their interests. Because people cannot have pure experiences, their beliefs are inextricably enmeshed with theories and traditions.

Two sets of concepts therefore provide the basis for thinking about the meaningful actions of actors. The first set includes concepts such as tradition, structure, and paradigm (Bevir 2013; Kuhn 2012: 43–51). These concepts explore the social context in which individuals think and act. They vary in how much weight they suggest should be given to the social context in explanations of thought and action. We define a 'tradition' as a set of understandings an actor receives during socialization. Although tradition is unavoidable, it is only ever a starting point, not something that governs later performances. We should be cautious, therefore, of representing tradition as an unavoidable presence in everything people do as this risks leaving too slight a role for agency. In particular, we should not imply that tradition is constitutive of the beliefs people later come to hold or the actions they then perform. Instead, we should see tradition mainly as a backdrop or underlying influence on people. Just because individuals start out from an inherited tradition does not imply that they cannot adjust it. On the contrary, the ability to develop traditions is an essential part of people's being in the world. People constantly confront, at least slightly, novel circumstances that require them to apply inherited traditions anew, and a tradition cannot fix the nature of its application. When people confront the unfamiliar, they have to extend or change their heritage to encompass it, and as they do so, they develop that heritage. Every time they try to apply a tradition, they reflect on it, whether consciously or not, to bring it to bear on their circumstances, and by reflecting on it, they open it to innovation. Thus, human agency can produce change even when people think they are sticking fast to a tradition they regard as sacrosanct.

The second set includes concepts such as dilemma, anomaly, and agency (Bevir 2003b; Kuhn 2012: 52–65). The concept of 'dilemma' provides one way of thinking about the role of individual agency in changing such traditions. People's capacity for agency implies that change originates in the responses or decisions of individuals. Whenever someone adopts a new belief and associated action, they have to adjust their existing beliefs and practices to make way for the newcomer. To accept a new belief is thus to pose a dilemma that asks questions of one's existing beliefs. A dilemma arises for an individual or institution when a new idea stands in opposition to existing beliefs or practices and so forces a reconsideration of these existing beliefs and associated tradition. Traditions change as individuals make a series of variations to them in response to any number of specific dilemmas. A related point to make is that dilemmas do not have given, nor correct, solutions. Because no set of beliefs can fix its own criteria of application, when people adopt new ideas they change traditions creatively. It might look as if a tradition can tell people how to act; how to respond to dilemmas. At most, however, the tradition provides a guide to what they might do. It does not provide rules fixing what they must do.

It is important to recognize that social scientists cannot straightforwardly identify dilemmas with allegedly objective pressures in the world. People vary their beliefs or actions in response to new ideas or perceived situations. They do so irrespective of whether that new idea reflects real pressures, or, to be precise, irrespective of whether it corresponds to a pressure perceived real by social scientists. In explaining change, there is no reason to privilege academic accounts of the world. What matters is the subjective and intersubjective understandings of local actors, not scholarly accounts of real pressures in the world. The task of the social scientist is to recover the shared intersubjective dilemmas of the relevant actors.

A decentred approach highlights contests among diverse and contingent meanings rooted in different traditions and the dilemmas faced by actors in particular contexts. As a result, it privileges specific new empirical topics with a particular focus on the context-specific practices enacted by actors and the meanings that inform them. In looking at the interplay between traditional, dilemma and meanings in action, a decentred approach focuses on narratives, rationalities, and resistance (Bevir 2010). 'Narratives' convey complex sets of meanings, rooted in historical circumstances, and providing a shared framework for meaning making and social practices. Narratives assist actors in sense-making and confronting novel situations and dilemmas, and in turn narratives are made and re-made through social practice. Narratives are inherently political or ideological, conveying not only meanings, but also moral imperatives. A decentred theory suggests that social scientists should pay more attention to the traditions against which elites construct their worldviews, including their views of their own interests. Moreover, the central elite need not be a uniform group, all the members of which see their interests in the same way, share a common culture, or speak a shared discourse. Our decentred approach suggests that social scientists should ask whether different sections of the elite draw on different traditions to construct different narratives about the world, their place within it, and their interests and values.

Relating these ideas to the study of networks and networking in healthcare, it encourages analysis to move beyond the reified notion of networks as technical instruments of top-down government within which different actors and agencies see their worlds reconfigured, Rather we need to see networks as sites of multiple, shared and contested meaning, where diverse actors engage in network-related activities based upon their prevailing traditions or systems of belief. This means that the practices of networking for one group can be radically different from another, and from the prescribed vision of policy or social science theory. Furthermore, the introduction or imposition of networks as a policy instrument might be seen as creating the types of disruptions and changes that create the dilemmas for social actors. In these situations, actors and groups of actors draw upon their prevailing meanings, such as what networking means to them, and at the same time develop new meanings in the face of contradictions. Through enacting traditions and dealing with dilemmas, actors create the social reality of networks and networking that can depart from and resist the narratives of policy-makers. In short, networks and networking is made real through the situated and meaningful practices of health and care actors as they enact or resist a networked model of care.

## The Contributions to This Collection

In different ways, the chapters in this collection develop a critical and decentred analysis of the ways networks and networking have re-shaped, or at least tried to re-shape, the organisation and governance of health and care services. They each focus on a particular examples of networking in contemporary health and care reform, such as integrated health and social care models (Bishop), research collaborations (Ledger, Vickers), inter-organisational mergers and buddying (Millar), regional stroke networks (Baeza), and networks for stakeholder or patient involvement (Williams); as well as focusing on different dynamics of networking, such as the role of technology-mediated networks (Pope), the role of stories and storying-telling (Turner), and the motivation of actors to engage in networking (Hyde). In different ways, they show how policy narratives often present an idealised or reified understanding of networks that downplays both the underlying ideology or rationality of policy, and neglects the ways networks and networking is enacted through the situated and meaningful practices of actors; and how the situated practices of networking often divergent from or resist the intent or assumptions of policy.

Furthermore, the collection offers extensions to the application of decentres theory in the study of health and public policies. Given their focus on networks and networking, it is perhaps unsurprising that many chapters bring to light the inter-active and relational dynamics of networks, especially the idea of inter-subjective meaning located in shared webs of belief (Bishop, Hyde, Turner), but also the potential for new relationships to form around dilemmas (Baeza, Hyde, Millar). The chapter also show how dilemmas might not simply arise in the context of new or changing circumstances, but how they can be cultivated and used to advance certain agendas (Baeza, Bishop). In other ways, the chapters give closer attention the spatial, affective, and motivational dimensions of traditions and meaningful action (Bishop, Hyde, Vickers). That is, meaningful action is always located in a space to which different traditions ascribe meaning, and where new policies seek to create new meanings around which dilemmas emerge (Bishop). They also show how the emotional consequences of networking can shape how actors make sense of and seek to act in the context of reforms (Turner), especially in terms of how this shapes the motivations and intents of actors (Hyde). More broadly, the chapters reveal how juxtaposition between local traditions of networking and policy narratives for networking can create dilemmas but also opportunities for resistance or creative mediation of interests (Ledger, Turner, Vickers).

In other ways, the chapters draw on additional theoretical perspectives to enrich or critique the decentred approach. This includes, for example, concepts and ideas derived from Actor Network Theory to understand how intended or expected modes of organising work become thwarted and resisted in the everyday practices human and non-human networks (Pope). Theories of inter-subjective storytelling and meaning making complement the decentred interest in narratives to rethink the processes of learning and innovation in the context of dilemma (Turner). In addition, the ideas of Foucault are invoked to thinking about the relational dynamics of power and governance in healthcare networks, especially the role of pastoral power in the implementation of evidence-based care (McGivern). And as outlined above, theories of space and place also offer additional ways of thinking about tradition and dilemma (Bishop).

## References

Ansell, C., & Gash, A. (2008). Collaborative governance in theory and practice. *Journal of Public Administration Research and Theory, 18*(4), 543–571.

Barnes, J. A. (1954). Class and committees in a Norwegian Island Parish. *Human Relations, 7*(1), 39–58.

Bevir, M. (2003a). A decentred theory of governance. In H. Bang (Ed.), *Governance as social and political communication*. Manchester: Manchester University Press.

Bevir, M. (2003b). Notes toward an analysis of conceptual change. *Social Epistemology, 17*, 55–63.

Bevir, M. (2010). Interpreting territory and power. *Government and Opposition, 45*, 436–456.

Bevir, M. (2013). *A theory of governance*. Berkeley: University of California Press.

Bevir, M., & Waring, J. (Eds.). (2017). *Decentring health policy: Learning from British experiences in healthcare governance*. London: Routledge.

Brady, H., & David, C. (Eds.). (2004). *Rethinking social inquiry: Diverse tools, shared standards*. Lanham, MD: Rowman & Littlefield.

Burt, R. S. (2009). *Structural holes: The social structure of competition*. Cambridge: Harvard University Press.

Castells, M. (2011). *The rise of the network society* (Vol. 12). West Sussex: Wiley.

Cooksey, D. (2006). *A review of UK health research funding*. London: The Stationery Office.

Crossley, N. (2010). Networks and complexity: Directions for interactionist research? *Symbolic Interaction, 33*(3), 341–363.

Ferlie, E., Fitzgerald, L., McGivern, G., Dopson, S., & Bennett, C. (2013). *Making wicked problems governable? The case of managed networks in health care*. Oxford: Oxford University Press.

Fulop, N. J., Ramsay, A., Perry, C., Boaden, R., McKevitt, C., Rudd, A., et al. (2015). Explaining outcomes in major system change: A qualitative study of implementing centralised acute stroke services in two large metropolitan regions in England. *Implementation Science, 11*(1), 80.

Granovetter, M. S. (1973). The strength of weak Ties1. *American Journal of Sociology, 78*(6), 1360–1380.

Hajer, M., Hajer, M. A., Wagenaar, H., Goodin, R. E., & Barry, B. (Eds.). (2003). *Deliberative policy analysis: Understanding governance in the network society*. Cambridge: Cambridge University Press.

Kickert, W. J., Klijn, E. H., & Koppenjan, J. F. (Eds.). (1997). *Managing complex networks: Strategies for the public sector*. London: Sage.

King, G., Robert, O. K., & Sidney, V. (1994). *Designing social inquiry: Scientific inference in qualitative research*. Princeton, NJ: Princeton University Press.

Kislov, R., Wilson, P. M., Knowles, S., & Boaden, R. (2018). Learning from the emergence of NIHR Collaborations for Leadership in Applied Health Research and Care (CLAHRCs): A systematic review of evaluations. *Implementation Science, 13*(1), 111.

Klijn, E. H., & Koppenjan, J. F. (2000). Public management and policy networks: Foundations of a network approach to governance. *Public Management an International Journal of Research and Theory, 2*(2), 135–158.

Klijn, E. H., & Koppenjan, J. (2012). Governance network theory: Past, present and future. *Policy & Politics, 40*(4), 587–606.

Klijn, E. H., Steijn, B., & Edelenbos, J. (2010). The impact of network management on outcomes in governance networks. *Public Administration, 88*(4), 1063–1082.

Kuhn, T. (2012/1962). *The structure of scientific revolutions*. Chicago: University of Chicago Press.

Lowndes, V., & Skelcher, C. (1998). The dynamics of multi-organizational partnerships: An analysis of changing modes of governance. *Public Administration, 76*(2), 313–333.

McGuire, M. (2006). Collaborative public management: Assessing what we know and how we know it. *Public Administration Review, 66*, 33–43.

McGuire, M., & Agranoff, R. (2011). The limitations of public management networks. *Public Administration, 89*(2), 265–284.

NHS England. (2015). *Five year forward view*. London: NHS England.

Owen-Smith, J., & Powell, W. W. (2008). Networks and institutions. *The Sage handbook of organizational institutionalism* (pp. 596–623). London: Sage.

Pollitt, C. (2009). Bureaucracies remember, post-bureaucratic organizations forget? *Public Administration, 87*(2), 198–218.

Rycroft-Malone, J., Wilkinson, J., Burton, C. R., Harvey, G., McCormack, B., Graham, I., & Staniszewska, S. (2013). Collaborative action around implementation in collaborations for leadership in applied health research and care: Towards a programme theory. *Journal of Health Services Research & Policy, 18*(3_suppl), 13–26.

Scott, J. (Ed.). (2002). *Social networks: Critical concepts in sociology* (Vol. 4). London: Taylor & Francis.

Sheaff, R., & Schofield, J. (2016). Inter-organizational networks in health care: Program networks, care networks, and integrated care. In E. Ferlie, K. Montgomery, & A.-R. Pedersen (Eds.), *The Oxford handbook of health care management* (pp. 434–458). Oxford University Press.

Strong, P., & Robinson, J. (1990). *The NHS under new management.* Milton Keynes: Open University Press.

Waring, J., & Crompton, A. (2019). The struggles for (and of) network management: An ethnographic study of non-dominant policy actors in the English healthcare system. *Public Management Review, 22*(2), 1–19.

Waring, J., & Currie, G. (2009). Managing expert knowledge: Organizational challenges and managerial futures for the UK medical profession. *Organization Studies, 30*(7), 755–778.

Waring, J., Bishop, S., & Roe, B. (2017). Network contra network: The gap between policy and practice in the organisation of major trauma care. In M. Bevir & J. Waring (Eds.), *Decentring health policy* (pp. 102–120). London: Routledge.

Waring, J., Crompton, A., Overton, C., & Roe, B. (2020). Decentering health research networks: Framing collaboration in the context of narrative incompatibility and regional geo-politics. *Public Policy and Administration.* https://doi.org/10.1177/0952076720911686.

# The Contested Practice of Networking in Healthcare Management

Paula Hyde, Damian Hodgson, Simon Bailey, John Hassard, and Mike Bresnen

## Introduction

> There is a danger in network analysis of not seeing the trees for the forest. Interactions, the building blocks of networks, are too easily taken as givens… Yet why interactions exist cannot be ignored when considering the role of networks in a theory of organization. (Salancik 1995: 346)

P. Hyde (✉)
Birmingham Business School, University of Birmingham, Birmingham, UK
e-mail: p.hyde@bham.ac.uk

D. Hodgson · J. Hassard
Sheffield University Management School, University of Sheffield, Sheffield, UK

S. Bailey
Centre for Health Service Studies, University of Kent, Canterbury, UK

M. Bresnen
Manchester Metropolitan Business School, Manchester Metropolitan University, Manchester, UK


M. Bevir and J. Waring (eds.), *Decentring Health and Care Networks*, Organizational Behaviour in Healthcare,
https://doi.org/10.1007/978-3-030-40889-3_2

Writers on organizations have long emphasised the need to understand their increasing complexity in relation to the environments in which they operate (Child 1972; Lawrence and Lorsch 1967; Perrow 1972; Marchington et al. 2005). The recent history of the UK National Health Service (NHS) offers several illustrations of how, in this case, a rapidly fragmenting and increasingly market-driven institutional context (Kirkpatrick 1999) has had dramatic effects on organisational complexity, exacerbating long-recognised divisions between professional groups (Currie et al. 2009) and between managers and professionals (Currie and Procter 2005; Noordegraaf 2011). In attempting to respond to such integration challenges, increasing attention has been paid to ways in which healthcare as a system can be reconnected and such boundaries traversed, including using distributed forms of leadership (Buchanan et al. 2007), knowledge brokerage (Burgess and Currie 2013), communities of practice (Bate and Robert 2002), and, notably, managed networks (Addicott et al. 2007; Ferlie et al. 2010). The current financial pressures upon public services including healthcare (Fulop et al. 2012; McKee et al. 2002) have lent weight to calls for the kind of network-enabled transformative change which can integrate across boundaries (6 et al. 2006). While much has been written about the nature of networks and network relations since the seminal work of Granovetter (1973), the focus has predominantly been on the structure, nature and composition of the network itself, rather than the act of networking. As a consequence, 'we know surprisingly little about the strategies individuals employ when networking, and in particular the underlying agency mechanisms involved' (Bensaou et al. 2014: 29). The result is a call for more 'fine-grained analysis of the social practices and ongoings in relational networks' (Faulconbridge 2007: 926). This illustrates a return to more longstanding anthropological perspectives on the interactive dynamics of kinship and community networks (Bott 1955), together with more contemporary decentred policy perspectives that emphasise the situated meanings and practices of interacting social actors (Bevir 2013).

In this chapter, we address this gap by examining the practices of networking, both formal and informal, engaged in by a range of healthcare managers across three organisations in the English NHS. We examine how they go about building network relationships and the meaning they attribute to their networking activities, we focus upon the multiplexity of networking (Heebels et al. 2013) and also the emotional and moral commitments implicit in the practice of networking (Casciaro et al. 2014). We argue that the motivations and skills of network actors contribute directly to the ability of networks to deliver organisational value in the form of efficiency or flexibility and raises questions about the potential for effective governance.

## Networks in Healthcare Organisations

From the late twentieth century, social, managerial and organisational research has focused on the concept of the network. In *The Rise of the Network Society*, Castells argues that 'networks constitute the new social morphology of our societies' (1996: 500) and points to emerging recognition of the importance of knowledge and knowledge flows across all aspects of society, business and culture. The strengths of 'the network' as a highly dynamic and open system of interrelated nodes lies in the fluidity of this phenomenon–one capable of rapid expansion or adaptation in the face of complex and fragmented social and organisational arrangements. Network concepts have been used to represent and analyse a vast array of social phenomena; as methodological tools to understand the functioning of communities and society (Putnam 2001), as designs for new and more effective organisations (Miles and Snow 1986), as solutions to the failings of markets and bureaucracy (Powell 1990) and as models to account for the vital flows of knowledge within and between contexts, organisations and communities (Brown and Duguid 2000). As we elaborate below, there is a tendency within the literature on networks, especially policy networks, to present a reified notion of networks as discrete entities or 'things' that can neglect the situated meanings and interaction dynamics of networking (Waring et al. 2017).

The concept of network also bears some similarity to the notion of 'community of practice' (CoP) (Lave and Wenger 1991), which refers to a bounded and focused phenomenon associated with delimited groups of practitioners, bound by communal relationships, with common understandings of the world, and with a shared enterprise or mission (Wenger 1998). Unlike networks, CoPs are founded upon a set of practices, through participation in which members collectively learn (and at the same time are socialised into) a common way of thinking and acting. Through frequent and intense social interaction, CoPs serve to enhance knowledge sharing and creation among members, but also tend to inhibit knowledge exchange and learning *between* such communities, due to epistemic and social boundaries (Ferlie et al. 2005; Swan et al. 2002). By contrast, networks (in principle) represent a more open set of relationships without the homogeneity of membership, knowledge and identity. They are less cohesive, consisting of relatively weak links and more distant or infrequent interactions, leading some to explore the consequences for knowledge sharing of 'networks of practice' (NoPs) (Agterberg et al. 2010).

Furthermore, we would argue, networks do not inevitably suffer from the same functionalist bias now associated with CoPs. It has been noted that despite enthusiastic support for the concept of CoPs in research on knowledge utilisation, their effectiveness as a means of knowledge sharing and innovation often remains unproven (Crilly et al. 2013). In terms of possible explanations for this failure, the same authors suggest: 'There is lack of clarity about the concept apart from acting as some form of organic informal network. Little is known about how power influences such networks. Nor are there any instruments to measure the performance of such practice based learning to promote accountability' (Crilly et al. 2013: 146–147). This explanation neatly captures the implicit contradiction in the use of CoPs. On the one hand, CoPs are valued as an 'organic informal network'. On the other, their deliberate adoption within organisations persistently requires that they be rationalised, performance-measured, and rendered accountable; in short, formalised and instrumentalised (Ferlie et al. 2005; Swan et al. 2002). Hence the deliberate and strategic formation of management networks neglects the point, noted by Anderson-Gough et al., that 'the most enduring networks are those which are relatively organic rather than instrumental' (2006: 243). We will return to issues of instrumentality/organicity in networks in the discussion below. For the moment, our point is to draw attention to the ambiguous terrain of activities and relationships that constitute the practice of networking, and the persistent gravitational pull of instrumentality in research in this area.

In order to better explore and understanding the dynamic complexity of network relationships, our analysis is not limited to formal and managed networks. Rather, we are interested in the more informal, infrequent, accidental and spontaneous links that are forged between individuals in this sector, such as friendship and affinity groupings, or highly dispersed communities bound by 'weak ties' (Granovetter 1973). In keeping with the earlier work of Lave and Wenger (1991), we are concerned here not so much with a formalised definition of what a community or network might be, but rather with the relations, motivations and actions that shape, sustain and constrain an individual's participation in a network.

Shifting attention from the network to the individual inevitably brings us closer to the equally influential concept of 'social capital', which is frequently drawn upon to explore the characteristics of the individual in a network, in terms of their 'social connectedness', rather than in the properties of the network itself (Coleman 1988). Again, though, there is a powerful undercurrent of instrumentalism in much of the writing. Social capital has been defined as 'the sum of the actual and potential resources embedded within, available through, and derived from the network of relationships possessed by an individual or social unit' (Nahapiet and Ghoshal 1998: 243). The value of this concept is summarised effectively by Burt (2005: 3), who argues that:

> Social capital explains how people do better because they are somehow better connected with other people. Certain people are connected to certain others, trusting certain others, obligated to support certain others, dependent on exchange with certain others. One's position in the structure of these exchanges can be an asset in its own right.

The danger, however, of prioritising social capital is that the notion of capital prioritises the economic aspects of social relationships (Tlili and Obsiye 2014), and frames these primarily in terms of 'economic exchange, possession and organisational effectiveness' (Anderson-Gough et al. 2006: 236). Hence 'when social capital is viewed as a completely rational form of a resource' (Vorley et al. 2012: 82) there is a tendency to neglect or disregard the less instrumental reasons why individuals forge relationships. This may be for emotional closeness (Kennedy 2004), for the affirmation of self and identity (Hey 2005), for the reassurance of belonging in a community (Grabher and Ibert 2006), or in order to become 'a full participant in a sociocultural practice' (Lave and Wenger 1991: 29). In many accounts, social capital remains too broad and holistic a concept, being reduced to the network position occupied by individual actors and signified merely by the average tie strengths of their relations (Bensaou et al. 2014: 29).

This tension between instrumentality and organicity is reflected in the ambiguous status of 'the social' in social capital (Tlili and Obsiye 2014). One the one hand, social capital can be seen as an aggregation of individual human capital via social relations. On the other hand, the inverse may be the case, and it is the individual who seeks a capital gain via social connectedness. If we consider the concept of knowledge as an example of this action, then the latter case results in a concept of knowledge as something which can be possessed by an individual or group and used as a regulatory device upon others (Contu and Willmott 2000). In effect this is a restatement of the problem of over-embeddedness *within* and lack of translation *between* communities of practice (Ferlie et al. 2005; Swan et al. 2002), a problem that has particular relevance in the context of healthcare (Currie et al. 2010; Currie and White 2012; Noordegraaf and Van Der Meulen 2008), and one we return to in discussion.

Focusing on the space between the individual and the network, then, we are primarily interested here in the *process* of networking—following the call of Gheradi (2009) to shift the focus from the concept of community of practice (CoP) towards the practices of the community. In examining these practices, we would not and do not limit such acts of interpersonal relating to 'proactive attempts by individuals to develop and maintain personal and professional relationships with others for the purpose of mutual benefit in their work or career' (de Janasz and Forret 2008: 630). Although we are attentive to the impact of networks on individual and organisational effectiveness, we do not assume a priori that this is the sole purpose or predominant consequence of networks. In taking this approach, we hope to address the critique of Heebels et al (2013: 702) and others, who point to the neglect in organisation studies of 'the emotional aspects or the multiplex motives for the formation and maintenance of personal ties'. This draws attention to issues of ethics and instrumentality in networking, an activity which "contain(s) powerful moral understandings and personal commitments" (Bensaou et al. 2014: 53).

Our focus in this chapter therefore is explicitly on networking–that is, the actions of individuals to establish and maintain enduring relationships–understanding this as the process by which networks are created, supported and sustained. While our study encompasses the analysis of both formal and informal networking, given the predominance of the former in management research (especially in healthcare) we pay particular attention to the latter. In other words, we focus ideographically on the processual character of emergent networks and the motivations of the actors involved in their formation.

## Methodological Approach

This chapter reports findings from a qualitative (100+ interview and observation based) study of management networks within three healthcare organisations in the UK NHS. The organisations participating in the study included a general hospital (Acute Trust), a mental health and community-based organisation (Care Trust), and a hospital providing dedicated tertiary care (Specialist Trust). Within each organisation, managers were differentiated between three specific types: *clinical, functional* and *general. Clinical managers* had an active clinical component to their role and responsibilities, while *functional managers* occupied specialist but non-clinical positions (such as heads of finance, human resources, etc.). Between these extremes, *general managers* had operational positions with generic titles such as 'operations manager' or service manager' but which did not require specific professional or clinical backgrounds. Within each category, the managers had mid- to senior-level responsibilities and characteristically had at least one managerial layer above and below them. The research process involved qualitative inquiry of an interpretive and ethnographic nature, including a combination of interview- and observation-based methods. The research presented here focuses only on the themes relating to networks and network relationships.

Rather than identifying networks in advance, and exploring their nature, configuration and use, the approach adopted in this study was to ask individual practitioners themselves about their network relationships, emphasising a broad rather than a narrow scope of enquiry. In this way, the aim was to avoid the widespread assumption, particularly prevalent in certain literatures such as health management, that 'tight' (i.e. 'managed') networks are those most worthy of investigation (Ferlie et al. 2010). Similarly, for reasons set out above, the research does not adopt a sociometric approach to networks, which attempts to quantify and objectify network relationships by measuring the frequency and duration of contact (Conway 2014). Instead, it pays attention to the emotional intensity and intimacy of such ties (which is arguably closer to Granovetter's original work). The intention here is to understand the 'situated and contextual quality of relationships' (Anderson-Gough et al. 2006: 236) in terms of the significance and nature of networks and the specific practices of networking undertaken by our interviewees. We attempt to capture the varied and complex meanings of networking in order to highlight the richness of relationships often overlooked by research which seeks simply to quantify them or measure their effectiveness.

## Diversity of Networks Across Organisations and Groups

In all, 15 types of networks were identified. These were differentiated along a number of dimensions, such as: degree of coordination, strictures on membership, ways in which the network was formed, and its location within or across organisational boundaries (see Table 1).

With few exceptions, each of these categories contained a diverse set of networks. To take two examples, we found that *alumni networks*

**Table 1** Typology of networks

| Nature of network | Description |
|---|---|
| Academic/scientific | Links to universities, research or scientific bodies |
| Alumni | Connections made through participation in a specific training or educational programme which persist beyond end of programme |
| Peer/cohort | Relationships formed with others who joined this (or another) organisation at the same time |
| Commercial/3rd sector | Links to private sector organisations or charities |
| Elite | Connections to senior decision makers, within the trust/organisation or at a regional/national level |
| Functional specialist | Relationship or collectivities bound by a shared work specialism |
| Government | Relationships with individuals within regional or national government |
| Managerial | Relationships between groups of managers, including both occupational networks and more operational groups |
| Mentor | One-to-one relationships with a formal or informal mentor, typically but not necessarily outside the organisation |
| NHS | Connections to individuals in other NHS organisations, including Department of Health, SHAs/PCTs, GPs/CCGs, etc. |
| Operational/clinical | Day-to-day relationships typically formed through the day-to-day execution of responsibilities |
| Personal | Friendships, non-work relationships, family connections, etc. |
| Professional | Links with general or health-specific formal professional bodies, in accounting, HR, facilities, health and safety, etc. |
| Public sector | Non-governmental public connections, with for instance schools, legal bodies (e.g. coroners), prisons, armed forces, BBC |
| Political | Networks specifically cultivated to develop influence—typically diverse in composition, hence not captured by other categories |

ranged from the very formal (e.g. prescribed action learning sets) to the entirely informal (e.g. loose affiliations of friends who socialised), whereas *elite networks* might be described as highly instrumental (e.g. built on engineered introductions and self-promotion) or relatively organic (e.g. resulting from a shared interest or accidental social

**Table 2** Dimensions of networks

| | | |
|---|---|---|
| Structure | Formal | Informal |
| Co-ordination | Tight | Loose |
| Membership | Closed | Open |
| Formation | Instrumental | Organic |
| Position | Internal to organisation | External to organisation |

connections). Personal networks, however, were generally organic, informal, loose and external in scope, while most professional networks were closed and relatively formal. Nonetheless, the dimensions provided a useful means of differentiating networks, and also of identifying similarities between them—given that on the surface they were very different in composition and nature (see Table 2).

Differences also were evident between the organisations studied. So, for example, in the Care Trust managers referred most frequently to external networks, reflecting the multiple connections within this organisation between different primary, secondary and community health bodies. Conversely, fewer references to networks of any kind, internal or external, were made within the Acute Trust, reflecting the overall size of the organisation and perhaps the more functional and rigid organisational structure of a general hospital (which contrasted with the more fluid conditions of service delivery in the Care Trust). In terms of the patterns of networking emerging from the research, it was perhaps unsurprising to see the clinical and functional managers in our study relying most heavily upon their particular professional or medical/scientific networks. They appeared to enjoy connections to elite networks either through these associations or through representation of a professional area at board level. In some cases, this networking was clearly active and involved high levels of commitment—as in the case of medical directors. In others, it was more latent and more implicit—where respondents retained membership of a nursing body as a fall-back career, or where they drew upon their clinical experience to enhance their legitimacy in managing clinicians. While the background of some general managers enabled them to participate in clinical or professional networks, typically they would rely upon networks established through day-to-day operations, which were bound to individual organisations and necessarily less formal and enduring due to the disruptions brought about by recurrent organisational change. A large number of the general managers interviewed however spoke of the perceptible *absence* of supportive networks in their role, when compared to their clinical and functional peers, a point returned to below.

## Who Networks, and Why?

### Networking for Knowledge

The primary purpose of networking for almost all managers was to acquire or share knowledge. Widely discussed across all three trusts and all management groups, this was mentioned with particular regularity by managers with clinical backgrounds. There were, however, significant differences in how this was understood or practiced, a key distinction being that between passive and active networking for knowledge. Passive networking in this respect was largely related to (i) partaking in events, or membership of formal or informal groups, networks or associations; (ii) being broadly informed about new or potential changes in policy; (iii) scanning a community for new ideas which might be transferable; or (iv) learning lessons from failed initiatives elsewhere. We refer to this more passive activity as 'Peripheral Awareness', primarily to differentiate it from the more active networking for knowledge.

> The secret is always having the ability to look over the garden fence and see what's happening in somebody else's garden. Because that's the only way you learn. And (…) from all this variety, as I've said before, why reinvent the wheel, why do it? (Functional manager, Specialist Trust)

Managers discussed, in particular, the value of networks and networking in terms of providing a resource for the pursuit of intentional enquiries or searches for information in order to fix a particular challenge in everyday practice, i.e. problem-solving networks. Such targeted networking was typically related to networks based around a particular specialism, operational or clinical. In many cases, such networks were purposefully formed to facilitate such activities.

> The Clinical Leaders' network tends to start off with a sort of a general presentation and then you'll get into your area networks, so there'd be perhaps (Town A, B & C) might sit as a sort of subgroup within the network and then you'd bounce off your problems from your colleagues and sort of see whether you could learn anything from others experiences. (General manager, Acute Trust)

Less formal, structured problem-solving networks include the action learning sets established on many development programmes. Those formed during the NHS Graduate Management Training Scheme for instance were highlighted by a number of managers. They were foundational for building on the strong group relationships formed during extended training and induction programmes.

This knowledge sharing, then, is supported strongly by the establishment of trust, underpinned frequently by long-term personal relationships and affiliations outside of the day-to-day work environment. Although in principle networking for knowledge is the most instrumental and practical mode of networking, it could frequently have a complementary relationship with other, less pragmatic modes. This is an issue we return to below.

## Networking for Support

Networking for support represented the second most cited motive for forming and maintaining networks; the reliance on such relationships for emotional reassurance, personal validation, or consolation. The incidence of this theme was noteworthy, as it was mentioned by almost half of those interviewed. It was especially common in Care Trust, yet relatively rare in the Acute Trust. This substantial variation may result from the perceived importance and legitimacy of 'therapeutic discourses' in care settings, as against the relative formality of the culture at the Acute

Trust, where such discussions may be seen as inappropriate, and thus may not fully reflect the actual incidence of this form of networking. However, discussions of networking for support were complicated at times by the reluctance of some interviewees to define such relationships as a 'network'. Indeed, for some informants this seemed to attribute an inappropriate sense of instrumentality to such friendships.

Also striking was the importance attached to such networks. Managers frequently discussed how difficult it would be to survive in a pressurised and often emotionally challenging role without a strong support network. Such networking might include current or former colleagues, friends, family members or more formal and explicit arrangements with mentors, peers, members of action learning sets, etc.

> We meet weekly, we talk about what's going on or have a moan about something, but often it's helpful just to have a moan about something with someone that you're comfortable to do that, rather than it becoming winding you up (…) we bring each other back down at times. (Functional manager, Care Trust)

Descriptions of this form of networking ranged from the clearly emotional—as a safe place for 'venting' emotions or 'having a moan' outside of the work context, or as a relationship which enabled someone to remain 'grounded'—to the more functional—as a kind of 'informal coaching', or a place to get 'objective comment' on your decisions and actions. This distinction was not a clear cut one, however, which reinforces the importance of relational attributes such as trust and interpersonal understanding in enabling effective knowledge sharing or meaningful advice. Equally, some descriptions emphasised the performative benefits of this emotional support, in the sense of enhancing their own resilience and therefore their ability to do the job well, or stay in the job at all.

Often the importance of external networks—separate from the organisation or immediate working surroundings—was stressed, given the need for confidentiality and to maintain a professional bearing with work colleagues.

> No matter how well you've set your network up, there are occasions when you can feel quite isolated in a trust as big as this. And you can't imagine who you could go to and just actually say that without it escalating into something that's really taken out of all proportion. (General manager, Care Trust)

This aspect of networking tends frequently to be ignored or under-represented in research in this area, but is clearly one that a substantial number of managers interviewed found invaluable, given the increasing tensions and pressures of their everyday roles (McCann et al. 2008).

## Networking for Career

Networking in support of career advancement was discussed by just under one third of managers. For this form of networking, the need to be informed about new opportunities and openings coexisted with the perceived importance of being known by key decision-makers. Given the diversity of positions, organisations and career structures, it was noticeable that this was cited consistently across all three trusts and across all management groups. A number of managers also pointed to the emphasis placed upon encouraging this mode of networking by key management and leadership development programmes in the NHS.

> One of the big things they tell you pretty much on day one is that one of the main focuses on the Graduate Scheme is networking. We attended loads of events where there'd be the directors of finance there, chief execs, and it was always like you're encouraged to network. (Functional manager, Specialist Trust)

Networking for career development was practiced either collectively or individually. Collectively, career networking typically operated through membership of particular communities or participation at key events such as research conferences or senior training programmes, whereby a manager could raise her/his profile and establish a reputation while at the same time making personal connections with individuals. Individually, career networking ordinarily builds upon a kind of formal or informal mentorship arrangement. Several interviewees were quite open about the importance of approaching career networking tactically, to ensure mentoring connections were made with influential individuals and with a long-term career strategy in mind.

> I was very keen to come back to this organisation after the training scheme. And as a ploy, as a tactic in trying to do that, (I noted) my mentor whilst I was on the training scheme was X, who's now the acting Chief Exec here. And I kept my contacts from when I was working here previously… I think it's also about networking with the right people at the right time, and it's just picking your opportunities and just being a little bit cute about who you speak to and who you make your networks with. (General manager, Acute Trust)

Importantly, career networking has value not just for the individual but also for the group or organisation, in that some managers described how their strong networks enabled them to identify and attract higher quality recruits.

> You need a network, you can't function without a network (…) I've got a lot more from doing things and building up those networks. It's like the graduate trainees, I've had a lot who've ended up here, in years past, without even me actually applying, because they know that the training they'll get is the right training and they know that I'll look after them (…) If you look at it another way, and this sounds quite cold, I've got a free member of staff for three years, virtually, who is going to add value to the organisation (and) who, ultimately, could be a permanent member of staff. And that's just from spending a little time networking. (Functional manager, Acute Trust)

Overall, this practice was highly valued, despite deep ambivalence about it in some quarters and a widespread recognition among those who engaged in career networking that it required sophisticated interpersonal skills to enact successfully.

## Networking for Influence

The deliberate use of networking in order to secure some influence over a decision or behaviour in another organisational location is an especially instrumental conception of networking. This was discussed at length by a minority of respondents who emphasised it as important for themselves and their field of activity. This proved particularly so in Care Trust, possibly as several service areas overlapped with social care or other governmental agencies (e.g. forensic services), which meant that Care Trust services had more complex and fluid relationships with other organisations. It is also a possible consequence of the inherent political dimension of some of these service areas, such as the treatment of drug and alcohol addiction, which required the Care Trust to be more involved with public debate about the 'right way' to treat particularly vulnerable or socially excluded groups. Additionally, one could argue that while the deliberate pursuit of influence was mentioned by relatively few respondents, influence has a broader applicability to the activity of networking than was either consciously recognised or articulated in interviews. Networking for influence was typically undertaken deliberately, consciously and strategically.

> It's not just some kind of pleasurable experience, I engage with a network approach to management, because I think it gives you the best chances of delivering things. (General manager, Care Trust)

In terms of networking practices, a distinction could be made between networking based upon a reciprocal exchange of favours and a broader attempt to push or represent a particular agenda through links with senior management, key role-holders or influential external parties. One manager defined these as parallel activities, describing one part of his approach as building reciprocal favours (e.g. 'just scratching each other's backs') and the other as strategically representing a set of interests (e.g. 'having a cup of tea with the chief exec [and] making sure he doesn't forget the agenda here'). In each case, this involved deliberately maintaining a list of useful and influential contacts across a wide network. Some managers for example mentioned having 'a little secret map in my mind of who I think is sound around this place', or boasted of having 'the fullest black book of contacts of any of my peers'.

Effective networking for influence, then, relies partially upon a detailed personal understanding of organisations and relationships, a specific set of interpersonal skills to effectively build up influence and, crucially, time working in a particular field, as all involved describe the process of building up contacts as one which is lengthy and time consuming. Unlike career or knowledge networking, this practice was unreservedly described as deliberate, strategic and consciously instrumental.

## Multiplexity of Networking

It is important to note that, although these descriptions of networking were identifiably distinctive, in practice managers' networking were driven by a combination of motives. Indeed, the same activity resulted in a combination of outcomes which do not fit neatly into any one of the categories described above. So, for instance, managers described personal relationships outside of their organisation as valuable for support in times of stress, but also that these provided knowledge (in the form of advice) as well as reassurance or comfort. In this sense, we are examining 'multiplex' networking, understood as 'the extent to which social network ties involve different roles, exchanges and/or affiliations. Multiplexity involves a link between two actors in a network that consists of more than one kind of relationship' (Heebels et al. 2013: 704).

A number of networking complementarities appeared central in managers' accounts. Firstly, they identified a strong overlap between networking for support and for knowledge. What is striking here is not only the mutual confidence which is formed as colleagues become informal counsellors, but also how personal knowledge enables more informed and insightful advice to be offered. This is based on a deep understanding of each other's personalities and respective situations. Similarly, managers discussed the potential complementarity between networking for support and influence, again based on the establishment of a personal relationship of trust, explaining how for example 'doing a favour' for someone could provide an opening to ask for help in the future. A similar complementarity, between support and career networking, implicitly underpins many mentoring relationships, where it is difficult to draw line between a personal relationship of coaching and counselling and a more strategic and political relationship with a senior colleague initiated to raise profile and generate career opportunities. A more pragmatic complementarity would connect networking for knowledge and for influence. The organic continuity between these two activities was underpinned by an implied and established mutual interest. Similarly, a complementarity was often observed between networking for knowledge and for career progression, with the former being the overt motivation and the latter being an unspoken yet deliberate by-product of the relationship.

Overall, then, the motivations or indeed the eventual outcomes of networking are not necessarily discreet, deliberate or strategic. Managers engage in networking for a complex variety of reasons. Relationships change and often mature over time, and individuals often find the benefits of networking are wider than initially expected. Critically, though, there are various synergies between networking activities which encourage a broader conception of networking and its collective benefits, individually and organisationally.

## Challenges to Networking

Among these overlapping and interconnected motivations for networking, a number of issues were raised consistently as obstacles to forming effective networks. In particular, time pressure, competitive tensions and the practical challenge of building, managing and benefitting from networks represented the most substantial difficulties faced. The most consistently cited challenges to effective networking were time pressures and intensive work demands. The issue of work intensification and stress was raised as a theme by over two thirds of those interviewed, and often discussed at length. The impact of substantial and often increasing pressures of work was experienced when managers attempted to engage in less formal networking, such as establishing a relationship with a mentor, or maintaining learning sets after the completion of a training programme.

> We had learning sets with people from similar roles, backgrounds, etc., which I found really, really useful. The minute that programme finished and we tried to carry those on, it lasted about a month. And everybody got subsumed again into their daily grind. (…) I make a commitment that I'm going to start doing that again. And then the next time I look up, it's been 6 months and I've just been sat in the office and never left the hospital. And it's terrible; really terrible how that happens. We just all get totally consumed by our individual organisation's problems. (General manager, Acute Trust)

More formal networks, such as practice-related or professional associations, could also have their effectiveness undermined by the difficulty in maintaining active engagement levels.

> There is the Allied Health Professional network but it's not always that well attended. Everybody is under such huge pressure now, there is just no time to do anything. (General manager, Acute Trust)

The potential for knowledge exchange through external networking was most clearly impeded by the presence of competitive tensions between trusts. This obstacle was affirmed by a number of managers, but particularly among general and functional managers and most frequently in Acute Trust and Care Trust. The conditions described by managers illustrated a 'normalized' work intensity (McCann et al. 2008), and the 'titration' of information through competitive relations are shaped by an organisational and institutional context which limits the extent to which individuals can make and sustain connections with others outside their immediate operational horizon, and also limits the gains to be made from those connections, in terms of sharing, supporting, advancing and influencing.

## Networking in Context

Finally, we locate managers' motives, experiences and views of networking in the wider context of health and care management. All managers worked in organisations attempting to find a 'third way' between markets and hierarchies in healthcare, often through participation in more formal or mandated networks. Arguably these produce the worst of both worlds (Kirkpatrick 1999), with complex, hierarchical and routinised bureaucracies, highly regulated by targets and under considerable public scrutiny, being also subject to the unpredictable dynamics of 'the market'. The resulting combination of financial insecurity, managerialist regulation and professional embeddedness can create risk averse organisations, bounded and siloed and with little ability to generate or capitalise on the 'interstices' of collaborative networks and communities (Fox 2000; Swan et al. 2002). The individual and their 'will' to network, therefore is situated within an organisational context which is divided by conflicting demands, which simultaneously creates ambivalence.

Many of managers were committed and self-conscious networkers able and willing to speak at length about their networking strategies and practices, and often able to identify the benefits of networking for their own effectiveness and for their organisation. As noted, many had been effectively socialised as 'networked managers' (de Janasz and Forret 2008), through training programmes, advice and encouragement from leaders and mentors, and through membership of professional and clinical associations and groups.

Others, however, displayed an acute sensitivity to suggestions that networking behaviour was in some sense inauthentic, instrumental or even manipulative. Several managers expressed deep reservations about the perceived need to network, or discomfort engaging with what they understood as self-promotional or inauthentic behaviour. Reflecting this sensitivity, several managers were at pains to reject the implication that they had benefitted from networking, or that their own networking itself was intentional or strategic.

The challenge was often to engage in this activity 'organically' rather than 'instrumentally', and thus avoid the appearance of manipulative or self-serving behaviour. However, the line between 'instrumental' and 'organic' networking is often difficult to draw, in part because 'instrumental' networking is only effective if it is presented as 'organic' networking. Frequently this fails when the instrumental intent in forming a relationship is made explicit. The most effective networked managers therefore presented themselves as skilled social performers who could network deliberately and strategically with a focus on a goal, while ensuring that this appeared natural. Others, however, expressed substantial unease with the pressure placed upon them to network and the consequences of this in terms of integrity and authenticity in the workplace.

## Conclusions

Formal or mandated networks, much like CoPs, have enjoyed considerable popularity in the management literature and particularly so within healthcare contexts (Kirkpatrick 1999; Ferlie et al. 2010). In developing a decentred perspective on networks (Bevir 2013) our chapter shifts the focus away from the preoccupation with creating and managing formal networks as advocated in policy narratives, to consider instead the informal relationships and infrequent interactions (Agterberg et al. 2010) that comprise the everyday practices of networking within and between health and care organisations. In doing so, we focus less on the structure of networks and more on the situated meanings and activities of networking itself, recognising that research must address 'both an actor's social network (noun) and an actor's social networking (verb)' (Bensaou et al. 2014: 30). In doing so, we identify a range of challenges to both formal and informal networking (which serve to shape, sustain and limit the nature and incidence of relationships).

We argue that informal networking involves analysing a *multiplex* set of motives (Grabher and Ibert 2006; Heebels et al. 2013) that go beyond the desire to share and access knowledge for professional and career development. We note in particular how support and influence also feature strongly in such arrangements. Importantly, we identify various synergies between networking activities which encourage a broader conception of networking and its collective benefits, individually and organisationally. A narrow focus on formal networks and communities of practice, or indeed concentrating on deliberate and instrumental networking practices, can therefore prevent access to the richness of relationship-building and human interaction of which networking forms a part.

We note the wider perceived pressures to network in this context—the vast majority of managers saw networking as something they needed to do, and were strongly encouraged to do. However, only a small sub-set were able to overcome the constraints shaping the experience of networking in healthcare—whether due to the time and stability within organisations required for network development and maintenance, or due to competitive tensions that reinforced the isolation of individual organisations and promoted the belief that healthcare knowledge was highly situated and 'inimitable' (Crilly et al. 2013). This could tend to wed general managers to local operational demands and deny the opportunities to forge proactive, forward-looking links with other organisations. Moreover, this represents a significant problem in the context of current challenges facing managers i.e. to create radical efficiencies in healthcare which require strategic and transformational change.

At the same time, recognising the multiplexity of meanings and motives brings into sharp focus the tension between instrumentality and authenticity when networking. Multiplexity presents a deep challenge to attempts to establish "a clear conceptual distinction between instrumental networking driven by individual agency versus spontaneous networking reflecting the constraints and opportunities of the social structure" (Casciaro et al. 2014: 726). The moral dimension to networking, neglected in much of the more functional research in this area, is palpable to several of our respondents, and even the enthusiastic and committed networkers appear sensitive to the 'taint' of instrumentalism, if only insofar as this risked undermining the effectiveness of their networking activities (Anderson-Gough et al. 2006).

In sum, there is clearly perceived value for managers in networks of interaction which extend beyond the immediate demands of work. Indeed, for some clinical and functional groups, such networks are crucial to professional and career development. For others they also have value—particularly for gaining knowledge and support. However, a focus on formal networks for knowledge mobilisation and utilization is beset with problems. These often stem from the multiplex set of meanings and motivations associated with networking. Developing networks may therefore be desirable and even necessary, but a fuller engagement with the meanings and practices of networking is essential to address not only the feasibility of networking but also the moral commitments and challenges to integrity posed by networking.

## References


6 P, Goodwin, N., Peck, E., et al. (2006). *Managing networks of twenty first century organisations*. Basingstoke: Palgrave Macmillan.

Addicott, R., McGivern, G., & Ferlie, E. (2007). The distortion of a managerial technique? The case of clinical networks in UK health care. *British Journal of Management, 18*, 93–105.

Agterberg, M., Van Den Hooff, B., Huysman, M., & Soekijad, M. (2010). Keeping the wheels turning: The dynamics of managing networks of practice. *Journal of Management Studies, 47*, 85–108.

Anderson-Gough, F., Grey, C., & Robson, K. (2006). Professionals, networking and the networked professional. *Research in the Sociology of Organizations, 24*, 231–256.

Bate, P., & Robert, G. (2002). Knowledge management and communities of practice in the private sector: Lessons for modernizing the national health service in England and Wales. *Public Administration, 80*, 643–663.

Bensaou, B. M., Galunic, C., & Jonczyk-Sédès, C. (2014). Players and purists: Networking strategies and agency of service professionals. *Organization Science, 25*, 29–56.

Bevir, M. (2013). *A theory of governance*. Berkeley: University of California Press.

Bott, E. (1955). Urban families: Conjugal roles and social networks. *Human Relations, 8*(4), 345–384. https://doi.org/10.1177/001872675500800401.

Brown, J., & Duguid, P. (2000). *The social life of information*. Boston, MA: Harvard Business School Press.

Buchanan, D. A., Addicott, R., Fitzgerald, L., Ferlie, E., & Baeza, J. I. (2007). Nobody in charge: Distributed change agency in healthcare. *Human Relations, 60*, 1065–1090.

Burgess, N., & Currie, G. (2013). The knowledge brokering role of the hybrid middle level manager: The case of healthcare. *British Journal of Management, 24*, S132–S142.

Burt, R. (2005). *Brokerage and closure*. Oxford: Oxford University Press.

Casciaro, T., Gino, F., & Kouchaki, M. (2014). The contaminating effects of building instrumental ties: How networking can make us feel dirty. *Administrative Science Quarterly, 59*, 705–735.

Castells, M. (1996). *The rise of the network society: Vol 1. The information age.* Oxford: Blackwell.

Child, J. (1972). Organizational structure, environment and performance: The role of strategic choice. *Sociology, 8,* 1–22.

Coleman, J. (1988). Social capital in the creation of human capital. *American Journal of Sociology, 94,* S95–S120.

Contu, A., & Willmott, H. (2000). Comment on Wenger and Yanow. Knowing in practice: A 'delicate flower' in the organizational learning field. *Organization, 7,* 269–276.

Conway, S. (2014). A cautionary note on data inputs and visual outputs in social network analysis. *British Journal of Management, 25,* 102–117.

Crilly, T., Jashapara, A., Trenholm, S., Peckham, A., Currie, G., & Ferlie, E. (2013). *Knowledge mobilisation in healthcare organisations: Synthesising the evidence and theory using perspectives of organisational form, resource based view of the firm and critical theory.* NIHR Service Delivery and Organisation Programme.

Currie, G., Finn, R., & Martin, G. (2009). Professional competition and modernizing the clinical workforce in the NHS. *Work, Employment & Society, 23,* 267–284.

Currie, G., Finn, R., & Martin, G. (2010). Role transition and the interaction of relational and social identity: New nursing roles in the English NHS. *Organization Studies, 31,* 941–961.

Currie, G., & Procter, S. (2005). The antecedents of middle managers' strategic contribution: The case of a professional bureaucracy. *Journal of Management Studies, 42,* 1325–1356.

Currie, G., & White, L. (2012). Inter-professional barriers and knowledge brokering in an organizational context: The case of healthcare. *Organization Studies, 33,* 1333–1361.

de Janasz, S., & Forret, M. (2008). Learning the art of networking: A critical skill for enhancing social capital and career success. *Journal of Management Education, 35,* 629–650.

Faulconbridge, J. (2007). Relational networks of knowledge production in transnational law firms. *Geoforum, 38,* 925–940.

Ferlie, E., Fitzgerald, L., McGivern, G., Dopson, S., & Exworthy, M. (2010). *Networks in health care: A comparative study of their management, impact and performance.* London: HMSO.

Ferlie, E., Fitzgerald, L., Wood, M., & Hawkins, C. (2005). The nonspread of innovations: The mediating role of professionals. *Academy of Management Journal, 48,* 117–134.

Fox, S. (2000). Communities of practice, Foucault and actor-network theory. *Journal of Management Studies, 37,* 853–867.
Fulop, N., Walters, R., & Spurgeon, P. (2012). Implementing changes to hospital services: Factors influencing the process and 'results' of reconfiguration. *Health Policy, 104,* 128–135.
Gheradi, S. (2009). Community of practice or practices of a community? In S. Armstrong & C. Fukami (Eds.), *Handbook of management learning, education and development* (pp. 514–530). London: Sage.
Grabher, G., & Ibert, O. (2006). Bad company? The ambiguity of personal knowledge networks. *Journal of Economic Geography, 6,* 251–271.
Granovetter, M. (1973). The strength of weak ties. *The American Journal of Sociology, 78,* 1360–1380.
Heebels, B., Atzema, O., & van Aalst, I. (2013). Social networks and cultural mediators: The multiplexity of personal ties in publishing. *Industry and Innovation, 20,* 701–718.
Hey, V. (2005). The contrasting social logics of sociality and survival. *Sociology, 39,* 855–872.
Kennedy, P. (2004). Making global society: Friendship networks among transnational professionals in the building design industry. *Global Networks, 4,* 157–179.
Kirkpatrick, I. (1999). Markets, bureaucracy and public management: The worst of both worlds? Public services without markets or bureaucracy. *Public Money & Management, 19,* 7–14.
Lave, J., & Wenger, E. (1991). *Situated learning: Legitimate peripheral participation.* Cambridge: Cambridge University Press.
Lawrence, P., & Lorsch, J. (1967). *Organization and environment.* Cambridge, MA: Harvard University Press.
Marchington, M., Willmott, H., Rubery, J., & Grimshaw, D. (2005). *Fragmenting work: Blurring organizational boundaries and disordering hierarchies.* Oxford: Oxford University Press.
McCann, L., Morris, J., & Hassard, J. (2008). Normalized intensity: The new labour process of middle management. *Journal of Management Studies, 45,* 343–371.
McKee, M., Healy, J., Edwards, N., et al. (2002). Pressures for change. In M. McKee & J. Healy (Eds.), *Hospitals in a changing Europe* (pp. 36–58). Buckingham: Open University Press.
Miles, R., & Snow, C. (1986). Network organizations: New concepts for new forms. *California Management Review, 28,* 62–73.

Nahapiet, J., & Ghoshal, S. (1998). Social capital, intellectual capital, and the organizational advantage. *Academy of Management Review, 23,* 242–266.
Noordegraaf, M. (2011). Risky business: How professionals and professional fields (must) deal with organizational issues. *Organization Studies, 32,* 1349–1371.
Noordegraaf, M., & Van Der Meulen, M. (2008). Professional power play: Organizing management in health care. *Public Administration, 86,* 1055–1069.
Perrow, C. (1972). *Complex organizations.* New York: McGraw Hill.
Powell, W. (1990). Neither market nor hierarchy: Network forms of organization. *Research in Organizational Behavior, 12,* 295–336.
Putnam, R. (2001). *Bowling alone: The collapse and revival of American community.* New York, NY: Simon & Schuster.
Salancik, G. (1995). Wanted: A good network theory of organization. *Administrative Science Quarterly, 40,* 345–349.
Swan, J., Scarbrough, H., & Robertson, M. (2002). The construction of 'communities of practice' in the management of innovation. *Management Learning, 33,* 477–496.
Tlili, A., & Obsiye, M. (2014). What is Coleman's social capital the name of? A critique of a not very social capital. *Critical Sociology, 40,* 551–574.
Vorley, T., Mould, O., & Courtney, R. (2012). My networking is not working! Conceptualizing the latent and dysfunctional dimensions of the network paradigm. *Economic Geography, 88,* 77–96.
Waring, J., Bishop, S., & Roe, B. (2017). Network contra network: The gap between policy and practice in the organisation of major trauma care. In M. Bevir & J. Waring (Eds.), *Decentring health policy: Learning from British experiences in healthcare governance.* London: Routledge.
Wenger, E. (1998). *Communities of practice: Learning, meaning, and identity.* Cambridge, UK: Cambridge University Press.

# Analysing the Micro Implementation of Health Care Reforms: A Decentred Approach

Juan I. Baeza, Alec Fraser, and Annette Boaz

## Introduction

The network governance narrative of public management reform sponsored by post New Public Management (NPM) authors (Pollitt and Bouckaert 2011; Christensen and Lsgreid 2007) promoted more integrated and systemic approaches to the delivery of public services designed to address the fragmenting effects of earlier NPM reforms (Ferlie et al. 2016). The different streams of governance have created

J. I. Baeza (✉)
King's Business School, King's College London, London, UK
e-mail: juan.baeza@kcl.ac.uk

A. Fraser
London School of Hygiene and Tropical Medicine, University of London, London, UK

A. Boaz
St. George's, University of London & Kingston University, London, UK


M. Bevir and J. Waring (eds.), *Decentring Health and Care Networks*, Organizational Behaviour in Healthcare, https://doi.org/10.1007/978-3-030-40889-3_3

what Jones (2018) terms a complex sedimented governance architecture. While the NPM approach emphasises managerial authority and top-down implementation, network governance works through collaboration and partnerships. In this binary theoretical field, the decentred theory of governance offers a different perspective that focuses on how 'people see the world' (Bevir and Rhodes 2001). In this paper we use a bottom-up decentred lens to understand how local actors perceive reforms and use their agency to make sense of the changes in the delivery of stroke services.

The decentred theory highlights the importance of key actors' beliefs and traditions, crucial aspects that are rarely analysed. It does not seek to 'tame an otherwise chaotic picture of multiple actors, creating a contingent pattern of rule through their conflicting actions', instead it embraces this messy experience and uses it to explain how governance occurs in this disordered reality (Bevir and Richards 2009). Bevir and Richards (2009) see everyday practices arising from situated agents whose beliefs and actions are informed by traditions and that these traditions can be detected as habits and practices. The decentred approach sees 'practices' as the sets of actions pursued by actors, which are influenced by their beliefs. Within organisations, these practices come to be viewed as 'traditions'; the accepted ways of doing things. It is from these traditions that situated agents select their broad beliefs concerning the appropriateness of certain actions. In turn, these beliefs may change when confronted by 'dilemmas'. A dilemma can be defined as an idea which—if it stands in contradiction to another established belief, practice, or tradition—poses a problem for individuals or groups. According to this approach such dilemmas can only be resolved by either accommodating or discarding the new idea (Bevir and Rhodes 2007; Geddes 2014). We add to Bevir's approach by exploring the roles of context, audit and leadership at the micro level.

We consider the decentred approach as particularly well suited to analysing and explaining the micro implementation of a health care reform. The aim of this chapter is to use this perspective to better understand how a major health care reform was implemented 'on the ground' in two contrasting National Health Service (NHS) Foundation Trusts. Foundation Trusts are semi-autonomous hospitals within the

National Health Service (NHS) in England that have various managerial and financial freedoms and relative independence from the Government's Department of Health and Social Care. Through two qualitative case studies we investigated the implementation of reforms to NHS stroke services that began in 2007 in England, which were the result of a culmination of a longer effort from within the sub-specialism of stroke. The stroke reforms can be characterised as a 'disruptive innovation' in that it challenges existing stakeholders (commissioners, providers, and other interested parties) to rethink their current practices through the introduction of new ideas. These potential challenges to the prevailing arrangements, may conflict with the existing beliefs and traditions of local actors. This requires us analytically to identify the dilemmas (both operational and clinical) and existing traditions (as faced by the different actors but principally, clinicians) and the situated agency of these individuals within their organisations respectively. A decentred approach to governance (Bevir and Rhodes 2007; Bevir and Richards 2009) allows us to highlight the importance of situated agency and local traditions in the face of such dilemmas (Fraser et al. 2019).

Through our study, we want to prompt new thinking around the decentred concept of 'dilemmas'. Can dilemmas only result in intractable tensions between two sets of beliefs, practices and traditions that individuals hold and then must resolve? Our findings offer an empirical base on which to build on Geddes (2014) call for "a more comprehensive articulation of the concept of 'dilemma'." However, unlike Geddes whose focus is on the macro political level, we examine the micro level of policy implementation. Before we go on to explain our methods, we provide a contextual summary of how stroke care has been transformed in the past decade or so.

## Developing Stroke as a Specialty

Globally, stroke (referred to as apoplexy until the middle of the twentieth century) has been a leading cause of death and disability for many years (Johnston et al. 2009). The disease predominantly affects the elderly and historically there has been a lack of effective treatments (Pound et al. 1997). Drawing on Foucault's (1973) work on the 'spatialisation' of disease, Daneski et al. (2010) give a detailed history of the treatment of apoplexy and stroke, highlighting in particular, the different ways this disease has been conceptualized over time, the complexities around different types of stoke (ischemic and haemorrhagic) and its development as a condition dealt with by geriatricians through the twentieth century. It is only over the last 30 years, through the establishment of a distinctive body of knowledge and the accumulation of evidence of treatment and effectiveness that stroke medicine has become an important clinical specialism in its own right. Two significant evidence-based developments have been notable in the fashioning of modern stroke care from the late twentieth century. The first is essentially organisational—the development of specialised Stroke Units (SUs) and Hyper-Acute Stroke Units (HASUs), where stroke patients receive specialised multidisciplinary care (first in a HASU and then ongoig treatment and rehabilitation in an SU) (Stroke Unit Triallists' Collaboration 2007) rather than on general medical or care of the elderly wards. The second, is diagnostic and linked to the proven effectiveness of thrombolysis—a drug that offers a radical improvement in outcomes for certain stroke types (NINDS 1995). This international best-practice was translated into NHS policy through the National Stroke Strategy launched in 2007 (Department of Health). This transformation around the medical discourses of stroke was part of an international trend over the last two or three decades (Baeza et al. 2016) leading to stroke being categorised as 'a preventable and treatable disease' (RCP 2008) with new pathways for stroke patients inscribed in government policy over the past decade in the English NHS (Department of Health 2007). These developments posed complex organisational challenges for individual hospitals, clinicians and strategic level managers across England and Wales. Essentially the stroke reforms focused on the maxim of 'time is brain', resulting in stroke being regarded as an emergency and not an elective condition (Department of Health 2007). People with a suspected stroke should be immediately transferred to a hospital providing hyperacute services throughout the day and night—this includes expert clinical assessment, rapid imaging and the ability to deliver thrombolysis. They should receive an early multidisciplinary assessment and have prompt access to a high-quality stroke unit

(Department of Health 2007). Regional strategic stroke plans were rolled out in different locations from 2008, influenced by the Royal College of Physicians (RCP) and guidance from the National Institute for Health and Care Excellence (NICE). By 2008 the transformation of stroke care was such that the RCP and NICE stated that:

> Over the last two decades, a growing body of evidence *has overturned the traditional perception* that stroke is simply a consequence of aging which inevitably results in death or severe disability. (NICE 2008, emphasis added)

It is also important to stress that the proposed stroke service changes were implemented in full, on time and faced very little opposition from the relevant stakeholder institutions, clinicians or the wider public, this is unusual, marking the case as a 'positive outlier' (Flyvbjerg 2006; Fraser et al. 2017). The reforms enjoyed broad political and popular support (Boseley 2014). A number of studies have explored local developments linked to the strategic drivers of the 2007 national directives (see Fulop et al. 2015; Turner et al. 2016; Fraser et al. 2017; Fraser et al. 2019). The external forces of organisational (SUs) and technological (thrombolysis) innovations have prompted large change in the treatment of stroke, which has overturned the *traditional perception* of stroke that had been the norm. These innovations have produced potential dilemmas, and it is these that we want to examine at the micro level through two case studies whose methods we describe below.

## Our Study

As part of a European Commission seventh framework funding programme, a comparative study examined the implementation of evidence into practice in stroke services in England (2 hospital sites) Sweden (2 hospital sites) and Poland (1 hospital site). This multiple case study approach (Yin 2003) enabled us to develop credible case and cross case analysis to establish the internal consistency of the information gathered and use this analysis to develop theoretical constructs from the data (Eisenhardt 1989; Eisenhardt and Graebner 2007). Our aim was to collect rich descriptions about their perspectives of evidence-based practice and the stroke care reforms. This chapter only uses the data from the two English case studies in order to focus on divergence at the micro level. The two English sites differed in terms of urbanity; patient demography; influence and existence of competing hospitals; difficulties in attracting and retaining skilled staff; and differences in community care arrangements.

Informants were purposively sampled to represent the different managerial and professional groups involved in delivering stroke care. The purposive sample included a range of both clinical and managerial staff from the hospital based SU, emergency medicine, radiology, ambulance service, community rehabilitation services, including physiotherapists, occupational therapists, speech & language therapists, dieticians and psychologists, commissioners of services and GPs. A total of 45 interviews were carried out in these two case studies. Below we provide brief profiles of the two English case study sites.

## Case Study 1 (CS1)

This is a district general hospital in a non-metropolitan region which serves a population of 230,000 (with pockets of deprivation) and a staff of 3300. The hospital was established in 1981, has had foundation trust (FT) status since 2006 and is affiliated with the local medical school. It is in an unfashionable location and is less prestigious than other specialist hospitals that are in 'more attractive' areas of the region, however, these are too distant to compete in terms of stroke patients. On a macro level, the 2007 National Stroke Strategy provided a push for improvements in the delivery of stroke services, and at a meso level, the host commissioner has invested heavily in improving the hospital's stroke services.

## Case Study 2 (CS2)

This is an outer London teaching hospital, serving a population of 500,000 with a staff of 4000. The hospital's SU has been upgraded to a large combined hyper acute stroke unit and SU since 2008. Prior to this, the hospital had a comparably poorly staffed, non-exclusive 'proto-stroke unit' with 23 beds, often occupied by non-stroke patients, which meant that many stroke patients never made it to the SU until many days post-stroke. The hospital had to invest very heavily and rapidly in terms of medical and radiological resources as part of the London stroke plan to arrive at a point at which the minimum standards were achieved—more so than other, better established sites.

## Findings

The stroke reforms and the subsequent reconfiguration of stroke services resulted in a series of dilemmas that we explored in our two case studies. We followed the decentred approach to reanalyse these data and three important themes emerged that we develop below.

### The Importance of Context in Shaping Beliefs and Traditions

Contextual factors are important in shaping individual beliefs and traditions and so these need to be considered when we examine how a dilemma is dealt with by individuals. Here we consider the stroke reforms as a potential dilemma that could cause problems but also present opportunities that were dependent on contextual factors, which were very different in the two case studies.

The context for CS1 was of a hospital that was perceived as a poor performer in stroke care by the local service commissioner, whose medical director provided a damning assessment:

> *They weren't doing the right things, and the things they were doing, they weren't all doing right.* (Medical Director of the local service commissioners; CS1)

This hospital's location was also important, it was geographically isolated which impacted negatively upon its ability to recruit good staff, which was cited as a contributing factor to its historical poor performance:

> *We have huge difficulty recruiting, because we're on the edge of the world, you see.* [...] *half the catchment area that you would normally have people from, is sea here. So, unless there's oil rig workers that want to come and help us, we're stuck.* (Nurse consultant, CS1)

A context of historical poor performance and geographical isolation therefore shaped the local actors' beliefs and traditions and this has had an influence on how they responded to the perceived dilemmas to change their established way of working and improve the delivery of stroke care.

The context for actors in CS2 was quite different as the hospital saw itself in a strong strategic position as a result of the 2008 London Stroke Plan, which reconfigured stroke services in ways that favoured outer-London hospitals like this one. Winning the bid to have a HASU was perceived as vital for this hospital as it would enable it to gain more resources not only for stroke services but for the hospital as a whole. However, to achieve this, it would have to switch from its traditional management approach that was predominately operational to a new more strategic one. There was a recognition that changing the prevailing management traditions needed outside, specialist, strategic management expertise to develop a succesful HASU bid. The management consultant who was bought in explained the change in management that was needed:

> [M]*ost Trusts are heavily operational. They're not - they don't tend to be very strategic because it's all about the crisis today and next week... And what I was trying to say was, 'Look, you know, things are not going to be as they always were. They're going to move – special stuff is going to move to tertiary centres... So that's a key element to your strategy which they hadn't really been thinking about...* [A]*nd you get a kind of critical mass of those kind of services* [e.g. stroke]. *And then you become the default* [hospital for other services]. (Independent Management Consultant; CS2)

It is important to highlight the role of the regional stroke networks as a contextual factor, as a dominant theme for CS2 much more than in CS1. These provide a regional network for supporting regional innovation and improvement through supporting high-level strategic planning and sharing of best practice. It is also the case that the extent of the local reforms was much more radical in CS2 (because of its London location) than in CS1. This may be linked to the differences in demographic and geographical challenges faced in the two sites. In CS2 the regional stroke networks were integral, for example, in working with senior strategic managers around decisions related to not only the upgrade of existing services to deliver better stroke care through HASU provision—but also the downgrading and closure of some existing units (Fulop et al. 2015; Turner et al. 2016; Fraser et al. 2017). Deciding how many HASUs would be needed in CS2 and where they should be located provoked significant dilemmas for members of both the formal networks alongside other interested actors. This 'disruptive innovation' was skilfully managed in CS2 and provided an opportunity for a radical redesign, not only of how best to deliver stroke care to the regional population, but also a significant break from past models of stroke care as the disease was effectively redefined as a regional concern as opposed to an institutional concern (Fraser et al. 2017). Winning the HASU bid would positively change things for this hospital, thereby creating a new situation that can produce opportunities and problems. This might not fit exactly with the decentred concept of a dilemma but nonetheless it creates an interesting new reality that impacts on local actors, which produces positive and/or negative outcomes depending on the context. Another significant contextual aspect of the stroke reforms was the heavy use of audit, which we explore in the next section.

## The Role of Audit in Shaping Attitudes and Behaviour

Checking and inspection in the form of audit is often resisted by health professionals who tend to desire freedom of practice (Foster and Wilding 2000). However, our study suggests the audit regime ushered in by the stroke reforms was mainly welcomed by senior clinicians. Despite the pressure placed upon her, the senior stroke nurse informant in CS2 suggested that the new audit culture around stroke services had productive value for her as a manager because without it, '*things would slide and slip*'. This perspective chimes with Idedema and Rhodes'

(2010) idea of surveillance as an "ethic of care for self and other". Whilst the senior stroke nurse clearly disliked some elements of audit and the pressure which it placed upon her, at the same time she was very willing to embrace it in order to achieve the mandated goals of the new model of stroke care.

> *It's, first and foremost I think it's the patient care and safety. And also, they are standards that are set within the stroke network which have to be met. So according to these standards we are also actually being assessed according to the evidence that has been given that – so if you don't meet, if you don't practice evidence-based treatments, you're bound to fail on your standards, so it brings down the whole, the Trust as a whole. So, I think those are the motivations.* (HASU coordinator and nurse; CS2)

Networks were central in CS2 to the establishment and embedding of new audit practices and the pursuit of standardisation in stroke care. Networks encouraged competition through transparency alongside broader collaboration and emphasised the productive potential of disciplinary power (Foucault 1973; Martin et al. 2013). The networks encouraged an organisational focus of audit (as opposed to a focus on individuals or clinical teams). Because the networks were collaborations between professionals and managers, they drew on both viewpoints, and also, they were considered to be locally rather than externally constituted and hence had high levels of legitimacy.

A senior nursing colleague in CS2 agreed that despite being critical of elements of the 'bloated' audit regime, it is necessary because it 'pushes' them to improve care. The disciplined and pressurised nature of increased surveillance can be channelled in productive ways by senior clinicians in order to improve clinical practice. This is particularly so with respect to nursing, which was seen as a problem in this trust, a problem that a strict surveillance apparatus can address. These data consistently showed how respondents in this hospital highlighted the ways in which the external audit demands allowed them to monitor and govern the competence of the nursing staff locally, illustrating the strength and enduring nature of hierarchical governance, as well as the perhaps unexpected welcoming of an audit regime by health professionals.

For CS1 the new strengthened audit regime was also welcomed but for different reasons, it bought the prospect of more resources to tackle their historical under achievement in stroke care:

> *Yes, I mean we, our Sentinel audit* [audit of stroke service performance] *is never good and it hasn't been historically, because we've not had the right, you know, we've not had the right resources in place, we've not had the ward in the right area, enough beds. So, I'd be really interested to see what happens.* (Matron; CS1)

The role of national guidelines was cited as significant in CS1, and the support of the local service commissioner was also essential in terms of funding. There seemed to be enough capacity within the stroke service to meet the government targets for patients to be treated on an SU, indicating that new ways of doing things (ideas) can become traditions if there is a supportive environment (resources). When it came to why evidence-based practice and audit performance might be important to institutions, economic reasons were frequently cited:

> *Well obviously there will be quality issues, which are similar to what I would look at on a personal level. But also obviously there are financial drivers as well,* [...], *obviously, PCT* [local service commissioners] *who are providing a lot of our funding and stuff, you know, they will want to be seeing that we are giving best to our patients* [...] *But that obviously has an impact on the Trust at how much revenue that is bringing in, as to whether we don't get full payment if we're dropping below a level and then there are certain sort of carrots dangled if you meet certain extra criteria, that there is extra monies available, so obviously that's very important to the Trust as an organisation.* (Senior sister SU; CS1)

There are a number of carrots and sticks that add credibility to the new governance regimes brought in by the stroke reforms and finally, the implicit idea that failure could '*bring down the Trust*' in some way, adds a further pressure to conform or more accurately a pressure on senior managers to achieve conformity for the sake of the hospital as a whole. Somewhat paradoxically, these new contextual pressures can also be seen as enabling the clinical managers to use the new 'dilemma', in the shape of the stroke reforms, to motivate and/or demand staff to change their beliefs and practices.

The new context of digitally delivered and data heavy requirements of audit led to a performative disciplinary framework (Spicer et al. 2009) centred on professional reflexive action as this nurse manager explains:

> *It's our professionalism and we also need to feed back to the Department of Health the things we're actually doing. So, we're actually achieving governance within our own unit. We're actually monitoring ourselves, we're actually achieving targets, and we're quite open if we're not achieving, and what we actually do to change. You can have eight very good weeks or something and then very bad week. So, what happened in that bad week? How do we tackle that week? How we are doing and prove what we're doing and it's about developing ourselves.* (Ward manager and nurse; CS2)

The stroke reforms, with their 'audit heavy' aspects of practice also managed to disrupt and challenge the previous beliefs and traditions of professional autonomy. Professional autonomy is now reframed as the 'freedom' to provide excellent treatment:

> *I think people will talk to you about, you know, are you allowed to have autonomy to do things badly? And that's ultimately the bottom line, is do you allow people to give suboptimal treatment? And I think what we've established is, no you're not allowed to give suboptimal treatment.* (Doctor; CS2)

This is an interesting quote because it presents the view of a senior consultant highlighting the problems with previous traditional beliefs of clinical autonomy. Essentially, if autonomy means freedom to deviate from the new agreed way of delivering stroke care, then such autonomy has become unacceptable and so this belief needs to be changed and recast in the new reality.

The issue of this new autonomy was illustrated by another doctor in the hospital who felt that the power of the stroke reforms was rooted in the fact that they chimed with his longstanding clinical beliefs and traditions, as opposed to other regulations that challenged them, again the stroke reform dilemmas were producing positive organisational and individual outcomes:

> [I]*n some ways* [I feel my autonomy is] *augmented* [by the stroke reforms], *because I have the authority of the Trust to basically drive through things that I feel are urgent, urgently. So, I suppose if you didn't agree with it, I suppose my autonomy is threatened by the four hour* [A and E target] *wait, but it's probably not threatened by* [the stroke reforms], *but that's because* ***this aligns with our clinical priorities, whereas the other thing doesn't.*** (Doctor; CS2) (emphasis added)

This was also the case in CS1, with the Early Stroke Discharge (ESD) initiative that this therapist describes as a positive innovation:

> *It's* [ESD] *coming from on high, I guess, inasmuch as it's part of the accelerated stroke improvement programme from the Department of Health downwards, and so I guess it's come from on high. But obviously the clinicians on the ground have always known that the patients would benefit from rehab* [rehabilitation] *in their own home, rather than in the hospital.* (Senior lead of therapies; CS1)

These data illustrate how traditions and beliefs can be successfully challenged and reshaped if the proposed modification fits with actors' individual and professional longstanding beliefs. They also show the enabling and productive possibilities of organisational surveillance (Iedema and Rhodes 2010; Martin et al. 2013).

## The Importance of Leadership in Implementation

Finally, we used the decentred approach to explore the role of leadership, an aspect that wasn't found in the existing decentred literature. Our data show that leadership was another key factor in shaping how the stroke reforms were perceived and implemented by actors within the two trusts. Leadership was significant at different levels, firstly, in CS1 it was seen as important by the local leaders that the national stroke reforms were accompanied with resources that would enable them to address their historical deficiencies in stroke care.

However, the local leaders also pointed to the fact that the drive for a change in local practice came from outside and not from them internally. The push factors were characterised as emanating from national guidelines and regional initiatives that they needed to implement:

> *It's an external, very external driver, so because we didn't do it, the research proved that, the research trial that had been done proved that patients who had the thrombolysis did very well.* (Stroke nurse specialist; CS1)

This evidence presented these nurse leaders with a dilemma, the dilemma being that their current stroke care was not producing good outcomes for their patients, the patients were being failed and these nurses were motivated to lead a change in practice to confront this dilemma. It is usually powerful hospital consultants as clinical leaders that can enact change but there was a perceived lack of this type of medical leadership in CS1, which was a crucial problem that needed attention for improvements to occur. Another stroke nurse specialist stressed the need to improve the internal leadership capacity in order to enact change:

> *Leadership within the stroke team has been perceived as a problem historically. And it was one of the things that we really tried to tighten up on in the last six months.* (Stroke nurse specialist; CS1)

The problem that the nurse cited was that there was a lack of leadership from the senior consultants in the trust and this was a causing a blockage to change. Using the decentred approach, we can explain how the dilemma that the stroke specialist nurses were experiencing (delivering a poor level of care) led them to use their situated agency to lead a change in practice, to modify traditions in response to a dilemma.

A consultant explained how the fact that the leaders in this change process were nurses and had been recruited into the trust was an important factor in 'winning others over', particularly other nurses, in the hospital:

> *most of the leadership has come from elsewhere. And it's come from a very motivated stroke nurse specialist that we brought in from elsewhere and who had been doing this before, who is, you know, just one of those people that*

> *knows their subject, is passionate about their subject and communicates well. And that just sort of sells it to half the Trust. And I think, to some extent, I think the fact that it's been a nurse specialist that's not quite been, let's say, not actually been leading, but to a large extent has been driving the agenda, I think has made it a lot easier to sell, certainly to the A & E nursing staff. I think if it was a stroke consultant coming down to this department trying to tell them what to do, they'd be saying, 'Oh I don't understand that, that's all above my head, you clever doctors, you know, off you go and speak to our consultants.* (A&E Consultant; CS1)

The data from case study site 1 illustrates that the traditional power of the medical profession can be sidestepped by motivated nursing professionals in order to achieve change. However, this internal hospital view contrasted dramatically with that of the medical director of the local service commissioner who felt that it was only strong managerial and medical leadership that would be able to drive the necessary changes in the hospital's stroke services, nursing leadership on its own, in his opinion, was not enough. Here, he sums up what he saw as the hospital's continued failure and explains what he sees as the reasons and possible solutions:

> *They* [the hospital] *didn't set up an acute* [stroke] *service for some time. They managed to set up an in hours thrombolysis service. But not at weekends* [...] *The business case was to deliver 24/7 thrombolysis.* [...] *My principal focus is service transformation, and one of the things I've observed is that getting service transformation without a clearly definable clinical leader is very, very difficult.* [...] [T]*here is a vacuum of clinical leadership in stroke at the hospital.* [...] *Now, I think if they had had a clinical champion, it would have gone faster, but there was nobody with a voice at middle or senior management team level...* (Medical director of the local service commissioner; CS1)

This view from this medical director was that change was difficult without senior **medical** leadership and that **nursing** leadership on its own was unlikely to be as effective. Which, contrasts with the hospital's senior consultant's view that the nursing leadership was why thrombolysis was implemented at all and would not have succeeded if it had been led by doctors. In terms of the decentred approach the key question is, what type of leadership is the most effective way of reshaping beliefs and traditions, and these data suggest that the answer is very dependent on the micro context. However, the medical director also recognised the limits of simple hierarchical governance at the micro level:

> *I guess the other aspect of that is the issue of being held to account, so it's clear that it's a regional priority, it's clear that it's a national priority, the DH* [central government] *kicks the SHA* [regional health planner], *the SHA kicks the PCT* [local service commissioner], *the PCT kicks the provider* [hospital]. *The boot that's on the DH's foot is big and spiky and it hurts the bottom of the SHA when it makes contact. The boot of the SHA is big and spiky, and it hurts the bottom of the chief executive when it makes contact, because both of these spikes are P45* [a notice of dismissal]. *There is no P45 issue that one can reason with the* [hospital]. *It's contractual, it's difficult, and it's highly complex.* (Medical Director of the local service commissioner; CS1)

This quote vividly illustrates the perceived limits of simple top-down implementation. From the perspective of informants within the hospital, influence from respected leaders (specialised nurses in this case) seemed to be successful, while the local service commissioner informant feels that hierarchical authority is the only way to achieve radical, lasting change.

The decentred approach is useful as it sees beliefs and traditions as resilient to simple top-down governance, instead the different actors' beliefs and traditions need to be considered and understood by local leaders. In the first case study the hospital consultant felt that this was best done by a stroke specialist nurse, rather than by medical leadership. The medical consultant's views of nurses from CS1 are in total contrast to those in CS2. There was a notable tone of disdain around the competencies and abilities of nurses from internal senior figures at the CS2 hospital. Senior doctors expressed a desire for their nurses to get back to basics—'not touchy-feely stuff'—based on 'hard facts' and 'testing' and increased discipline through the use of audit. This type of language was also used by other respondents and perpetuated a narrative and belief in which nursing in this hospital was seen as failing, which was noted as being a historical belief that was resistant to change:

> *The* [general] *nursing has got a lot better, but they're still our weakest link and we have, I mean it's really difficult to know what to do about that…*

> *Again, I think there's a difference between the professions. The therapists are very self-motivated. They will ask questions, they will go and look up answers, they will set up teaching groups for themselves, they will make themselves aware of what's going on. The nurses don't seem to do that. Again, I may be being very nasty to the nurses, it may well be that they spend so much time wiping bottoms and cleaning up vomit and that sort of thing that actually they don't have the energy and that is fine, because when push comes to shove nobody else does that work and that's their ultimate goal.* (Doctor; CS2)

The above quote from a senior consultant illustrates some very clear, generalised and entrenched beliefs of the perceived competences, skills and goals of different professional groups. These beliefs have developed over several years and so are difficult to alter which led to general nurses in this hospital being closely regulated and controlled by the clinical leaders, who were primarily doctors. When compared to the situation in CS1, it shows that power is contextually situated, and the decentred approach encourages us to examine these contextual micro factors. The internal hospital leadership of the stroke services in CS2 was by contrast very aspirational and eager to develop their services as this manager made clear:

> [I]*t was very clear from Darzi's* [a leading surgeon who was appointed by the Labour government in 2007 to undertake a review of the NHS] *work that he wanted these specialist centres and then little sort of polyclinics in a little part. So, what we did not want to be was* [unimportant]*; we really wanted to become one of the players.* (Clinical Services Manager for stroke; CS2)

Driving the change process here was a desire from a senior manager to become 'one of the players' and the default option to colonise further specialisms on the back of the success of securing stroke specialist status. These new competitive beliefs clashed with the previous traditions that were more collaborative and network based. Post-reconfiguration stroke services would have an explicit and quantifiable value to the management of this hospital because it would need multiple ancillary services in order to function at the requisite 'gold' standard designated by national and local guidelines and the funds for these services would be guaranteed by the commissioners. This would make stroke service delivery central to the successful clinical, economic and organisational functioning of the hospital as a whole. The importance and significance of the stroke services and their workers would all increase. Although these are positive changes for the stroke services and for the whole hospital, they are also disruptive and challenging. For example, this was evident with respect to the collegial nature of consultant decision making and workforce planning within the hospital. Notwithstanding the increased importance of stroke to the organisation, the lead stroke consultant had no direct power to force other hospital services such as radiology to change their traditional practice in line with his own desire that radiology offer consultant on-call coverage for thrombolysis decisions which is linked to the explicit requirements of the London stroke care model. There was a need to change the consultant radiologists' longstanding traditions which could not simply be achieved through hierarchical governance, but instead would need careful negotiation and understanding.

Again, the regional stroke networks in CS2 were also important as they combined clinical and managerial knowledge, power and legitimacy, and thereby provided a focal point for leadership and strategic direction. The stroke networks here existed in a unique space between the senior strategic management at a regional level, the local commissioners and the local hospitals. Simultaneously however, they drew on elements of all three through their diverse membership. Whilst none of the network actors derived hierarchical jurisdiction, or line management authority over other members of the network, they were able to harness their 'soft' powers of pursuation and collegiality to encourage change.

## Discussion

The implementation literature notes that policy and innovation implementation are not rational, top-down and linear processes (Nutley et al. 2007; Hill and Hupe 2002). This chapter highlights this assertion and sheds light on the reality of policy implementation at the micro level. Firstly, we found that several contextual factors of each hospital had a significant influence on how the stroke reforms were received and implemented by key actors in the two instituitions. Although macro policy is important, the data suggest that top-down implementation is limited, as governance is locally reproduced through context-based narratives and frames. This was illustrated by the different types of leadership in the two case studies, in CS1 it was the nursing leadership that led to changes and improvements in stroke care, something that would have been impossible in the CS2 context where nursing was considered weak by the key actors. Secondly, it was surprising to find that the introduction of greater surveillance in the form of audit was welcomed by staff in general, and senior staff in particular who used it to govern junior staff and highlight the need for more resources in stroke care. Lastly, in terms of leadership, our findings begin to question the traditional view of medical supremacy in local leadership as already mentioned. Below, we expand on these three findings and discuss the strengths the decentred approach offers to health policy analysis.

We used the 'decentred' governance approach (Bevir and Rhodes 2007; Bevir and Richards 2009) to analyse whether, and if so, how, and to what extent, specific micro traditions were challenged by new ideas and beliefs that the NHS stroke care reforms introduced in two English hospitals. The decentred approach offered an illuminating way to analyse health reform by highlighting the importance of dilemmas, beliefs, traditions and the local political contests that arise from these, which allowed us to unpack the context of policy implementation at the micro level. Our micro level data show the importance of local context in both shaping and then adapting local actors' traditions and beliefs and thereby influencing their responses to the resulting dilemmas. These contextual influences are then important in understanding how a macro level policy directive is locally interpreted and implemented, as Bevir and Rhodes (2009: 31) state:

> The workings of any policy or institution depend on the ways in which all sorts of actors interpret and respond to the relevant directives.

Our data suggest that dilemmas are individually constructed, and the decentred approach indicates the importance and influence of micro level actors in how reform is governed and emphasises the need for a bottom-up approach to implementation. A top-down, centrally driven approach to reform is unlikely to consider local context within which individual actors will *interpret and respond to the relevant directives.* Furthermore, these individual responses will be collectively reinforced at the micro level and thus influenced by the local context, where the leadership will be important.

Our analysis contributes to how we might view and define the decentred concept of a dilemma. For example, the heavy use of audit in the stroke reforms could have posed a dilemma for the stroke clinicians, as it potentially challenges their clinical autonomy to direct their practice (Timmermans and Berg 2003). However, both doctors and specialist nurses in CS2 used audit to govern both the work of junior staff and other colleagues. They used a potential dilemma (audit) to challenge and shape other local actors' existing beliefs of professional freedom. In CS1, audit helped highlight the deficiencies of stroke care, which could have caused a dilemma for the stroke care clinicians, but instead they used the audit data to successfully argue for extra resources, an example of disciplinary power being used as a productive force (Martin et al. 2013).

Elsewhere, we have discussed how professional jurisdictional power does not simply rest with the medical profession but is more nuanced (Baeza et al. 2016) and this chapter illustrates the importance of leadership in local implementation. Our data demonstrate how stroke specialist nurses can be effective leaders and can be more influential than some senior doctors in implementing change at the local level. In CS1 we found that the specialist nurse successfully took on a leadership role that was left by a medical leadership vacuum and this enabled her to make significant changes to improve local stroke care. This local leadership was crucial in shaping and reshaping the beliefs and traditions at the micro level.

Our paper shows, through empirical data, the promise of the decentred approach to health policy analysis. This approach could be used to analyse large scale, complex health reforms, for example, NHS England is encouraging health and social care leaders across local systems to come together to produce sustainability and transformation plans (see: https://www.england.nhs.uk/integratedcare/stps/view-stps/) to cope with the twin challenges of intense productivity pressures and reductions in funding. These new partnerships involve a wide array of local actors who have diverse perspectives of how their local health services should respond to the productivity and funding dilemmas. By analysing the various actors' beliefs and traditions within the different local contexts the decentred approach can offer a rich examination of these large-scale service reforms.

## References

Baeza, J. I., Boaz, A., & Fraser, A. (2016). The roles of specialisation and evidence-based practice in interprofessional jurisdictions: A qualitative study of stroke services in England, Sweden and Poland. *Social Science and Medicine, 155*, 15–23.

Bevir, M., & Rhodes, R. (2001). *A decentered theory of governance: Rational choice, institutionalism, and interpretation* (UC Berkeley Working Papers). University of California, Berkeley.

Bevir, M., & Rhodes, R. (2007). Decentred theory change and network governance. In *Theories of democratic network governance* (pp. 77–91). Palgrave Macmillan UK.

Bevir, M., & Richards, D. (2009). Decentring policy networks: A theoretical agenda. *Public Administration, 87*(1), 3–14.

Boseley, S. (2014, August 5). Centralised stroke care saves more lives, says study. *The Guardian*. Available at: http://www.theguardian.com/society/2014/aug/05/centralised-stroke-care-study-hospitals.

Christensen, T., & lsgreid, P. (2007). *Transcending new public management: The transformation of public sector reforms*. Aldershot: Ashgate.

Daneski, K., Higgs, P., & Morgan, M. (2010). From gluttony to obesity: Moral discourses on apoplexy and stroke. *Sociology of Health Illneess, 32*, 730–744.

Department of Health. (2007). *National stroke strategy*. London: Department of Health.

Eisenhardt, K. (1989). Building theories from case study research. *Academy of Management Review, 14*, 532–550.

Eisenhardt, K., & Graebner, M. (2007). Theory building from cases: Opportunities and challenges. *Academy of Management Journal, 50*, 25–32.

Ferlie, E., Baeza, J., Addicott, R., & Mistry, R. (2016). The governance of pluralist health care systems: An initial review and typology. *Health Services Management Research, 30*, 61–71.

Flyvbjerg, B. (2006). Five misunderstandings about case-study research. *Qualitative Inquiry, 12*(2), 219–245.

Foster, P., & Wilding, P. (2000). Wither welfare professionalism? *Social Policy and Administration, 34,* 143–159.

Foucault, M. (1973). *The birth of the clinic: An archaeology of the human sciences.* New York: Vintage.

Fraser, A., Baeza, J. I., & Boaz, A. (2017). "Holding the line": A qualitative study of the role of evidence in early phase decision-making in the reconfiguration of stroke services in London. *Health Research Policy and Systems, 15*(1), 45.

Fraser, A., Tan, S., & Mays, N. (2019). To SIB or not to SIB? A comparative analysis of the commissioning processes of two proposed health focused Social Impact Bond financed interventions in England. *Journal of Economic Policy Reform*, 1–16. https://doi.org/10.1080/17487870.2019.1572508.

Fraser, A., Baeza, J., Boaz, A., & Ferlie, E. (2019). Biopolitics, space and hospital reconfiguration. *Social Science and Medicine.* https://doi.org/10.1016/j.socscimed.2019.04.011.

Fulop, N. J., Ramsay, A. I., Perry, C., Boaden, R. J., McKevitt, C., Rudd, A. G., et al. (2015). Explaining outcomes in major system change: A qualitative study of implementing centralised acute stroke services in two large metropolitan regions in England. *Implementation Science, 11,* 80.

Geddes, M. (2014, April 14–16). *Posing a Dilemma for Dilemmas: Where do they come from and why do they matter?* Paper presented to the Political Studies Association Annual Conference, Manchester.

Hill, M., & Hupe, P. D. (2002). *Implementing public policy: Governance in theory and in practice.* London: Sage.

Iedema, R., & Rhodes, C. (2010). The undecided space of ethics in organizational surveillance. *Organization Studies, 31*(2), 199–217.

Johnston, S., Mendis, S., & Mathers, C. (2009). Global variation in stroke burden and mortality: Estimates from monitoring, surveillance, and modelling. *The Lancet Nephrology, 8,* 345–354.

Jones, L. (2018). Sedimented governance in the English National Health Service. In M. Bevir & J. Waring (Eds.), *Decentring health policy.* Oxon: Routledge.

Martin, G. P., Leslie, M., Minion, J., Willars, J., & Dixon-Woods, M. (2013). Between surveillance and subjectification: Professionals and the governance of quality and patient safety in English hospitals. *Social Science and Medicine, 99,* 80–88.

Nice. (2008). https://www.nice.org.uk/guidance/cg68/resources/guidance-stroke-pdf. Last accessed 30 August 2018.

NINDS—The National Institute of Neurological Disorders and Stroke rt-PA Study Group. (1995). Tissue Plasminogen activator for acute ischemic stroke. *New England Journal of Medicine, 333,* 1581–1587.

Nutley, S. M., Walter, I., & Davies, H. T. O. (2007). *Using evidence: How research can inform public services.* Bristol: The Policy Press.

Pollitt, C., & Bouckaert, G. (2011). *Public management reform: A comparative analysis* (3rd ed.). Oxford: Oxford University Press.

Pound, P., Bury, M., & Ebrahim, S. (1997). From apoplexy to stroke. *Age and Ageing, 26,* 331–337.

RCP. (2008). *National clinical guidelines for stroke.* London.

Spicer, A., Alvesson, M., & Kärreman, D. (2009). Critical performativity: The unfinished business of critical management studies. *Human Relations, 62,* 537–560.

Stroke Unit Triallists' Collaboration. (2007). Organised inpatient (stroke unit) care for stroke. *Cochrane Database Systematic Reviews* (4), Cd000197.

Timmermans, S., & Berg, M. (2003). *The gold standard: The challenge of evidence-based medicine and standardization in health care.* Philadelphia: Temple University Press.

Turner, S., Ramsay, A., Perry, C., Boaden, R., McKevitt, C., Morris, S., et al. (2016). Lessons for major system change: Centralization of stroke services in two metropolitan areas of England. *Journal of Health Services Research and Policy, 21,* 156–165.

Yin, R. (2003). *Case study research. Design and methods.* Thousand Oaks, CA: Sage.

# Buddies and Mergers: Decentring the Performance of Healthcare Provider Partnerships

Ross Millar, Russell Mannion, and Robin Miller

## Introduction

Networked modes of organising continue to be promoted by policy makers as a lever for improving the performance of healthcare services. The development of inter-organisational partnerships, such as public–private partnerships, federations, mergers, and alliances signify this trend with the widespread adoption of joint working arrangements across a range of service areas (Lewis et al. 2008; Sullivan and Skelcher 2002; Orr and Vince 2009; Glasby et al. 2011). Over recent years particular interest has been given to how partnership working can be better used to improve the performance of the hospitals and community services in the English NHS (NHS England 2018, 2019a). Recent scandals highlighting poor and deficient care in provider organisations (Francis 2013; Kirkup 2018) have led to regulatory approaches that

R. Millar (✉) · R. Mannion · R. Miller
University of Birmingham, Birmingham, UK
e-mail: r.millar@bham.ac.uk


M. Bevir and J. Waring (eds.), *Decentring Health and Care Networks*, Organizational Behaviour in Healthcare,
https://doi.org/10.1007/978-3-030-40889-3_4

mandate partnership arrangements, such as mergers and acquisitions, between underperforming and high performing NHS provider organisations. Running in parallel with these developments have been initiatives designed to promote new partnerships with the aim of better integrating health and social care services (NHS England 2014).

Reflecting on the rise of partnership and collaborative working, Dickinson and Sullivan (2014) locate these trends within the tradition of performance improvement in the public sector. Heavily influenced by the principles of New Public Management, inter-organisational collaboration has tended to centre on techno-bureaucratic approaches to improvement through the use of performance targets and measures narrowly defined by measures of efficiency and effectiveness that ignore the cultural performances of collaboration that are deeply rooted in the meanings, values, norms that reside within a particular organisational and cultural milieu (Dickinson and Sullivan 2014).

Current interest in inter-organisational partnership working as a mechanism to stimulate turnaround in failing organisations can also be situated within a broader tradition of public service reforms related to the 'management for excellence': the construction of organisational best practice examples that are translated into prescriptions for high-performing organisations (Jas and Skelcher 2005). Jas and Skelcher (2005) note that while the pursuit of excellence may encourage isomorphic processes and secure legitimacy with key stakeholders, the approach cannot, in isolation, be used to explain improved performance when other factors associated with the organisation and management of services are taken into consideration. Management of excellence theory presupposes that public-sector organisations can be differentiated in terms of their performance, yet definitions of performance are inevitably multiple, contingent, and dynamic, reflecting a mixture of measurement possibilities and contested discursive constructions (Jas and Skelcher 2005).

The purpose of this chapter is to critically engage with these traditions of public sector improvement with a decentred account of inter-organisational partnership working in the performance improvement of NHS providers. Situated within a context of continuous restructuring and 're-disorganisation' of NHS provision (Smith et al.

2001; Pollitt 2007; Walshe 2010), partnership working in the NHS is often promoted as a means of achieving performance improvement, yet these often fail to achieve the large-scale change anticipated. This is due, for example, to a failure to sufficiently engage the workforce, patients, and the public in any improvement efforts (Best et al. 2012). By paying particular attention to the situated agency of those charged with making such collaborations work, the chapter moves beyond techno-bureaucratic understandings of partnership structures and functions with an interpretive account of how NHS provider partnerships are constructed through the ability of individuals to create meanings in action, particularly how situated agents construct their beliefs about NHS provider partnerships against the background of traditions and often in response to dilemmas or problems (Bevir and Richards 2009). We argue that decentring the performance of NHS provider partnerships has the potential to shed new light on the dynamics of collaborative practice, the role of regulatory hybridity, and the contingent nature of organisational turnaround.

## Partnering for Improvement

Interest in partnership working has been on the NHS policy agenda for a number of years. The approach came to particular prominence during the Labour government (1997–2010) often in the context of supporting cross agency working across health and social care boundaries (Dickinson and Sullivan 2014; Glasby and Dickinson 2008; Glasby et al. 2011). Since 2010, the Coalition and Conservative governments have similarly promoted partnership working with The *Five Year Forward View* strategy setting out a range of proposals to support 'radical upgrades in prevention and public health' that called for 'better partnerships' and the 'breaking down of barriers between health and social care' (NHS England 2014). The agenda called for new forms of organisation, particularly multi-disciplinary community organisations to enable better integration of primary and secondary care services. The Dalton Review (DHSC 2014) commissioned by the government to support the *Five Year Forward View* assessed a range of collaborative, contractual, and consolidated models that NHS providers could draw on to improve the quality of care (Fig. 1). These options were intended to avoid 'top down solutions' for local health economies, but were encouraged in situations of organisational failure and turnaround by providing 'opportunities for successful organisations to bring their proven leadership, processes and expertise into organisations which are unable to demonstrate clinical and financial viability' (DHSC 2014: 4).

Emphasis on partnership working has continued with declarations that collaborative options become 'the new norm' (NHS England/NHS Improvement 2016) with the more recent NHS 10-year plan promoting service integration and 'genuine partnerships' across healthcare systems (NHS England 2019a). This is now articulated through the creation of Sustainability and Transformation Partnerships (STPs) which bring NHS and local government together within a defined locality to 'run services in a more coordinated way, to agree system-wide priorities, and to plan collectively how to improve residents' day-to-day health' (NHS England 2019b). The intention is for STPs to become

| Partnership type | Partnership function |
|---|---|
| **Merger:** | Where two or more organisations combine their resources to form a new organisation. |
| **Acquisition:** | Where an organisation becomes subsumed by an acquiring organisation |
| **Buddying:** | Where individuals or organisations with more experience help, mentor, advise or train others |
| **Federation** | Where several organisations come together to collaborate to deliver one or more type of service or back office provision. |
| **Joint Venture** | Where two or more organisations pool their sovereignty to create a new legal or contractual entity to manage a particular service |
| **Integrated Care Organisation** | An organisation that brings together some or all of the acute, community, primary care, social care and mental health services in a variety of forms |
| **Service Level Chain** | Where one organisation provides services for other providers through a contract, a service level agreement or a fee to use the policies and protocols of the first provider. |

**Fig. 1** Provider partnerships in the NHS (Adapted from Miller and Millar 2017; DHSC 2014)

fully Integrated Care Systems by 2021. Running alongside these developments have been ongoing concerns regarding the quality, safety and financial sustainability of hospitals and community services. The policy response here has seen attempts to enhance collaboration among NHS providers through the development of new models of care (Starling 2017). The launch of Acute Care Collaborative vanguards exemplifies an approach that encourages NHS providers to work together through the creation of hospital groups and networks to achieve the desired improvements in quality and efficiency (NHS England 2018).

Partnerships are also being sought to facilitate the organisational turnaround of NHS providers within broader regulatory frameworks designed to improve the performance of the provider sector. The Single Oversight Framework used by NHS Improvement (Fig. 2) details the variety of regulatory approaches being implemented to understand how and where providers may benefit from improvement support (NHSI 2017; CQC/NHSI 2017). The merger and acquisition of 'failing' NHS care providers by 'high performing' care providers has been promoted as a notable example of a mandated partnership that has achieved its objectives (CASS/NHSI 2017; Collins 2015). The promotion of buddying, mentoring and direct leadership relationships between executives and clinicians has also been recommended as a way to provide

*Levels of regulatory support (NHSI 2017)*

- Universal support: voluntary tools providers can draw on
- Targeted support: initiatives designed to help providers with specific areas e.g. intensive support teams
- Mandated support: e.g. appointment of an improvement director, agree a recovery trajectory in partnership with CQC; appointment of one or more partner (or 'buddy') organisations to provide support

*Longer term options for those in special measures for quality reasons (CQC/NHSI 2017)*

- Service reconfiguration across different services
- Management support or operational franchise agreements
- Transactions in the form of merger or acquisition of organisations to produce quality improvements

**Fig. 2** Summary of current regulatory support for performance improvement in NHS provider organisations

peer support and learning during mandated organisational turnaround efforts (Miller and Millar 2017).

These various interventions resonate with established approaches for understanding organisational failure and turnaround. Empirical work has identified a range of symptoms and organisational factors that often describe the process in terms of four or five basic phases (see Fig. 3; Walshe et al. 2004; Ravaghi et al. 2017; Harvey et al. 2014, 2010; Jas and Skelcher 2005; Boyne 2004).

Public sector regulatory regimes have sought to implement these approaches through a combination of 'watch dog' compliance and 'guide dog' support and development roles to performance improvement (Jas and Skelcher 2005). Current interest in NHS provider partnerships to turnaround organisational performance can be located within these regulatory approaches. In the analysis of UK healthcare systems, both Furnival et al. (2017) and McDermott et al. (2015) document a range of 'new hybrid regulatory models' that are using improvement support interventions, such as capacity building and quality improvement initiatives, in parallel with deterrence and compliance approaches that are embodied in directives, targets, and sanctions. These authors argue that regulatory hybridity can provide a

- Decline and crisis: a long and gradual period of performance decline characterised by a progressive loss of business, market position, resources, reputation and external support.
- Triggers for change: the events or circumstances which mean that the decline is recognised and acknowledged by internal and external stakeholders in the organisation, which may be a particular financial, operational or leadership crisis.
- Recovery strategy formulation: the production of a plan to deal with failure which explicitly acknowledges the scale and nature of the problems and sets out strategies or methods for dealing with them.
- Retrenchment and stabilisation: shorter term actions aimed at turnaround often concerned with dealing with operational management problems, finances, preventing further decline, and securing 'quick wins' in performance which will aid survival.
- Return to growth: longer term actions concerned with setting out the new vision for the purpose and objectives of the organisation

**Fig. 3** Stages of organisational failure and turnaround (Adapted from Walshe et al. 2004)

way to achieve performance improvement in healthcare organisations. However, they caution that a delicate balance of approaches is required which pays sufficient attention to engaging local organisations in regulatory changes. McDermott et al. (2015) note the importance of socio-historical contextual factors that both constrain and enable regulatory hybridity, drawing on the view of Reed (2011) that hybridized control systems often represent 'contested terrains' requiring successful coordination and communication of change narratives within 'precarious and contingent' contexts' (Reed 2011: 57 in McDermott et al. 2015: 339).

Such understandings of regulatory hybridity are based on the perspectives of those working within regulatory organisations. The perspective of those working in organisations that are responding to regulatory approaches to failure and turnaround have yet to be captured empirically, especially in relation to how local actors negotiate and navigate competing regulatory demands and contexts. Theorising about organisational failure and turnaround has focused on the private sector and has not taken into account the complexity of measuring and improving performance in public organisations (Jas and Skelcher 2005). Furthermore, the often rational-linear theories of turnaround predicting a successful return to growth are in tension with empirical evidence pointing to long term or permanent states of failure for some organisations (Walshe et al. 2004). Current mechanisms for partnership working to facilitate turnaround, such as mergers, are often susceptible to building on 'simplistic assumptions' about processes of organisational change that fail to take into account or engage with inter-organisational relationships, capabilities, norms and trust (Fulop et al. 2005; Sanderson et al. 2018).

New partnerships are likely to be shaped by local historical contexts and narratives that have emerged over time. Such conditions have been well documented when it comes to working across organisational boundaries in health and social care. Success depends on the presence of a number of factors, including the presence of a shared vision; clarity of roles and responsibilities; and appropriate incentives, rewards and accountabilities (Warwick-Giles and Checkland

2017; Dickinson and Glasby 2010; Glasby et al. 2011). Collaborative working may also encounter a range of barriers based on structural fragmentation of service responsibilities, conflicting professional ideologies, values and interests, as well as perceptions about threats to organisational status, autonomy and fears about being 'taken over' (Glasby et al. 2011; Mannion et al. 2011; Dickinson and Glasby 2010; Fulop et al. 2005).

## Case Studies of NHS Provider Partnerships

Recent mergers and acquisitions between under-performing and well-performing healthcare providers have received much attention by healthcare regulators (NHSI 2017). Studies of these show that while financial and clinical quality improvements have been identified, the time, cost, and complexity associated with 'turnaround' have led to challenging consequences for stakeholders involved (Aldwych Partners 2016; CASS/NHSI 2017; Collins 2015; NHS Improvement 2016). The creation of 'buddy' hospitals to provide support to struggling organisations and those in special measures appears to have aided turnaround and performance improvement, as measured by the CQC performance ratings (CQC 2017). New models of care appear to show promising signs with research suggesting they have stimulated organisational innovation and promoted system-wide collaboration (Naylor and Charles 2018; Starling 2017) Nevertheless, questions remain with regard to the resulting efficiency and effectiveness (Georghiou 2019).

Hitherto, research into provider partnerships has focused primarily on policy maker concerns with making efficiency savings and increasing service effectiveness. A decentred account of NHS provider partnership contexts has yet to be applied (Bevir and Richards 2009; Bevir and Waring 2018). Our research aimed to capture the perspectives of situated agents engaged in partnerships designed to remedy organisational failure and promote turnaround within current NHS policy environment. Between April 2016 and February 2017, 30 qualitative interviews were carried out with key individuals within each of following case study sites:

- A voluntary merger through acquisition between Greenpoint and Middleton Way specialist hospitals ($n = 7$)
- A mandated merger through acquisition between St Phillips and Rowheath Park hospitals ($n = 11$)
- A mandated buddying relationship between Green Bay hospital and Regency Vale hospital ($n = 12$)

Participants were executive directors, senior managers, clinicians and support staff who were identified as 'boundary spanning actors', i.e. they were directly involved in the development of these partnerships (Nicholson and Orr 2016). The interviews encouraged reflections on the 'partnering journey', focusing on what these partnerships mean and how they work with the view to eliciting insights into the experiences of, as well as assessments of opportunities and challenges for the future (Miller and Millar 2017). Data analysis paid particular attention to narratives regarding the formation and development of these partnerships: how boundary spanning actors constructed and understood these formations and the traditions and dilemmas associated with their enactment (Bevir and Waring 2018).

Those involved in NHS provider partnerships described the contexts and methods for identifying and turning around hospital performance. A voluntary merger of Greenpoint and Middleton Way hospitals was described as a culmination of events that brought them together. Middleton Way was described as experiencing financial difficulties due to a major capital investment project that had failed to come to fruition. A Care Quality Commission review of Middleton Way during this period also identified a number of areas requiring improvement leading the CEO and other members of the board to subsequently stepdown. The vacancies at Middleton Way triggered a 'window of opportunity' for the Greenpoint CEO to become the joint chief executive across both trusts with Members of the board at Greenpoint following afterwards. Running alongside these developments, Greenpoint had for some time been interested in moving into a new '21$^{st}$ century' building with a preferred location for any new development closer to other acute providers in the area. The most obvious partner out of the acute providers available was Middleton Way given the nature of their clinical services. These increasing interactions turned into discussions and actions to formally acquire Middleton Way.

> I guess we're about a year down the kind of formal process but in practical terms, we're probably about ten years down the informal journey so long, long before I came to the hospital there had been conversations about [us] coming together.

The mandated merger acquisition of Rowheath Park hospital by St Phillips hospital was instigated by the Care Quality Commission (CQC) regulator as a way to stimulate turnaround in an organisation that was 'slowly spiralling into a distressed organisation'. St Phillips was defined as a high performing hospital trust by the CQC that consistently achieved against performance targets and was rated 'outstanding' for finance, quality and safety. In contrast, the nearby Rowheath Park was failing against regulatory performance measures rated as 'inadequate' by CQC and given special measures status. This combined with a poor local reputation and continuous turnover at board level over recent years. The St Phillips board agreed to formally acquire Rowheath Park and were given a year to turn the organisation around by CQC. An additional driver for St Phillips to acquire Rowheath Park was to gain a larger footprint in the health economy. Strategically, there had been recognition that they needed to get bigger, either with an acquisition or a merger:

> I think if you're merging two corporate cultures, which are likely to be quite different, I don't know how you generate, at speed, a new corporate value culture … at least with us it was like, 'Fine. We're coming in, it's an acquisition. The St Phillips culture, the St Phillips corporate identity, the St Phillips values are going to come to Rowheath Park.

Following a CQC visit in 2013, Green Bay was put into special measures citing key issues with financial control and problems with its emergency care pathway. Those interviewed described a range of deep-rooted problems, including a poor local reputation, financial deficit and a 'treadmill' of stress for staff. As part of the special measures programme,

Green Bay was buddied with the high performing Regency Vale as a way to improve quality and financial performance of the organisation. For Green Bay, buddying with Regency Vale was supported largely because of existing relationships they had with their executive members. Buddying provided much valued advice as well as opportunities to test out ideas. This feeling was reciprocated with Regency Vale who were happy to provide help and support where needed.

> the Chief Executive of Regency Vale and I worked together in the past so we knew each other very well, and the approach by this Trust wasn't to invite another organisation to take us over or to send in all their troops because that wouldn't help them, they have a job to do as well. It was to test whether the approach we were taking was actually sensible, pragmatic and would stand up to scrutiny. And so apart from mentoring, they helped with networking us into potential candidates to come here.

## Dilemmas in Leadership and Management

A variety of different leadership styles and approaches were employed to achieve the desired turnaround and improvement. At Greenpoint, the Chief Executive was considered central to making the change happen, with the visibility of the wider executive helping to set the tone of commitment and direction. Committed leadership by the St Phillips board and its clinical directors was also deemed central to the successful acquisition of Rowheath Park. Described as an 'unusually tight organisation' the relatively stable executive and clinical body meant they had established a coherent team with credibility and belief that the acquisition would be a success.

> the whole engagement piece was central to everything that we did and above that was an absolute belief that the leadership, the quality of the leadership was going to be the single most influential factor in strengthening the culture. So, again, we had a very clear objectives and milestones around that area.

it's actually the ability of the senior people to have constructive, trusting dialogue with each other. [The Chief Executive] is brilliant on that and he sets the tone for the executive.

Green Bay appointed board members to introduce a different leadership style that encouraged greater engagement with staff. Central to the approach taken by the board was 'opening up' the organisation to new ideas and practices to generate service improvements.

An insular culture had developed so one of the key things the board were looking to do was open up the organisation to new ideas, and to going and looking and finding out what's going on elsewhere… there's no doubt that partnerships for organisations who need some mentoring, coaching and showing what good looks like is essential, and I think we got a lot of support from a range of partnerships, as opposed to specifically from the buddying relationship.

Those involved in leading the partnership arrangements described the importance of developing a corporate vision through the use of collective language to nurture partnership working. The Greenpoint board, for example, promoted a shared vision of 'we are one trust', where 'integration' rather than merger or acquisition was the preferred term. St Phillips introduced clinical buddying arrangements within Rowheath Park as way to build relationships and gather intelligence about cultures, behaviours and, management relationships. While those leading this buddying described initial reluctance and scepticism to the exercise, clinical buddying was able to create safe spaces for conversations and reflections on current practice.

as soon as we took over Rowheath Park … we had to use the language of we rather than them and us, and a sense that we are in this problem as a collective, so your problem is now our problem, and we can't walk away. So unlike buddying, this is a Catholic marriage, it's one way. So we made that really clear, that our futures were now bonded, … So that, I think people realised. So we also had a vision about what we wanted to do.

Changes to operations management were often tied to a range of HR-led initiatives to support implementation. At St Phillips this included 'cultural diagnostic' work to find out about the organisation using staff surveys, turnover rates, disciplinaries, and grievances. Work on translating values and behaviours into Rowheath Park also included changes to the recruitment questions and performance appraisal systems, and a realignment of policies, procedures, grading structures. The Greenpoint merger similarly involved bringing together corporate functions such as the payroll provider, ordering system, communication systems coming together to make efficiency savings.

> we want to pick up all the stones, we learnt a lot about the organisation by doing that kind of forensic look at stuff.

> you look at our transaction, we have got a projected £7million saving by coming together, most of that's back office and corporate... You know, you get rid of one board, you probably save a £1million and so on and so forth. ... there's bits of clinical but it's really around the margins so pathology and diagnostics, you know?

While there was much optimism and belief in the approaches being taken, notable limits to these efforts were highlighted. The implementation of redesigned management structures was thought to have underestimated the challenge, time and energy required to deliver the required changes, with IT systems and infrastructure remaining the biggest frustration. The emotional labour of leading change took its toll:

> for the first like six months I was bloody knackered because every time I wanted to interact with somebody I thought, I don't know them, I'll just pop in and see them.

> I think we misunderstood the complexity of running a three-site operation and that still continues to stretch us, so we got two DGHs 20 miles apart and we're trying to run it on an integrated basis so that's a big challenge.

Concerns were also expressed about the ability to fully engage staff in the process of partnership development. Time constraints associated with implementing the merger meant that discussions and engagement across the organisations was not possible.

> Maybe there was a bit too much of a focus on the actual mechanics of the transaction and the, you know, the beasts that had to be fed and, you know, getting all of that right and the money sorted and all of that, and not so much on the softer, you know, how are the teams feeling about this? What are the things that people really value that they want to see continue into the new organisation? A bit more around that, I think, would have probably made people here feel a bit more like they were on the journey as well rather than they were almost just passengers.

Leadership efforts to forge a new collective identity proved at times to be contentious as the language and corporate visions of staff engagement were in tension with the apparent dominance of high performing organisational values:

> the perception is it's about adopting the Greenpoint way rather than what the CE says, which is you take the best of both and then you bring them together. So, I think, again, maybe because we haven't had those sessions with staff, you know, just to actually say, "Okay, so how are we going to do this in future? What's the combined way of doing it?" There's just been a bit of a, "Well, we're going to start doing it this way". I think staff here have probably felt a little bit put out about that

Concerns were raised, for example, of disconnect in quality improvement work not 'filtering down' to service levels, along with the time and resources being invested into these initiatives were being taken away from elsewhere.

> What we do here is we have all different people come in with different theories and we just keep chopping and changing so nobody ever buys into it because you think, well, it's McKinsey's this week, it's GE next week, it's VMI this week, it's KPMG… we know what we're going to do, we've got the change management theory, and then we always do it across the summer, and then we get into winter, the support has gone, the Green Bay have failed again. So, it's about sustainability of any help or buddying that we get, in my mind. It's not just about doing it for a short period of time.

Within such a context, questions were raised about whether the partnership arrangements being proposed were appropriate for the organisation:

> I think buddying up is good but it's got to be with the right organisation and our staff are very sceptical because of all the help that's come in... you have to think what are we asking our staff to do? We are asking them to work in one of the busiest hospitals in the country, the biggest EDs in the country, and we're asking them to partner with another hospital that's completely different .... It's about the same size but the attractions are completely different. ....

## Dilemmas in Performance Measurement

Across the interviews was a shared anticipation that the partnerships entered into would result in shared improvements in regulatory performance, especially targeted measures of improvement.

> I think we will be judged by the regulators against things like KPIs and finance. That's what will happen. But we obviously, just because of the nature of our organisation, I'm not saying they're not important because they're really important but we also want to have some of the other measures like experience of staff, patient experience getting better but then in reality, that's not what we're going to get measured on externally.

Green Bay attributed improvements in their CQC scores with the changes introduced within the organisation as a consequence of their partnership. Rowheath Park similarly reported a change in CQC measures from 'inadequate' to 'good' within a year of acquisition, with some services identified as 'outstanding'. Rowheath Park now met all quality standards and a year on from being in the bottom 20% of the staff survey, was rated in the top 20% organisations for staff satisfaction.

> I think it was about three months ago when we had a totally green dashboard, that's never happened at Rowheath Park before.

With the implementation of the merger still to go through, Greenpoint were predicting benefits with their merger with Middleton Way, especially around the proposed move to one physical site providing financial stabilisation, clinical improvements, and workforce benefits evidenced in key performance indicators such as staff satisfaction, appraisal rates.

> the financial ones are relatively easy I think to kind of capture and to measure so pre-transaction, you've got [Middleton Way] that's financially non-viable. They've declared they're a non-viable organisation in their deficit, they can barely afford to pay the staff… what we set out in the business case was essentially a kind of four-year journey of strengthening that financial position. So, that's an easy one. You can measure that; it's quite- obvious, it's quite quantitative.

Softer intelligence in the form of conversations and feedback from patients and the public was also being used to gauge performance. Feedback from staff feeling more valued and engaged in the process provided a measure of how things were changing. Greenbay pointed to greater 'visibility and presence' of senior clinicians at clinical governance meetings as a measure of improvement.

> when I started here the staff in A & E narrated a story that they felt they were the only people that were interested in patients that were coming in off ambulances, and now we've got the whole hospitals, all both hospitals, interested in the importance of making sure the emergency pathway is as quick and as high quality as possible. And that's a massive mindset shift, which I think the staff in A & E feel has been the biggest difference for them.

The voluntary merger between Greenpoint and Middleton Way highlighted the emergent nature of performance measurement within these partnerships. Plans were being put in place to develop a holistic view of performance that was able to bring together and translate the various regulatory requirements associated with the partnership. To do so required improved triangulation of existing organisational routine data with other forms of HR intelligence gathered as part of the merger.

> We're in the process of putting together an OD strategy that will encompass our performance framework, looking at what our organisational vision, goals and our metrics will be. So, once we've got that developed we'll be able to then be tracking that over time and looking at, "Okay so how were we performing around particular targets or finance targets or workforce data" and be able to keep tracking that over time. So, and we also want to bring into that some of those cultural measures like our staff engagement levels and our friends and family test and those kind of things.

While these performance improvements would continue to be captured, the sustainability of these efforts was brought into question. There was recognition that most mergers and acquisitions 'have a dip' in the first year, but combined with a context of increasing patient demand for services meant there was likelihood that performance measures would be further breached in the future. Staff readiness for change was questioned with concerns raised about the time to embed and sustain improvement efforts across the workforce.

> if I'm really honest, I think we're in the most dangerous bit of it, because this is the point at which we could go one of two ways. We can either carry on pushing forward, and truly generate what everybody wants to come out of it, which is a combined organisation that all works in one way... Or that will all be too difficult, require too much energy, and we'll divert down what is the path of least resistance. Which is we'll end up with two or three different sub-cultures.

## Dilemmas in Stakeholder Relationships

The ability to engage with different stakeholders in and around these partnerships was central to interpretations of partnership success. The relationship with regulators was crucial in this regard. Central to the successful acquisition of Rowheath Park was the additional financial investment, autonomy and governance support for the regulator to implement the acquisition

> Rowheath Park was an organisation that had no ambition for many, many years, they had no money. And so to actually say, that actually what we want on this site, we're going to bring these clinical services, these are going to be new buildings that you're going to have that was just really one of the most uplifting things for them.

> I think not being bombarded by external organisations is really, really important… you have to demonstrate that level of trust. …You have to be left alone to get on with it, and they have to understand you might break a few eggs.

Greenpoint had contrasting experiences of working with the regulatory requirements for merging services. Those leading the merger described confusion and ambiguity as they encountered a number of changes in broader NHS policy and regulatory frameworks mid-way through their application:

> People at the NSHI are slightly schizophrenic really because one end of NSHI is telling us one thing and another end is telling us another… we've been jumping to both tunes and actually that's been incredibly high maintenance in terms of the Chief Exec's time, the CFO's time, the Finance Team's time.

The 'special measures' status given to Green Bay by CQC brought with it a number of additional challenges related to the time and resources taken up to adhere to the reporting and assurance arrangements as well as reputational damaged being inflicted:

> We were one of the first so it really affected our recruitment and retention. People left, people didn't want to come and work here. Especially within the Emergency Department, the reputation went before it… Being in special measures really affected people coming in.

> When you're in special measures, the other side of that is that everybody's scrutinising you and you can't get away from it. So there are, I don't know how many, meetings a month where people are holding you to account, whether or not you're doing what you should be doing to get out of special measures. And that is hugely time consuming….

Relationships with other organisations in the health economy were often strained and at times fractious. Ongoing tensions were expressed about the lack of engagement and accountability of other organisations in the local health economy:

> I don't believe especially for some areas, and this economy included, that there's been enough scrutiny, enough thought into the reasons why you go into special measures because you could stop and say where was the oversight?
>
> We need to understand not just as organisational issues but actually as placed-based issues and infrastructure issues, which will require some way of holding a ring about some of these issues and accountability....

That said, changes in the health economy which placed greater emphasis on systems integration provided opportunities for growth and stability. The arrival of STPs provided opportunities to have greater influence over health economy activities. Organisations anticipated greater collaborations and involvement in the delivery of primary and community services

> we're trying to use that [STP] scale so everyone benefits. I think that will be a good step forward. We're a big advocate of GP hubs we want them to work.
>
> we had to reassure the staff here that actually a) it's a bigger health economy, you can no longer be a shining star in a sea of failing organisations, it's about, "How do we survive together as a system, not as an organisation?" which – and we've had to take this organisation through that journey really and actually demonstrate that actually we're asking for external funding too for the transaction so that it can be doable and we can do it well.

## Discussion

Inter-organisational partnerships have been promoted in health policy narratives as a means for sharing lessons and promoting performance improvements between care provider organisations. Our study looks at how this narrative is enacted and experienced through the situated and meaningful actions of people involved in creating new partnership arrangements, inter-organisational structures and working practices in response to regulatory demand. A preliminary point for discussion is that, in different ways, the studied partnerships (mergers, acquisitions, buddying) were mandated or strongly recommended by regulatory bodies in the context of recent regulatory inspections and assessment. Even where stakeholders were receptive to inter-organisational partnerships working, this needs to be set in the context of top-down regulatory pressure.

In realising these partnership arrangements, we found key actors draw on a range of approaches often rooted in established characteristics of executive leadership for quality improvement (e.g. Millar et al. 2013, 2015; Mannion et al. 2016). In particular, situated agents often worked to craft and communicate a local narrative of a merged organisational 'future' with visibility and staff engagement viewed as central to translating strategy into practice. Leaders often relied upon different forms of intelligence often combining harder forms of performance data with softer insights gathered from interactions with staff, patients and the public. These leadership practices sat alongside the implementation of parallel human resource management initiatives that were intending to better understand workforce differences, align processes to support the turnaround of poor performance, whilst also introducing a series of cost saving measures through the rationalisation of 'back office' services.

These situated agents provided insights into the emotional labour involved in meeting these regulatory requirements while seeking to engage organisations in the change process. The implementation of these organisational changes also highlights gaps within the strategies and management practices for achieving regulatory goals. Uncertainty and anxieties were expressed about the supporting infrastructure and sustainability of these partnerships. Working with external stakeholders influenced these efforts, where partnership success was shaped by relationships with regulatory bodies and the potential to work with the local health economy to manage and sustain any performance improvements.

Taken together these findings illustrate the dilemmas of working collaboratively, yet they also highlight the opportunities brought about by situated agency. Engagement with the partnership working agenda was motivated by opportunities for acquiring organisations to expand their power and influence across local health economies. While these partnerships were triggered by regulatory demands, the idea of partnering had been on the agenda for some time. Actors were actively engaging in these partnerships to expand their estate and gain further influence in health economy decision making and priority setting.

In this sense, these findings offer a way for understanding the situated agency of collaboration beyond a commitment to improving quality and financial outcomes. The partnerships acted as both instruments of opportunity as well as a constraint. Rather than proceeding through a series of linear stages from identification failure and the implementation of turnaround, these findings capture the active influence of corporate governance, management and the wider environment influencing these organisational settings (Walshe et al. 2004; Jas and Skelcher 2005), with accounts of performance rooted in different narratives of problems, solutions and proposed outcomes for these partnerships.

These findings capture the difficulties of re-creating regulatory hybridity within single organisations. McDermott et al. (2015) note that while having a combination of bottom-up and top-down approaches to improvement is desirable, this is difficult to achieve as some approaches have the potential to crowd-out others (Fig. 4 adapted from McDermott et al. 2015: 340). Our findings suggest that situated agents face ongoing dilemmas working across these approaches. They highlight how situated agents are engaging with top-down approaches within these partnerships as displayed in their accounts of fulfilling regulatory performance requirements and the presence of board level leadership promoting culture change. However, engaging with bottom-up approaches in the form of capacity and resources for change proved to more variable with limited evidence of empowering the workforce to generate local improvements at the time of the research.

These inter organisational partnerships were receptive to boundary spanning actors based on the mandated regulatory requirements

| | | | |
|---|---|---|---|
| Approaches to improvement | | National organisation | Local organisation |
| | Top Down | Q1: Ensuring | Q4: Embedding |
| | | Evidence of provider partnerships engaging in performance and process standards and accountability mechanism (e.g. targets, guidelines, scrutiny, inspection) | Evidence of provider partnerships engaging with developing cultures of improvement (e.g. Board policies, clinical governance, support and resourcing, celebrating improvement) |
| | Bottom up | Q2: Enabling | Q3: Empowering |
| | | Gaps apparent in capacity building (e.g. Training in improvement methods, change resource, peer networks) | Gaps apparent in local improvement efforts (e.g. encouraging bottom up innovation, problem solving, evaluation) |

Improvement

**Fig. 4** Integrative governance model (Adapted from McDermott et al. 2015: 340)

combined with the opportunities to expand and sustain services in the local health economy. However, these findings highlight gaps in regulatory hybridity, with a lack sufficient resources and collaborative stakeholder relationships to achieve the desired improvements. McDermott et al. (2015) note that hybridisation is likely to need time to develop. Indeed, these other domains might well be evident within these organisations or have been introduced subsequently as a process of hybridisation. These findings also suggest there is still work to be done to engage with provider organisations in order to achieve the desired improvements from these partnership efforts.

The concept of regulatory capitalism is a useful lens to view regulatory performance. Levi-Faur (2017) introduces this idea to understand the rise of the regulatory state as the continuing expansion, adaptation and transformation of commodity accumulation via markets as well as the 'patchwork of institutions' that constitute and govern markets, society and state. While current policy discourses around integration and partnership working suggest a move away from market competition in the NHS, regulatory capitalism would suggest that these developments represent the further institutionalisation of markets via regulatory designs shaping incentives and choices for NHS providers. Further research in this area offers the opportunity to explore this concept within NHS settings, decentring the analysis of regulatory systems as a hybrid of different systems (public, private, civil) of control.

## Conclusion

For the English NHS, inter-organisational partnerships can be positioned within broader narratives of organisational failure and turnaround. Our findings highlight the traditions and dilemmas facing those working in the NHS and reveal how situated agents navigate the complex and contradictory narratives calling for quality and service improvement and organisational development in the context of increasing cost constraints and efficiency savings. As interest in healthcare provider partnerships and integration continues to grow, further decentred research is needed to explore these developments. Our research provides a range of insights into the formation of provider partnerships yet further analysis is needed regarding the social embeddedness of partnership working: how situated agents within these provider contexts embed these practices across different organisational actors and contexts.

Partnership working as an approach to organisational performance improvement captures the hybrid nature of regulation that combines watch dog and guide dog roles and functions. Hybridity in this sense provides a valuable perspective to understand how situated agents navigate these contexts. While its normative element has been played down (McDermott et al. 2015), further research is required to consider and problematise hybrid regulatory forms and provide critical insights into the performances of partnership working within these arrangements. Partnerships are reflective of network formations in representing technologies of performance measurement, therefore further research is needed to reflect the neoliberal and managerial rationalities underpinning them (Bevir and Waring 2018). Such perspectives are particularly relevant given the predicted £22 billion shortfall in NHS spending by 2020/2021, and continuing calls for efficiency savings and increasing workforce shortages. Such a context is likely to present further dilemmas for those faced with the challenge of partnership working, and integration more broadly.

**Acknowledgement** The authors would like to thank The Health Foundation for funding this research.

## References

Aldwych Partners. (2016). *Benefits from mergers: Lessons from recent NHS transactions*. London: NHS Improvement.

Best, A., Greenhalgh, T., Lewis, S., Saul, J. E., Carroll, S., & Bitz, J. (2012). Large-system transformation in health care: A realist review. *The Milbank Quarterly, 90*(3), 421–456.

Bevir, M., & Richards, D. (2009). Decentring policy networks: A theoretical agenda. *Public Administration, 87*(1), 3–14.

Bevir, M., & Waring, J. (2018). *Decentring health policy: Learning from British experiences in healthcare governance*. Abingdon: Routledge.

Boyne, G. A. (2004). A '3Rs' strategy for public service turnaround: Retrenchment, repositioning and reorganization. *Public Money & Management, 24*(2), 97–103.

Care Quality Commission. (2017). *Driving improvement: Case studies from NHS trusts*. London: CQC.

Care Quality Commission/NHS Improvement. (2017). *Special measures for quality reasons: Guidance for trusts*. London: CQC/NHSI.

CASS Business School and NHS Improvement. (2017). *Mergers in the NHS: Lessons learnt and recommendations*. Update 2017. London: NHS Improvement.

Collins, B. (2015). *Foundation trust and NHS trust mergers: 2010 to 2015*. London: Kings Fund.

Department of Health and Social Care. (2014). *Examining new options and opportunities for providers of NHS care: The Dalton Review*. London: Department of Health and Social Care.

Dickinson, H., & Glasby, J. (2010). Why partnership working doesn't work. *Public Management Review, 12*(6), 811–828.

Dickinson, H., & Sullivan, H. (2014). Towards a general theory of collaborative performance: The role of efficacy and agency. *Public Administration, 92*(1), 161–177.

Francis, R. (2013). *Report of the Mid Staffordshire NHS Foundation trust public inquiry*. London: The Stationery Office.

Fulop, N., Protopsaltis, G., King, S., Allen, P., Hutchings, A., & Normand, C. (2005). Changing organisations: A study of the context and processes of mergers of health care providers in England. *Social Science and Medicine, 60*(1), 119–130.

Furnival, J., Walshe, K., & Boaden, R. (2017). Emerging hybridity: Comparing UK healthcare regulatory arrangements. *Journal of Health Organization and Management, 31*(4), 517–528.

Georghiou, T. (2019, January 31). Little evidence that integrated care initiatives deliver. *Health Services Journal*. Available at https://www.hsj.co.uk/integration/little-evidence-that-integrated-care-initiatives-deliver/7024298.article. Accessed 24 July 2019.

Glasby, J., & Dickinson, H. (2008). *Partnership working in health and social care*. Bristol: Policy Press.

Glasby, J., Dickinson, H., & Miller, R. (2011). Partnership working in England—Where we are now and where we've come from. *International Journal of Integrated Care, 11,* 1–8.

Harvey, G., Jas, P., & Walshe, K. (2014). Analysing organisational context: Case studies on the contribution of absorptive capacity theory to understanding inter-organisational variation in performance improvement. *BMJ Quality and Safety*. https://doi.org/10.1136/bmjqs-2014-002928.

Harvey, G., Skelcher, C., Spencer, E., Jas, P., & Walshe, K. (2010). Absorptive capacity in a non-market environment: A knowledge-based approach to analysing the performance of public sector organizations. *Public Management Review, 12*(1), 77–97.

Jas, P., & Skelcher, C. (2005). Performance decline and turnaround in public organizations: A theoretical and empirical analysis. *British Journal of Management, 16*(3), 195–210.

Kirkup, B. (2018). *Report of the Liverpool community health independent review*. Liverpool Community Health Services Review Report

Levi-Faur, D. (2017). Regulatory capitalism. In P. Drahos (Ed.), *Regulatory theory: Foundations and applications* (pp. 289–302). Canberra: Australian National University.

Lewis, J. M., Baeza, J. I., & Alexander, D. (2008). Partnerships in primary care: Network structures, dynamics and sustainability. *Social Science and Medicine, 67*(2), 280–291.

Mannion, R., Brown, S., Beck, M., & Lunt, N. (2011). Managing cultural diversity in healthcare partnerships: The case of LIFT. *Journal of Health Organisation and Management, 25*(6), 645–657.

Mannion, R., Freeman, T., Millar, R., & Davies, H. T. O. (2016). Effective board governance of safe care: A (theoretically underpinned) cross-sectioned examination of the breadth and depth of relationships through national quantitative surveys and in-depth qualitative case studies. *Health Services and Delivery Research, 4*(4). https://doi.org/10.3310/hsdr04040.

McDermott, A. M., Hamel, L. M., Steel, D., Flood, P. C., & McKee, L. (2015). Hybrid healthcare governance for improvement? Combining top-down and bottom-up approaches to public sector regulation. *Public Administration, 93*(2), 324–344.

Millar, R., Freeman, T., & Mannion, R. (2015). Effective hospital board oversight of quality and safety: A stakeholder analysis exploring the role of trust and intelligence. *BMC Health Services Research, 15,* 196. https://doi.org/10.1186/s12913-015-0771-x.

Millar, R., Mannion, R., Freeman, T., & Davies, H. T. O. (2013). Hospital board oversight of patient safety: A narrative review and synthesis of recent empirical studies. *The Milbank Quarterly, 91*(4), 738–770.

Miller, R., & Millar R. (2017). *Partnering for Improvement: Inter-organisational developments in the NHS.* The Health Foundation & Health Services Management Centre, University of Birmingham.

Naylor, C., & Charles, A. (2018). *Developing new models of care in the PACS vanguards: A new national approach to large-scale change?* London: The King's Fund.

NHS England. (2014). *The five year forward view.* London: Department of Health and Social Care.

NHS England. (2018). *No hospital is an island—Learning from the acute care collaborations.* London: NHS England.

NHS England. (2019a). *The NHS long term plan.* London: Department for Health and Social Care.

NHS England. (2019b). *Local sustainability and transformation partnerships.* Available at: https://www.england.nhs.uk/integratedcare/stps/view-stps/. Accessed 14 April 19.

NHS England and NHS Improvement. (2016). *NHS operational planning and contracting guidance 2017–2019*. Available at: www.england.nhs.uk/wp-content/uploads/2016/09/NHS-operational-planning-guidance-201617-201819.pdf.

NHS Improvement. (2016). *Literature review: The experiences of healthcare providers in delivering merger objectives*. London: NHS Improvement.

NHS Improvement. (2017). *Single Oversight Framework for NHS providers*. London: NHS Improvement.

Nicholson, J., & Orr, K. (2016). Local government partnership working: A space odyssey. Or, journeys through the dilemmas of public and private sector boundary-spanning actors. *Policy & Politics, 44*(2), 269–287.

Orr, K., & Vince, R. (2009). Traditions of local government. *Public Administration, 87*(3), 655–677.

Pollitt, C. (2007). New labour's re-disorganization. *Public Management Review, 9*(4), 529–543.

Ravaghi, H., Mannion, R., & Sajadi, H. S. (2017). Organizational failure and turnaround in public sector organizations: A systematic review of the evidence. *Medical Journal of the Islamic Republic of Iran, 31*(76), 434–444.

Reed, M. (2011). Control in contemporary work organizations. In P. Blyton, E. Heery, & P. Turnbull (Eds.), *Reassessing the employment relationship* (pp. 41–70). Basingstoke: Palgrave Macmillan.

Sanderson, J., Lonsdale, C., & Mannion, R. (2018). What's needed to develop strategic purchasing in healthcare? Policy lessons from a realist review. *International Journal of Health Policy and Management*. https://doi.org/10.15171/ijhpm.2018.93.

Smith, J., Walshe, K., & Hunter, D. (2001). The "redisorganisation" of the NHS: Another reorganisation involving unhappy managers can only worsen the service. *BMJ: British Medical Journal, 323*, 1262.

Starling, A. (2017). *Some assembly required: Implementing new models of care. Lessons from the new care models programme*. London: The Health Foundation.

Sullivan, H., & Skelcher, C. (2002). *Working across boundaries: Collaboration in public services*. Basingstoke: Palgrave.

Walshe, K. (2010). Reorganisation of the NHS in England. *BMJ, 341*, 3843.

Walshe, K., Harvey, G., Hyde, P., & Pandit, N. (2004). Organizational failure and turnaround: Lessons for public services from the for-profit sector. *Public Money and Management, 24*(4), 201–208.

Warwick-Giles, L., & Checkland, K. (2017). Integrated care: Using "sense-making" to understand how organisations are working together to transform local health and social care services. *Journal of Health Organization and Management, 32*(1), 85–100.

# Space and Place in Network Governance: Putting Integrated Care into Place

Simon Bishop

## Introduction—Networks and Integrated Care

Integrated care exemplifies the spread of network governance within healthcare, and brings with it the promise of breaking down professional silos on one hand and counteracting the divisive effects of market competition on the other. Seamless coordination and collaboration between a wide range of health and social care agencies is a globally espoused ideal, promoted as necessary for the effective care of people with complex and cross cutting needs (Glasby 2012). Policy makers, professional bodies and researchers, as well as patients and service user groups have all identified opportunities to improve efficiency and effectiveness of services through greater integration in the form of collaborative inter-agency networks. Across Europe and North America, greater collaboration and integration between care providers is seen as a key way of addressing growing pressures on care services (Kodner and

S. Bishop (✉)
University of Nottingham, Nottingham, UK
e-mail: simon.bishop@nottingham.ac.uk


M. Bevir and J. Waring (eds.), *Decentring Health and Care Networks*, Organizational Behaviour in Healthcare,
https://doi.org/10.1007/978-3-030-40889-3_5

Spreeuwenberg 2002; Leichsenring 2004; Goodwin et al. 2014). In the UK, integrated care has been promoted by successive governments and is today top of the policy agenda. Announcing changes to the distribution of funds between the UK NHS and social care in 2013, the then Secretary of State for Health, Jeremy Hunt declared, "*As far as this government is concerned we believe in integrated care and this is something that has been talked about for decades*" (HSJ, June 2013). NHS England's 'Five Year Forward View' (2014) promoted integration at the centre of the government's plans for health and social care provision, reiterated in subsequent policy announcements.

> Our aim is to use the next several years to make the biggest national move to integrated care of any major western country. (NHS England 2017: 31)

At the time of writing, health and social care policy in England is focused on the creation of regional Integrated Care Systems (ICSs). These have met with significant controversy, as campaigners and academics have suggested these are part of a wider political project of privatisation 'by stealth' (Pollock and Roderick 2018), involving formerly public services being contracted out to private sector ownership. From the perspective of Bevir and Needham (2017) network policies are not necessarily a mask for privatisation, but rather markets and networks exist within the same modernist public policy paradigm characterised by faith in transferable concepts and theories above socially situated forms of knowledge tied to particular groups, traditions, people and forms of historically and geographically situated social life. To counteract the centralising tendencies of modernist thought, Bevir and Needham (2017) advocate for examination of social policy through decentred theory which 'explains shifting patterns of social policy by focusing on the actors' own interpretations of their actions and practices and by locating these interpretations in historical contexts' (Bevir and Needham 2017: 626).

This chapter examines how the narrative of integrated health and social care is experienced and enacted on the front line of service organisation and delivery, especially the way in which people interpret and give meaning to policies of integration in relation to their local contexts. In particular, I focus here on the way issues of place and space play into the realisation of integrated care, as a way of offering new insight to decentred theory (Bevir 2013). With reference to Lefebvre's (1991) tripartite conception of space, I consider the way in which regional projects of integrated care involve rationalising spatial aspects of care provision through geographical resource-redistribution and the creation of shared space to engineer new social connections across professional and organisational boundaries. This is seen to interact with both existing spatial practices, dependent on long-standing geographic distinctions and the build environment, as well the professionals' experiences of space shaped by wider institutions. In exploring these issues, I elaborate on the importance of place and space to decentred theory. I begin below by introducing some of the ambiguities within policies of integrated care, before moving on to consider debates on place and space may which inform the study. These ideas are then explored in a case study of integrated care in a single metropolitan borough in Northern England.

## Decentring Integrated Health and Social Care

As a particular manifestation of network governance, integrated care seeks to overcome recognized organizational and professional boundaries, with the aim of improving service efficiency and effectiveness. In the main, literature advocating integrated care implicitly or explicitly draws on theories within institutional economics to consider the reduced transaction costs associated with working across organizational boundaries. For example, Robinson and Casalino (1996) identify 'vertical' (acute and primary care organisations under the same ownership) and 'virtual' (contractual) integration as two potential forms of network organisation, each of which are said to bring benefits by allowing resource flows through trusting inter-organisational relations. While it is the logic of efficient transactions that dominates at the level of policy and regional management level, rationalising resource use has also been advocated as bringing assorted quality benefits to patient and service user groups including access, equity and continuity of care (Kodner and Spreeuwenberg 2002).

Within the UK, integrated care has been supported enthusiastically by both academic departments and charitable think tanks including the Nuffield Trust and Kings Fund, who have been involved in numerous influential pilots, evaluations and evidence reviews. To illustrate the connections between theory and practice, Professor Chris Ham, former director of the Kings Fund and strong advocate for integrated care, acted as Director of Strategy at the Department of Health during New Labour's reign in government, as well as advisor to the WHO and World Bank. During this period, integration between NHS and local authority care services became a key focus of UK government policy. New Labour placed heavy policy emphasis on partnership and inter-agency working, for example by establishing the basis for joint Care Trusts (DoH 2000) and a sponsorship of numerous integrated care programmes and pilot schemes (Rand Europe 2012).

Despite many well-funded investigations into integrated care, including the development of dedicated academic journals, reviews and meta-reviews (see e.g. Reed et al. 2005; Ouwens et al. 2005; Martinez-Gonzales et al. 2014), the boundary problems effecting the health and social care system are found to be highly resistant to policy interventions. Many regions within the UK have been through several iterations of integrated care, often through quite short-lived projects (Reed et al. 2005) with wide variations in the aims, nature and scope of integration. For example, a small number of regions have been celebrated as attempting to fully merge health and social care provision at the organisational level, for example with the creation of joint Care Trusts (Lavender 2006). In other cases, elements of management, governance or financial resources have been brought together in relation to particular services or conditions (Campbell and McLaughlin 2000). A greater number of projects have attempted to facilitate closer collaboration between health and social care teams at the front-line level, through sharing information, joint working and decision-making (Brown et al. 2003; Davey et al. 2005; Hudson 2006). There have also been wide differences in the breadth of the agencies involved in integrated care programmes, with different projects variously involving primary and acute care organisations, community nursing and GP practices and/or local authorities, private and third sector care providers (Armitage et al. 2009).

This variation is reflected in attempts to identify outcomes of integrated care. While certain benefits have been noted (Hudson 2006; Ham and Smith 2010), in many instances, researchers have concluded that outcomes are tied closely to particular features of the organisations and regions in which they are enacted. An evaluation of the North West London 'integrated care pilot' found no common reduction in hospital admissions or observable changes to patient experience, but did note improvements in the working lives of staff (although these improvements were also seen to be dependent on additional reforms within the organisations in which they worked (Bardsley et al. 2013)). A major UK government-sponsored evaluation of 16 integrated care pilots (Rand Europe 2012) identified improvements in the engagement of staff and the introduction of 'good practices', such as use of care plans, but failed to link organisational changes to improvements in patient outcomes. It was recognised that findings were influenced by the wide range of approaches to integration adopted within different sites, making comparative analysis problematic. Perhaps the most consistent message from previous studies is that the potential of integration is dependent on locally contingent factors (Cameron et al. 2014; Heenan and Birrell 2006, 2009; Petch 2012; Campbell and McLaughlin 2000; Hultberg et al. 2005; Maslin-Prothero and Bennion 2010). In other words, integration appears tied to the places in which programmes of integration are enacted.

## Place and Space of Integrated Care

Most studies and evaluation so of integrated care locate change and improvement in health and social care outcomes on the 'context' and various local or environmental 'contingencies'. Whilst these are interpreted as impacting on or conditioning the relationships between an integration initiative and its outcomes, context is often poorly theorised and rarely analysed in its own right. Warren (2017) argues this is true of the literature on networks and network governance more broadly; 'contextual and compositional arguments, whilst to a degree helpful, can be argued to be essentially attempting to account for a places' deviation from an idealised imagined norm'. To counteract this, Warren (2017) suggests paying closer attention to the regions in which network policies are enacted, linking the specific aspects of history, social relations, local institutions and social policy that make up a regions' 'biography of place'. Rather than merely the sites for policy enactment, particular places have their own history and geography, which are enacted in the meaningful and situated practice of local policy actors and entwined with the policy process.

A focus on regional diversity and locality away from the political 'centre' would appear to fit with a decentred approach (Bevir 2013), but there is no accepted consensus on the nature of place or its contribution to social theory or interpretative policy research. Cresswell (2014) suggests that social theory on place can be seen as aligned with three broad perspectives. The first is the 'ideographic' approach that we can recognise in Warren's (2017) notion of 'biography of place'. This reflects the common sense view of individual places as objectively distinct and seeks to examine places according to their unique history and characteristics. The second is the 'social constructivist' approach, which tends to see places as formed in relation to prevailing structural social forces, and subsequently as the conditioning setting for particular forms of social interaction. Like other social constructs, places certainly shape social life, but they can also be changed themselves by the social processes surrounding and within them. The third theoretical approach to place is the 'phenomenological' perspective. Drawing particularly on Casey (1996, 1997) and Malpas (1999), this takes the view that 'place' (rather than particular places) is intrinsic to all human experience and while place is certainly a social construct, it is a common and necessary one upon which understandings of society and culture are built. Our perceptions, memories, and the events and activities of daily life are always 'in place', with a sense of place always present in the formation of meaning, communication as well as individual and collective identity.

The societal and political construction of place 'from above' together with the emic experience of place 'from below' is also reflected in parallel debates over the relationship between place and space. Gieryn (2000) defines place in opposition to space, suggesting place is 'space filled up by people, practices, objects and representations' (463). This captures a commonly assumed distinctions between space as abstract, general and objective, and place as manifest through specific geographies, physicality, and investment with collective embedded meaning. This view of 'natural' space in contrast to 'meaningful' place has however been contested in studies of urban geography and social theory since the 1970s, illustrated here through the work of Lefebvre (1991). Founded in Marxist analysis, Lefebvre argues that 'social space' does not consist of intrinsic geometric properties, but is formed through social processes which structure understanding and uses of 'natural' or 'absolute' space. Lefebvre (1991) identifies social space as composed of three inter-related facets: (i) 'representations of space', emanating from central policies, plans and designs, by which space is quantified and abstracted in relation to prevailing capitalist social structure; (ii) 'spatial practices' found in routines and patterns of daily living in contemporary (capitalist and archetypically urban) environments, created within systems of power; and (iii) the 'representational' or 'lived' space of subjective experience and meanings of space, which can be influenced by wider social, symbolic and artistic culture, and can lead to spatial practices and representations being contested.

In Lefebvre's work, elements of both phenomenology and social constructivism can be recognised, but the inter-relationship between the social and spatial is also of central concern. Lefebvre argues sensory, embodied presence within space is central to experience, with lived space emerging 'through an ephemeral collection of symbols, experience and rhythms of daily life that responds to and resists the rationalized planning' (Zhang et al. 2008: 648). At the same time, the production of space is shaped by power relations imposed through processes of programs of urban reform, building and development, which can dominate space while creating sites of struggle and resistance (Harvey 2003). Public policies attempt to 'work on' place and restructure space in light of government priorities and forms of service provision (Castells 1977) and once formed, the spaces in which we live 'suture [us] into our everyday existence' (Burrell 2013: 12), but by the same token lived spaces are sites for both remaking and resisting the power relations imagined by policy-makers (Waring and Bishop 2018). Welfare and social policy, such as those promoting integrated care, can be read as one means through which spaces are (re)constituted in line with the aims of the capitalist state and the dominant neoliberal market agenda (Peck and Tickell 2002). While particular places are 'elastic' (Agnew 1987) and the meaning of place is subject to changing and contested interpretation, they should not be seen as a backdrop to enacting social policy, but are instead central to policy formation and conduct.

Building on the above, this chapter considers the relationship between the imposed reconfigurations of space within projects of integrated care, and both the spatial practices of work and the lived experiences of integrated care 'in place'. New service models of integrated care involve rational re-analysis of population needs, roles, resources and locations of service provision. They are also interpreted and enacted amongst disparate professional and managerial groups within their own locations of work. Here the aim is to consider how places and spaces of integrated care are formed between the plans, practices and experiences of work. To do this, the chapter draws upon a recent integrated care project within a single Metropolitan borough, described further in the sections below.

## Case Study Background

This chapter draws on data collected whilst I acted as an independent evaluation consultant for a community care NHS Trust operating across several metropolitan boroughs in the North of England. In 2012/2013 the Trust entered into an integrated care programme with the local authority (LA) of one of the metropolitan boroughs in which it was operating, intended at the commencement to be a comprehensive programme of reform to all community care and social services for adult, children and young people across the region. This was initially intended to include a comprehensive management restructuring, with joint management of combined health and social care teams. It was also intended to co-locate health and social care staff within combined teams, including the development of shared operating procedures, integrated IT systems and common points of communication with external stakeholders, including common referral systems. Further relevant details surrounding the project are described in sections below. It is worth noting at the outset that the outcomes of the programme were largely seen as mixed, even by those responsible for implementation. Over the 3 years of the project—from conception to initial 'roll out'—ambitions for integration between the NHS Trust and the LA had been both scaled back and in many ways overtaken by a further regional reforms, including an additional integrated care programme aiming to bring together a wider range of stakeholders.

The study involved in-depth qualitative interviews with 45 project stakeholders, including senior project managers (7), locality leads and team managers (9), occupational therapists and physiotherapists (4), nurses and nursing assistants (12), general practitioners (4), social workers (5) and locality administrators (3). I also attended and observed management and service development meetings across the three-year period to understand in more detail how the integrated care programme emerged over time in relation to other aspects of organisational and service development. Observed meetings included GP locality meetings across each of the five relevant GP practice clusters, in which GPs were asked to respond to relevant interview questions, distributed prior to the meetings. I regularly visited integrated care office sites and observed of multi-disciplinarily team (MDT) meetings in each of the four localities (approximately 75 hours). I also collected descriptive data on attendance of the MDT meetings, the source of referrals to the integrated care workload, the use of the 'single point of contact' [SPOC] contact lines, numbers of joint home visits and admissions to long term care from the integrated care programme.

## Getting Integrated Care off the Ground

The origins of the integrated care project can be linked to national policy changes that were translated and implemented through the re-organisation of care at the regional level. As part of policy change in NHS commissioning leading up to the market reforms of the 2012 Health and Social Care act, the Transforming Community Services (TCS) initiative sought to ensure that Primary Care Trusts (PCTs) separated responsibility for service commissioning from service provision. In short, the policy aimed to prevent PCTs from 'buying' services from themselves. The PCT within the case study borough had been unsuccessful in their bid to lead community services, and senior leaders at the PCT proposed that more integrated service between a (newly created) Community Care Trust, including close partnership with the council, was likely to have more appeal to commissioners. A stumbling block in early discussions surrounded the state of children's services within the region, with the local authorities' children services under national scrutiny following a serious incident, and the Trust and the council discussed the possible impact and risk associated with this on the potential bid. Despite this, a strategic partnership with the local authority was proposed and agreed by chief executives at both the community trust and the council.

During this transition period of heightened uncertainty, there were widespread rumours across the PCT surrounding a potential take-over by an external organisation. It was therefore announced with a degree of optimism, or at least relief, that the majority of staff had been successfully re-employed in the new community care trust and that the organisation remained in NHS hands.

> So, we could have ended up in a private organisation, a voluntary organisation, social enterprise or an NHS and a variety of NHSs vertically or horizontally integrated. We were just grateful we'd got an NHS organisation. (Nurse, Locality Team Leader)

As part of this transition, the employment contracts of staff within the PCT were transferred to the new Community Care Trust in April 2011. The former NHS regulatory body Monitor (now part of NHS Improvement) became the primary focus of activity for completing the Transfer of Undertaking (Protection of Employment) (TUPE) process for over 220 members of staff and fulfilling the associated requirements for financial regulator. The next step towards integration was the instalment of a Joint Governance Board (JGB) in late 2011 made up of chief executives/directors from stakeholder organisations including the acute trust and commissioner. In addition, a Joint Implementation Executive

Board (JIEB) was formed to provide oversight and steer for the project work-streams and operational elements of the roll out of integrated care. Finally, an operational project management team was created, largely composed of senior managers from the existing PCT.

The integrated care project was therefore the result of both policy push from central government policy and pull from leadership within the borough. The model of integration developed by the leadership team was successful in rhetorically presenting the Community Care Trust as legitimate, and allowed them to secure the contract for care services within the new market rules. However, aside from a general aim to dramatically change the relationship between front-line health and social care teams and promote joint working, it was widely recognised that there was still a large degree of ambiguity about what integration with the local authority was going to entail in practice.

> It was actually quite woolly I would say some of the informant because I don't think at the time there was actually that fixed model in people's heads about how it was going to look. So it was just very broadly speaking about integration. (Project Manager)

To translate national aspirations for integrated care within the region, project managers begin to put very general plans for integrated care 'in place'. Three aspects of spatial reform, are covered below (1) mapping the localities of service provision, (2) creation of shared space, and (3) shifting hierarchies between the centre and periphery of the borough.

## Re-mapping Localities

A first challenge for project managers was establishing how the intended service model would overlay the existing geography of the borough, including suburban neighbourhoods, towns and villages. Mapping and the demarcation of boundaries has been seen as central to the political control of space (Agnew 1996) and an important concern of the JEIB was dividing the region into geographic units amenable to the logistics and operations of integrated care. Early in the project's life, there were attempts to involve staff in shaping these localities, but as time progressed decisions had to be made about where the boundaries would fall. Five localities to mirror divisions already used for service provision within the council were originally on the table, but as the project plan was worked up, project managers attention focused on the need to minimise costs and agreement was reached to reduce the number of localities to four. A map was drawn up by the project management team that divided the borough into East, West, South and Central areas, each to be served by a new integrated health and social care team.

> It wasn't the whole of the East as we know it now. We had [Suburb A] and then we brought in the teams from [suburb B and Suburb C] and we started building up from there. (Project Manager)

> we had to draw the line somewhere. We tried to look at [electoral] wards and the type of mix of places, but ultimately we needed to make a decision. (Project Manager)

As these quotes suggest, managers recognised that the boundaries of the new Working Together locality were somewhat arbitrary and not aligned with current neighbourhood distinctions or other public services. Nevertheless, the service localities came to frame other elements of the integrated care project, for example with project plans, line management, performance metrics, and divisions of work organised around the four areas. When asked about Working Together, front line staff identified themselves as part of either the North, South East or West teams (amongst other professional and role identifications). A common understanding developed about the demographic variations across these areas, with West covering a largely rural area, South composed of formal coal mining villages, and Central and East including urban areas of high social economic deprivation.

> We can't do it exactly the same as in [West] because they've got [comparatively well-off villages], we've got to cover places like [inner city suburbs] so of course we have some different pressures. (Occupational Therapist)

> So East. We don't have much to do with West, Central or South. It's just because our clients don't really cross over them areas. (Social Services Manager)

The locality division of the integrated care teams was particularly important given that the practice of community care work is so intricately tied to the geographic 'patch' which defines the content of their job. For community health and social care staff, movement between home visits and office bases formed the central pattern of their day-to-day work, and their case load depended on the levels of service need (strongly influenced by levels of affluence/deprivation) of the neighbourhoods they covered.

> X is probably the most central because we're probably equal distance from [village 1] and [village 2] as what we are to [town], so it's kind of in the middle really, but in an ideal world we'd have health visitors here, all the health visitors here. (Occupational Therapist)

> in terms of the area that we now cover which is very different. It's almost like starting a new job because you've got different resources, different kind of service user groups across the area. (Occupational Therapist)

> We do cover a very geographical area, large area. So time [is a key issue in integration]. Moving base points. (Team Leader)

The newly imposed divisions shaped the routines of everyday work by altering the patterns of travel to and from visits, although not always in pre-planned ways. New localities also altered the spread of professional groups and the opportunities for interaction. As the above quotes highlight this was the focus of frequent reflection and discussion, with a particular point of contention being the equity in the division of neighbourhoods (hence workload) each group covered, as well as the relationship between WT localities with other service boundaries.

> The [integrated care project] localities don't really make any sense, and to be honest it is a nightmare as we are never sure where to find any district nurses. (GP)

> We share the building with GPs but funnily enough we don't actually cover those GPs area [...] Which did cause a bit of frustration for the GPs when we originally moved in because they just couldn't see the logic of it at all. (Community Nurse)

The workability and implications of the new locality structure remained a continued topic of debate over the course of the integrated care project, and appeared to play a key role in staff views on how the project was (or was not) working and part of the projects perceived failings by the commissioners.

## Creating Shared Space

A second key spatial element of the integrated care project was the co-location of health and social care staff within new locality bases. This was intended to be a central mechanism of integration, that leaders assumed to improve communication and multi-disciplinary working, reduce duplication and allow the re-allocation of roles and resources. The initial focus of co-location was in a single locality (East) that was intended to act as a 'pathfinder' for the other localities to imitate. This made use of a purpose-built office building, opened in time for the integrated care project and with health and social care teams moving in together.

> I think one of the things that we've had different to the other areas is that this building here was obviously brand new. So, shaping how this building here was being utilised and developed came hand-in-hand with the development of one team working and co-locating teams. (Community Matron)

However, co-locating staff became a major undertaking across the life of the project. A key challenge was finding suitable accommodation within places 'central' to each locality that would allow efficient travel to domestic appointments. Co-location happened on a largely ad hoc basis, with project managers spending considerable time searching for desk-space in an assortment of existing NHS and Borough Council owned buildings. Staff were moved into a variety of buildings, that varied greatly in terms of age, style, design and layout, often in locations that made little logistical sense to the model of integration.

> We ended up all moving into a small office because we had to vacate to facilitate the move of furniture. Move all into one office to then all move out again to be able to move into here and then not having the IT structure in place. (Project Manager)

> We were supposed to move in earlier than that but because it's an old building that was being if you like renovated and adapted to suit our needs, there were complications. (Social Worker)

This resulted in frequent office moves while building adaptations were made. The challenges of suitable accommodation played into the growing distinction between localities. In this way, the managerial dilemmas around resources and office accommodation led people to reflect on and elaborate traditional geographic distinctions across the borough.

> I think we have a different approach because we know it's going to be quite some time before we are co-located. (Social Worker)

Further, where buildings for co-located teams were secured, the social organisation of co-location differed significantly between the four localities. For example, team leaders attempted to purposefully mix the desks of nurses, social workers and occupational therapists to encourage joint working, but each site was composed of a different and changing mix of health and social care staff, due to staff shortages and the particularities of local services. A number of staff commented on the benefits of working in close physical proximity with other professionals, from whom they were previously separated.

> Oh, it's improved communication between us all dramatically. Obviously we meet on a weekly basis officially, but we talk on a daily basis every day to our colleagues. (District Nurse)

> That's a big change, that you get the face-to-face networking. (Physiotherapist)

The ability to mix staff was also highly dependent on the nature of spaces available, with much talk of making-do 'for now'. What was also notable was that over time, professional groups sought to move closer together and 'reclaim' areas of the buildings for their own use. In the sites that were co-located in the same building, professional groups increasingly gathered into separate areas, looking for areas to demarcate as their own.

> The resistance [amongst staff members] is that they're used to be in small teams to then coming together as one big team. (Team Leader)

> ...because there was not many social workers, they felt very isolated which I can probably imagine. So obviously they requested a move so that they could be together, but they're still in the same building and I think that's what's key. (Community Nurse)

> I have got a little space of my own now where I can spread out a bit and actually leave some things there and I feel that's helped because they know where I am. (Occupational Therapist)

Therefore, while co-location became to be the central feature of the integration project, there was considerable variation in the realisation of integration based on available space and peoples' reaction to it. Individual and small groups of staff themselves looked for ways of working within the new spaces based on working patterns and professional allegiances. This professional re-grouping could be seen as an attempt to regain control over their professional work, following the employment transfer and frequent organisational changes.

## Reshaping Hierarchy

The third spatial aspect of the integrated care project was in reconfiguring the relationship between the project 'centre' and the 'periphery'. The branding of the integrated care project attempted to emphasis the 'oneness' of the borough and promote a single place-based identity, for example with slogans such as 'Together for the people of [name]'. Yet, the integrated care project involved creating a new hierarchical structure between project managers based in 'central' offices and the locality teams spread across the borough. The vast majority of early project management meetings were held in the large boardroom in the landmark building of Trust HQ. These were well attended by senior managers from stakeholder organisations, as well as locality team leaders. In the initial stages, project managers spend much of their time driving around the borough, trying to secure the 'buy-in' of various neighbourhood teams, returning to 'base' to discuss progress at project management meetings. It was though recognised that communicating face-to-face with teams around borough would be difficult, so attention was initially focused on working with the pathfinder site.

> We did have a look round, but then we spent a lot of time working with the East Team about what would work and what would suit that area and put a lot of staff involvement into that, into then designing them model and doing the work. (Project Manager)

This created a clear sense of hierarchy amongst localities, with the pathfinder site seen as the centre of integrated working. Other localities found themselves often compared to this pathfinder site and several respondents reported feeling 'left out' of the project and under pressure to catch up and conform.

> [Our team leader] very much wanted us to kind of yes look at what they'd done but make it our own. What worked for them may not work for us, but [she] obviously moved into her new post. So, what actually happened is what got fed through them was that they wanted us [to do]. (Physiotherapist)

> One of my friends who qualified at the same time as me was a sister in the area at the time and she was kind of relaying back what was happening over there and it seemed a better way of working. (Nurse)

Closely tied to the geographic division of the integrated care localities was the role of the four community matrons, who had been selected from a group of senior nurses to lead the nursing teams in each of the areas. These were a vastly experienced group at the highest band of their professional pay scale, who had worked within the region for much of their careers. Within the organisational chart of the Community Care Trust, these sat under senior nursing leaders who were part of the integrated care project team. As the integrated care project took shape, it became clear that the four community matrons were crucial for implementing the decisions made in central project teams; moving from a centralised to a locality-based structure required leadership responsibility to be distributed geographically, creating a barrier between central project managers and integrated teams.

> Well, they've all got their own patches now haven't they – so in some ways it can be difficult for us [project managers] to get them all singing from the same sheet. (Project Manager)

> in each of the areas, nothing is the same. They've all got their own little ways of doing things that are very different from each other. So we had to do a lot of unpicking and we still are doing in each of the individual areas. (Project Manager)

Forming the project around new geographic divisions created a gap between the concerns of the project team within Trust HQ and the localities faced with working out details of new integrated practices in each of the neighbourhoods. Following turnover in the project management team, there was a growing realisation that new boundaries had been created and attempts were then made to try to gain back control from the locality teams. Community matrons were increasingly seen as holding their own 'local' agendas that potentially detracted from central managers project ambitions. In response, a new re-centralised nursing management model was tabled by the project management team that potentially undermined the original integrated care plan, with little emphasis on integrated teams.

This changing status of the integrated care project was reflected in the location of project management activities shifting over time. Toward the end of the project's life, meetings were increasingly held in the back offices of individual project managers dotted around the hospital campus, and attendance dwindled. Approximately two years after the integrated care project began, it could be seen that while a number of activities had been celebrated as a success, the focus of commissioners' and senior managers had moved away from the project. As the project fizzled out, there was clearly a high degree of frustration about the cyclical nature of policy reform.

> I can't count how many there've been. Integrated Management Teams, MDTs, away days, afternoons away. Even moving furniture, it's a cost and it's the mental cost to workers as well. Yet again, 'Well we've started something. We've spent all that money trying to sort something out and now it's not going ahead. What a waste of time and energy', and then you're back to square one. (Project Manager)

## Discussion and Conclusion

The findings highlight how the spatial aspects of an integrated care project were formed through the interaction of project plans, work practices, existing geographic and demographic distinctions, available buildings and professional institutions. The integrated care project was developed with ambitions to develop seamless working around the patients and remove unproductive social boundaries between the health and social care across borough, but ended with ambiguity over how much integration had been put 'in place'. Returning to Lefebvre's (1991) elements of space, attempting to put the vision of integrated care into practice involved new 'representations of space' created by regional leaders and project managers. Key planning decisions included the creation of a locality map of service provision, designs for new co-located workspaces and altering core-periphery relations between the project centre and localities. These plans were shaped by underlying imperatives within the new Community Care Trust around resource control and service rationalisation, themselves shaped by myriad contextual factors specific to the region. These representations of space were entwined with both the spatial practices and lived experiences of working within integrated care. The spatial practice of community health and social care workers was split between the domestic spaces of patients and clients and the office bases in which they interacted with colleagues and performed bureaucratic tasks. Significant time was taken by travel between these points across an individuals' 'patch'. Altering locality boundaries and moving offices partially reshaped these working patterns in important ways, but also significant was the demographic make-up of the borough and existing public service facilities into which the new co-located model needed to be inserted. These were largely beyond the control of the project managers but shaped the performance of integrated care.

Turning to the representational 'lived' space, the office space available to each of the localities played into peoples' understanding of the integrated care project, with those finding themselves in dedicated office facilities feeling more privileged than those continually moved. In addition, professional identities and professional ownership of space were unsettled through the introduction of the integrated care project (Waring and Bishop 2018). This was most evident in the resistance to managerial designs for shared workspaces, with professional groups claiming ownership of portions of office space. Burrell (2013) suggests amenability to change and recurring 'rupture' has become the defining character of NHS, particularly at managerial level. Here professional staff could be seen to seek continuity through creating their own professional space while coping with inevitability of change which was clearly taking an emotional toll (Waring and Bishop 2018). The contrast between the networked vision of integrated care and the lived experience of professional staff reflects Ingold (2016) description of the transformation of place through modernity:

> once a knot tied from multiple and interlaced strands of movement and growth, [place] now figures as a note in a static network of connectors. To an ever-increasing extent, people in modern metropolitan societies find themselves in environments build as assemblies of connected elements. Yet in practice they continue to thread their own ways through these environments, tracing paths as they go. (Ingold 2016: 75)

Ideals of integrated care suggest the dissolution of occupational, professional and organisational boundaries, which as the above case illustrates are intricately tied to issues of space and place. Regional integrated care plans also involve the creation of new boundaries between the places of service provision, and therefore seek to replace existing social boundaries with new place attachments based on service management priorities. As noted by Harvey (2001) a sense of place can be central to developing solidarities and building cooperative movements as well as creating social boundaries and emphasising social difference. Celebratory narratives of place have been constructed for example around Torbay and Sedgefield (Hudson 2006), to promote 'successful' integrated care; but these implicitly castigate regions 'failing' to keep up with change. Current healthcare policy clearly involves contradictions in this regard, seeking to encourage cooperation and sharing innovation, while also creating a competitive environment in which regions are expected to out-perform peers. This can be seen in periodic announcement of integrated 'pilots', 'vanguards', 'pathfinders' and 'pioneer' sites; political language which overtly valorises spatial flexibility above embedded practice and traditional boundary distinctions. What is also noticeable is the lack of stability these short-lived initiatives appear to afford; as in our study, policies imposing spatial reconfiguration are at threat in subsequent rounds of policy reform.

Decentred theory (Bevir and Rhodes 2003) is attentive to subjective meanings developed within diverse traditions and emergent through iterative dilemmas. Space and place clearly have an important role in shaping how people experience and give meaning to policy change, far beyond that of neutral backdrop to policy formation and enactment. Tradition is commonly considered as resting within—and in some ways constitutive of—place, with forms of social life associated with distinctions between particular countries, regions and towns. However, as identified in the findings above, boundaries of place are not stable delineations of abstract space, but continually reconstituted in light of policy reform on one hand and issues of 'bottom up' politics and practice on the other. This is not to say central policy can unilaterally rationalise space to pursue policy objectives; rather policy discourses invoking spatial reform play into, and with, existing attachments to place, which are themselves subject to reconsideration light of dispersed processes of political and social change.

The implications of this work for current policy and strategic changes in English healthcare can be considered. Integrated Care Partnerships (ICPs), currently being promoted by NHS England, are already struggling for legitimacy, having quickly cycled through different names including Sustainable Transformation Partnerships, Accountable Care Partnerships (ACPs) and now ICSs. The 'Integrated' label was only adopted following controversy (including the early stages of a legal challenge) surrounding the commercial intent of these new regional bodies. The work presented here suggests a different form of contestation facing ICPs, namely over the creation of places and spaces amenable to reforms.

The evaluation this research is based on did not include extensive engagement with service users, and therefore does not present the views of the population of the region on the reconfiguration of community services. However, the locality of services remains a key concern amongst service users, particularly those in need of on-going community health and social services (Exworthy and Peckham 2006; Comber et al. 2011) and place-based identities continue to be a core factor influencing public debate over service change. A further limitation here is the need to keep the area anonymous, which limits the scope to provide historical details of the place under investigation. In contrast, historical work can provide greater evidence on the way configurations of political and social forces have played into the emergence of particular regional care provision. Future research could consider approaches to blending historical analysis with contemporary social scientific data within ethical constraints.

In conclusion, disputes over the spaces and places of public service provision are certainly not new; indeed, Castells identified competing interpretation of place as a key issue for state services, and is central to urban politics (Castells 1977). Given the centrality of themes of integration in contemporary public policy—which involve direct attempts to work on and reimagine space—studies focusing on the way in which place and space shape the performance of contemporary reforms are suggested here as important. This chapter provides empirical evidence on the importance of space and place in the trajectory of an integrated care project, and particularly highlights the contestation surrounding attempts to reconceptualise geography and facilities along new service divisions. Space and place are therefore important concepts within a decentred theory of public policy formation.

## References


Agnew, J. (1987). *Place and politics: The geographical mediation of state and society*. Boston: Allen and Unwin.

Agnew, J. (1996). Mapping politics: How context counts in electoral geography. *Political Geography, 15*(2), 129–146.

Armitage, G. D., Suter, E., Oelke, N. D., & Adair, C. E. (2009). Health systems integration: State of the evidence. *International Journal of Integrated Care, 9*(2). https://doi.org/10.5334/ijic.316.

Bardsley, M., Steventon, A., Smith, J., & Dixon, J. (2013). *Evaluating integrated and community-based care*. London: Nuffield Trust.

Bevir, M. (2013). *A theory of governance university of California press*, Berkeley CA.

Bevir, M., & Needham, C. (2017). Decentring social policy: Narratives, resistance, and practices. *International Journal of Sociology and Social Policy, 37*(11–12), 626–638. https://doi.org/10.1108/IJSSP-02-2017-00.

Bevir, M., & Rhodes, R. (2003). *Interpreting british governance*. London: Routledge.

Brown, L., Tucker, C., & Domokos, T. (2003). Evaluating the impact of integrated health and social care teams on older people living in the community. *Health and Social Care in the Community, 11*, 85–94.

Burrell, G. (2013). *Styles of organizing: The will to form*. Oxford: Oxford University Press.

Cameron, A., Lart, R., Bostock, L., & Coomber, C. (2014). Factors that promote and hinder joint and integrated working between health and social care services: A review of research literature. *Health and Social Care in the Community, 22*(3), 225–233.

Campbell, J., & McLaughlin, J. (2000). The 'joined up' management of adult health and social care services in Northern Ireland: Lessons for the rest of the UK? *Journal of Integrated Care, 8*(5), 6–13.

Casey, E. (1996). How to get from space to place in a fairly short stretch of time. In K. Basso & S. Feld (Eds.), *Senses of place* (pp. 13–52). Sante Fe, NM: School of American Research Press.
Casey, E. (1997). *The fate of place: A philosophical history.* Berkeley: University of California Press.
Castells, M. (1977). *The urban question.* London: Edward Arnold.
Comber, A. J., Brunsdon, C., & Radburn, R. (2011). A spatial analysis of variations in health access: Linking geography, socio-economic status and access perceptions. *International Journal of Health Geographics, 10*(1), 44.
Cresswell, T. (2014). *Place: An introduction.* Chichester: Wiley.
Davey, B., Levin, E., Iliffe, S., & Kharicha, K. (2005). Integrating health and social care: Implications for joint working and community care outcomes for older people. *Journal of Interprofessional Care, 19*(1), 22–34.
DoH. (2000). *The NHS Plan: A plan for investment, a plan for reform.* London: The Stationary Office.
Exworthy, M., & Peckham, S. (2006). Access, choice and travel: Implications for health policy. *Social Policy & Administration, 40*(3), 267–287.
Gieryn, T. F. (2000). A space for place in sociology. *Annual Review of Sociology, 26*(1), 463–496.
Glasby, J. (Ed.). (2012). *Commissioning for health and well-being: An introduction.* Bristol: Policy Press.
Goodwin, N., Dixon, A., Anderson, G., & Wodchis, W. (2014). *Providing integrated care for older people with complex needs: Lessons from seven international case studies.* London: King's Fund.
Ham, C., & Smith, J. (2010). *Removing the policy barriers to integrated care in England.* London: Nuffield Trust.
Harvey, D. (2001). *Spaces of capital: Towards a critical geography.* New York: Routledge.
Harvey, D. (2003). The right to the city. *International Journal of Urban and Regional Research, 27*(4), 939–941.
Heenan, D., & Birrell, D. (2006). The integration of health and social care: The lessons from Northern Ireland. *Social Policy & Administration, 40*(1), 47–66.
Heenan, D., & Birrell, D. (2009). Organisational integration in health and social care: Some reflections on the Northern Ireland experience. *Journal of Integrated Care, 17*(5), 3–12.
Hudson, B. (2006). Integrated team working: You can get it if you really want it: Part I. *Journal of Integrated Care, 14*(1), 13–21.

Hultberg, E. L., Glendinning, C., Allebeck, P., & Lönnroth, K. (2005). Using pooled budgets to integrate health and welfare services: A comparison of experiments in England and Sweden. *Health and Social Care in the Community, 13*(6), 531–541.

Ingold, T. (2016). *Lines: A brief history*. London: Routledge.

Kodner, D. L., & Spreeuwenberg, C. (2002). Integrated care: Meaning, logic, applications, and implications—A discussion paper. *International Journal of Integrated Care, 2*(4). https://doi.org/10.5334/ijic.67.

Lavender, A. (2006). Creation of a care trust: Managing the project. *Journal of Integrated Care, 14*(5), 14–22.

Lefebvre, H. (1991). *The production of space* (D. Nicolson-Smith, Trans.). Oxford: Blackwell.

Leichsenring, K. (2004). Developing integrated health and social care services for older persons in Europe. *International Journal of Integrated Care, 4*(3). https://doi.org/10.5334/ijic.107.

Malpas, J. (1999). *Place and experience: A philosophical topography*. Cambridge: Cambridge University Press.

Martínez-González, N. A., Berchtold, P., Ullman, K., Busato, A., & Egger, M. (2014). Integrated care programmes for adults with chronic conditions: A meta-review. *International Journal for Quality in Health Care, 26*(5), 561–570.

Maslin-Prothero, S. E., & Bennion, A. E. (2010). Integrated team working: A literature review. *International Journal of Integrated Care, 10*, e43. https://doi.org/10.5334/ijic.529.

NHS England. (2017). *Annual business plan*. London: The Stationary Office.

Ouwens, M., Wollersheim, H., Hermens, R., Hulscher, M., & Grol, R. (2005). Integrated care programmes for chronically ill patients: A review of systematic reviews. *International Journal for Quality in Health Care, 17*(2), 141–146.

Peck, J., & Tickell, A. (2002). Neoliberalizing space. *Antipode, 34*(3), 380–404.

Petch, A. (2012). Tectonic plates: Aligning evidence, policy and practice in health and social care integration. *Journal of Integrated Care, 20*(2), 77–88.

Pollock, A. M., & Roderick, P. (2018). Why we should be concerned about accountable care organisations in England's NHS. *BMJ, 360,* k343.

Rand Europe. (2012). National evaluation of the DH integrated care pilots. *Rand Health Quarterly, 2*(1), 8.

Reed, J., Cook, G., Childs, S., & McCormack, B. (2005). A literature review to explore integrated care for older people. *International Journal of Integrated Care, 5*(1). https://doi.org/10.5334/ijic.119.

Robinson, J. C., & Casalino, L. P. (1996). Vertical integration and organizational networks in health care. *Health Affairs, 15*(1), 7–22.

Waring, J., & Bishop, S. (2018). Transforming professional and service user identities in the heterotopian 'hybrid spaces' of public-private partnerships. *Policy and Politics, 46*(4), 663–679.

Warren, J. (2017). "The way things get done around here..." Exploring spatial biographies, social policy and governance in the North East of England. *International Journal of Sociology and Social Policy, 37*(11–12), 655–666.

Zhang, Z., Spicer, A., & Hancock, P. (2008). Hyper-organizational space in the work of J. G. Ballard. *Organization, 15*(6), 889–910.

# Situating Practices of Human and Non-human Networks in the Delivery of Emergency and Urgent Care Services

Catherine Pope

## Introduction

Information and communication technologies (ICTs) are an important driver for network-based forms of governance. Computers, the internet, and digital media, in particular have shaped, and continue to shape, governance from the macro level of the nation-state to, through to markets, institutions, formal and informal organisations (Castells 1996, 2000; Ferlie et al. 2010). ICTs enable the storage, retrieval, manipulation and transmission of digital information at scale and at speed in ways that support the kinds of knowledge distribution and decentralisation that underpin networked governance. These technologies include computer decision support systems (CDSS) and software algorithms deployed to improve, optimise and manage service delivery and productivity across a range of institutions and industries. These particular

C. Pope (✉)
Nuffield Department of Primary Care Health Sciences,
University of Oxford, Oxford, UK
e-mail: Catherine.pope@phc.ox.ac.uk


M. Bevir and J. Waring (eds.), *Decentring Health and Care Networks*, Organizational Behaviour in Healthcare,
https://doi.org/10.1007/978-3-030-40889-3_6

technologies have a perspicuous and growing role in the delivery of health services and care, such that the nomenclature has undergone a subtle shift, to become *clinical* decision support systems. The case presented in this chapter concerns one CDSS, namely NHS Pathways.

In analysing the growth and impact of these new technologies on health care governance, the chapter focusses on micro-level networks and, in particular, on the role that non-human (machine, computer, digital) actors play in what are, increasingly, technologized modes of health services delivery. My starting position is to concur with other commentators that there has been a significant shift in public services organizations from hierarchical forms of governance towards network governance and that this is especially the case in developed country health care systems, such as found in the NHS, European and North American context. Indeed, Ferlie et al. (2011, 2013) argue network governance is perhaps the 'least bad' form of governance for tackling wicked problems surrounding complex health care needs and equally complex health service delivery systems. For the NHS, faced with an aging and multi-morbid population, and increasingly consumerist public and political expectations about health service delivery, the provision of urgent and emergency care has become just such a wicked problem. One response to these challenges, as with other areas of heath care, has been the enrolment of digital technologies to support the delivery of services; in the case presented in this chapter this has included a particular reliance on computerised decision support. These CDSS and software algorithms have increasingly been deployed to improve, optimise and manage health service delivery in the NHS and other health systems. While there have been empirical studies of the deployment and implementation of CDSS in health care delivery per se (Greatbatch et al. 2005; Hanlon et al. 2005; Pearson et al. 2009; Pope et al. 2013), there has been perhaps less attention to the unfolding of governance in the everyday situated practices and networks of care that involve non-human ICT actors as well as human ones.

One consequence of neoliberalism has been the creation of new networked forms of governance (Bevir 2011a, b), that replace more hierarchical forms of order with governance arrangements that rely on interdependency, negotiated decision making, collaboration, and the elaboration of locally constituted norms and rules. A decentred theoretical approach has emerged which focusses on how these governance networks are socially constructed and understood (Bevir and Richards 2009) and which emphasises the importance of understanding how people create meanings in action. This has provoked micro-level studies of the success and failure of network governance, examining what people in networks do, for example looking at the characteristics, skills and style of network managers (Ferlie and Pettigrew 1996; Ferlie et al. 2010). This work has been extremely valuable in illuminating the situated agency of people in networks. It has also played into the hand of ethnographers keen to use their methods to "explore the beliefs and actions not only of politicians, civil servants, public sector managers, but also street-level bureaucrats, non-governmental actors and citizens" (Bevir and Richards 2009: 11) in the study of network governance. To date however there has been little empirical work examining the role of non-human actors in networked governance.

Science and Technology studies (STS), and particularly the variant Actor Network Theory (ANT) provides a parallel approach to thinking about networks, less interested in governance per se, but concerned with the shifting relationships between humans and non-humans (Latour 2005; Law 1986). Like decentred theorising, ANT has roots in constructivist approaches, and encourages an empirical focus on the making and remaking of networks. ANT has been especially useful in alerting social scientists to the importance of non-human agents in these networks, and to the situated performativity of interactions between humans and machines. This approach too has encouraged the use of ethnographic methods to "follow the actors" (Latour 1987), however it has been keen to blur the distinction between the social and technical, and consider how things (be it machines, animals or other objects) as well as people, act and have causal effects.

This chapter brings together these two threads, the decentred approach to governance and an interest in the relationships between human and non-human actors in networks. It explores how local situated practices of interpretation and resistance unfold in networks of human and digital agents engaged in health service delivery for urgent and emergency health care. The aim is to show how these actors come together to make, remake and resist rules, and to explicate the different ways in which 'governance on the ground' is constructed when people work with CDSS. The empirical material draws on a series of studies of a CDSS in everyday use in the UK NHS conducted over the decade since 2008. While this chapter represents my thinking on these issues, the research on which these ideas are based was very much a collaborative activity and these ideas could not have taken shape without the efforts of the people and funders acknowledged at the end of this piece.

## Triaging Emergency and Urgent Care Using CDSS

Clinicians learn to diagnose by building up evidence from observed signs and symptoms, reported patient history and linking this to medical knowledge in a process that resembles the hypothetico-deductive method. Often referred to as differential diagnosis, this requires clinicians to run through multiple candidate explanations for symptoms and engage in a process of elimination to derive a diagnosis. Triage overlaps diagnostic processes, either pre-empting them by flagging some symptoms or presentations as more urgent (this patient is bleeding and unconscious so should be seen first) or following it (this patient has experienced a heart attack and needs to be treated immediately). The term triage is thought to have originated in Napoleonic wars and to be derived from the French word 'trier' (to sort or select), and this process of sorting and prioritising patients was pioneered in warfare and mass casualty situations but is commonly used in health service settings (Robertson-Steel 2006). On the battlefield triage was performed by the most expert or senior clinician but in contemporary health services it has increasingly been delegated to clerks, receptionists and nursing staff (Hughes 1989).

'NHS Pathways' is a CDSS designed to support telephone triage in emergency and urgent health care. First introduced in 2005 (Turner et al. 2008), NHS Pathways operates an algorithm, or set of rules for problem-solving drawing on an extensive repository of clinical information which can be searched using a logical process of elimination, that attempts to mimic the clinical decision making described above. As Beer has noted "algorithms are inevitably modelled on visions of the social world, and with outcomes in mind, outcomes influenced by commercial or other interests and agendas" but in addition they are "lived with, they are an integral part of that social world; they are woven into practices and outcomes" (2017: 4). This paper explores how the CDSS has been modelled on a particular vision of triage and diagnostic practice, and how it is woven into the practices of health care delivery. The core argument is that the CDSS operates on the basis of perfect governance, it is premised upon the idea that triage is a rational, rule-governed standardisable process. The reality, as we will see, is that this vision is thwarted, adapted, and resisted in the everyday situated practices, human and non-human networks of care.

About 14 million telephone calls are triaged each year using NHS Pathways within the NHS 111 urgent care and the 999 emergency ambulance services (NHS England 2016). All NHS 111 providers and around half of the NHS Ambulance service providers in England use the software. In both services non-clinical staff answer calls and, supported by doctors, nurses and paramedics, they assess symptoms, prioritise and direct callers to appropriate care. For 999 calls, Pathways is an adjunct to a geographical monitoring system that can deploy and track emergency response vehicles. The call handler is offered a series of logical algorithms (pathways) to underpin questions for the caller/patient that determine the care needed and time frame in which this should be accessed. The CDSS follows a decision tree logic or structure and includes questions that the call adviser is required to ask verbatim as well as suggested prompts that are used to gain additional information, for example getting callers to describe the nature of their pain (as 'crushing' or 'shooting'). At the end of each 'pathway' the CDSS offers a disposition or outcome, and this can include, for example, sending an ambulance, arranging an appointment with a GP or the provision of information on self-care. In the NHS 111 service, the system is combined with a real-time directory of services (DoS) which provides information on the location and scope of services, as well as opening and waiting times to support the urgent care dispositions. Ambulance crews have different target response times according to the acuity/severity of the case allocated. The Pathways software has recently been chosen to underpin the extension of the NHS 111 to an online service where patients and service users will access the software via an app, bypassing the call handler.

## The Empirical Studies

This paper reports findings from two large cross-case, comparative ethnographic projects looking in detail at the NHS Pathways CDSS, funded by the NIHR Service Delivery and Organisation and the Health Services Development and Research programme. These projects examined the implementation of the Pathways digital technology in different settings in England. In these studies, researchers spent time watching the situated practices and collecting narratives from the staff involved in using the software. In the first study the settings were three urgent and emergency healthcare settings—a 999 (emergency care) telephone service and two urgent care services referred to as single point of access (SPA) and out of hours (OOH). The first study comprised 500 hours of observation, interviews with 64 individuals, and a survey of 166 call handlers. The second study included five NHS 111 sites and data were collected during 356 hours of observation, accompanied by 6 focus groups, and an online survey of 529 staff. In all sites staff were observed taking calls from patients, their carers, and the public using the CDSS and data were also collected from interactions between staff, managers and patients in communal areas and clinic settings. The researchers were visible and interacted with those present, so the data collected include descriptions and near verbatim accounts. Observation periods included all or part of a shift and were conducted in blocks of approximately 6 hours, at different times of the day and different days, over several months. Detailed notes were taken overtly and transcribed soon afterwards. Interviews were used to explore narratives and meanings and to verify researcher understandings of observed practice. The interviews took 30–90 minutes and were recorded and transcribed. The focus groups included 47 staff in groups of six to nine people, sampled from call centres and urgent care centres. These the data were recorded, anonymised and transcribed also.

Analysis of these data highlight the interpretive gap between the promise of digital governance encapsulated in the attempt to deploy the CDSS as a way of managing demand for care. The remainder of the chapter seeks to show how the CDSS is predicated on a model of governance premised upon the idea that triage is a rational, rule-governed, standardisable process. The sections that follow are presented as 5 'rules' that frame the emergent themes from the analysis and serve to articulate the messy realities of governance in networks of care that involve human and non-human actors. These rules were derived from the interrogation of the data and from readings of the literature about triage and CDSS, and were enrolled to support and structure the analysis. Each rule reveals how the rule-governed rationalised vision of triage is adapted and resisted in the everyday situated practices and interactions between people and the CDSS. Governance is, contra to the neoliberal hierarchical narrative, very much constructed in and by networks, but, in a twist on the classic formulation of networked governance, I argue that we must consider and include an understanding of non-human network actors if we are to explain how triage really works (or, fails to). In the sections below the chapter presents a thematic analysis of a series of assumptive rules about disease presentation and decision-making, which demonstrate how digital governance is thwarted, modified and performed in these networks.

## Governing Rules and Networked Realities

### Rule 1: Clarity of Comprehension

Telephone triage requires that the human call handler obtain information from the caller that can be mapped onto the 'pathway' algorithm. At its most basic this requires a conversation to elicit a description of the body areas affected, the nature of the symptoms (type, duration and severity) and any additional details that are relevant (such as a pre-existing condition or known risks). The Pathways system opens with a body map and a series of questions designed to elicit whether the case requires immediate medical attention (i.e. an ambulance). In the example below the call handler pushes the caller for detail to help make this decision:

> CH20: 'There's a slight drop on the right hand side of the face? Has that started within the last 3 hours … you don't know …? [] From the information you have given me, we would advise an ambulance because your friend said your face and body are dropping on one side'. [] 'That's up to the paramedics to decide … [an ambulance is] the quickest way to get you assessed'. (Observation, call centre, 111)

However, in many calls the clarity of speech required to follow the 'comprehension rule' is lacking. Some calls are incoherent, due to technical problems with the telephone line quality or background noise, or because of language difficulties, as in this quote:

> The first call is from a man whose first language is not English. He is calling on behalf of his son. He is OK with most of the words but has difficulty with some of the medical/health words such as "slurring". It takes [call-handler] quite a long time to get through the questions. (Observation 999)

Other callers are intoxicated. Communication may further be compromised by local dialects and colloquial expressions that are not shared by the call handler and the caller. One of our sites was in the North of England where idiosyncratic sayings were used, such as 'spelk' meaning a splinter, 'dunch' for hit, and 'nappa' used for head. This could prove problematic if the call handler was unfamiliar with this regional dialect. Whilst the Pathways questions use lay language rather than clinical terminology there were translation challenges that made adhering to the rule difficult. In another observation a much more mundane language problem was made visible, namely the need for shared meanings:

> Someone [is] phoning on behalf of a 95 year old woman who has had a "funny turn". This phrase is commonly used by callers – particularly when used to describe elderly people. [This] non-specific description

> means that the call-taker has to probe to try and understand what the underlying health problem is. In this instance, it proves quite difficult and after attempts to clarify what "funny turn" means here, she chooses the "dizziness or vertigo" pathway. (Observation 999)

In another case shared meaning was created from additional probing, overlain with the call handlers tacit knowledge, as she explained in this interview:

> You've got to probe a lot because if you don't, you can end up with an inappropriate 999. For instance, I took a call and it was a lady.... She was in Boots, the chemist in town, and she had walked up to the top floor, because that's where the pharmacy is. Well, she would be a bit out of breath, won't she? [] ... I had to go back ...I had to say, now, are you always breathless like this? Is this your normal condition? ...then I could proceed. (Interview, OOH call-handler)

One of the most interesting areas where clarity of comprehension was made problematic was in the important questions concerning blood loss. These questions occur early in the pathway algorithm and are designed to 'catch' cases where blood loss is potentially catastrophic and life threatening. Estimating blood loss, it turns out, is a difficult accomplishment. Over time the questions in the algorithm were adapted to assist call handlers in getting an answer, and the probe for this question was "would the blood fill a mug?" (large cup). Conceptually this appeared to be tricky for callers, who often the hesitated before responding, and sometimes they responded yes but without much conviction. Often the call handlers had to do additional probing to confirm the answer before moving on to the next question.

In order to comprehend the calls, the call-handlers were forced to draw on a range of communication skills that lay outside the formatted questions offered by the CDSS. Following the rule here required more than simply reading out the prompts from a screen, and the practice was more complex than envisaged by the software developers.

## Rule 2: Assume Singularity

A key claim for the CDSS is that it 'contains' abstracted but expert clinical knowledge and this supports standardised clinical decision by the clerical staff who operate the software. This knowledge base comprises details of conditions, following differential pathways designed to arrive at diagnoses. The idealised pathway follows a single condition and eliminates the 'wrong' diagnosis along the way—chest symptoms are either a heart attack or indigestion, a rash is potentially meningitis and needs immediate medical attention or is something more benign. Everyday practice, it turns out, is much more messy:

> CT10 also tells me about the ways in which he feels pathways doesn't work so well: "It doesn't work well for dementia, cause you can't ask the questions. It doesn't work for chest pain, chest pain from a cold or cough, because any breathing difficulties end up with an ambulance and that's not needed mostly". (Observation, call centre 111)

Some callers phone in with multiple, potentially interlinked problems. Discerning which of these is the core symptom or condition can prove difficult. This was most marked in the case of 999 phone calls from road traffic accidents that involved multiple injuries to one or several people. For such events the rules simply cannot work as intended—and the call handler has to exit the algorithm and refer to clinical advisors in the room. A more mundane version of this rule adaptation also occurs when callers are unsure which symptom is the most important. The headache or the stomach pain? The rash or the blurred vision? As a result, the call handlers have to do a lot of interactional work to fix the pathway, sometimes backtracking:

> I have an interesting conversation with CT9 after the call, where he tells me that there are certain scenarios like the last call, where Pathways doesn't work as well. He explains 'the system has flipped to the chest pain pathway' when he asked the patient about sever chest pain and the caller said yes; but actually the chest pain had come from breathlessness. The chest pain pathway then started asking about any breathlessness, 'which

> doesn't make sense'. CT9 tells me that 'it is best in that situation to ask the supervisor which pathway to follow. If you continue down the chest pain pathway and it's severe chest pain (which it wasn't) then you may end up with a disposition of an ambulance, which the patient would likely have said no to, which would be the right thing to say'. CT9 is clear that it's his experience and knowledge of the system that prevented getting the wrong disposition; he had to say to the patient 'it's not severe chest pain' and follow his hunch that it wasn't that severe. I'm interested here that CT9 is using his own judgement seemingly to steer the disposition? (Observation, call centre 111)

## Rule 3: Linearity

Algorithms or pathways, as the latter name suggests, are conceived as linear sequences of activity. Their construction and logic is a decision tree of lines that branch off along a track to arrive at the triage disposition or end point. Question 1 leads to question 2 and so on. The reality is less straightforward. Frequently call handlers were observed following a pathway and then backtracking in response to additional details. This required 'asking different questions', potentially leading the answers,

> CallA10 says, 'I rarely follow a pathway to the end. You can't. You'd never get to a disposition. You have to go off of the exact questions and ask them slightly differently. Depending on how you ask the questions ... you can ask them in such a way as to change the response and convince someone'. (Observation, call centre, 111)

and sometimes call handlers instinctively 'worked' the system to get onto a desired path:

> CallA12 says that 'with some ambulance despatch calls, you get a sense an ambulance is not needed', reiterating that sometimes he 'goes back' to re-ask a question and 'sometimes you get a different response then, or sometimes a caller will recognise themselves they don't need an ambulance and will say'. (Observation, call centre, 999)

This process could also involve a wider network than just the call handler and caller, as in this example, when the clinical advisor steps in:

> I notice again how involved the clinicians are with the call handling. At around 17:45 one of the clinicians is standing by Maggie's side whilst she takes the call. It seems that she was listening into the call and came over when she thought she could offer some help to assist with the call. My sense is that it looked to be heading off down a more serious or emergency route but the clinician steps into offer some assistance which means that the call results in "speak to doctor". (Observation, call centre, 999)

The clinical overrides, in essence an adaptation of the pathway rules, may also be made when patients as network actors express counter-preferences. Thus, when the final disposition ends as 'send an ambulance' and or 'attend a doctors surgery within 2 hours' patients may decline the proposed option and 'governance' embodied in the triage 'rules and rational logic breaks down.

## Rule 4: Expertise in the Machine Not the Mind

At the outset of the research, it was repeatedly claimed that the expertise and knowledge required to triage was 'in' the software. Call handlers and developers reinforced this view:

> The only responsibility you have as a call-taker, is to listen exactly to what [the caller] is saying, and you make sure what [the caller] is answering is right. You don't have the kind of final decision. (Observation, call centre, 111)

However, when call handling practices were observed it became clear that call handlers acquired experience and expertise necessary to make NHS Pathways work. Experienced call advisers internalised the knowledge and clinical expertise and often 'worked ahead' of the algorithm, anticipating answers and clicking through the pathways before the patient had answered a question:

> I observe that CT11 speaks very fast when he is triaging calls and as soon as he comes off the phone he tells me 'he probably goes a little bit fast because he knows the pathway so well'. He tells me 'it's probably not a good habit to be in - sometimes I might miss something, but I'm so used to the pathway now'. (Observation, call centre, 111)

> We have staff upstairs who can probably, on a lot of calls, go through it without using pathways because they are so used to it. ..... it could be that actually they've gone through 15 questions with them and they haven't even opened it [CDSS] up yet. (Interview, call centre manager)

> I think now that I've been here longer, and I understand more about certain conditions..... because you can read the supporting information. Um, you can kind of understand the different ailments and symptoms and the effects that they have on the body, so that if someone is describing a symptom to you, it kind of triggers in the back of your mind, oh, they're talking about jaundice, or something like that, which you wouldn't necessarily know about beforehand. (Interview, Call Handler)

> Um, ah, that's... I think medical knowledge is something you just pick up as you go along. I mean, I'm not a doctor, but I'm pretty... I would say I'm pretty sure of most signs and symptoms of quite a lot of illnesses now. So, generally speaking... me mam thinks I'm a doctor. She always rings us when there's something wrong with her. (Interview, Call Handler)

Call handlers discussed ways that they used their professional networks, interactions with clinical and non-clinical colleagues, as well as personal and familial experience, to build up medical knowledge to help them manage the calls. At one site it was fascinating to observe just how far outside the machine the expertise travelled, as a call handler demonstrated how during break times he used a training version of the pathways software, that was not connected to live system to check dispositions and build his knowledge of the pathways.

## Rule 5: No Gaming

Standardised algorithmic systems assume that people will follow the rules. They rely on compliance. Our observations showed a number of ways that the rules were broken, often deliberately, by a range of different human actors in the network.

There was evidence that some general practice surgeries were advising patients to call NHS 111 during the daytime as an alternative to providing appointments during core practice hours (for example when they were busy). This caused some tension between those working within NHS 111 and primary care providers,

> When CallA1 finishes the call, she says [with sarcasm] 'they're good these doctors surgeries! This guy phoned up for a visit and was told by the surgery, 'we can't get someone out now, so phone out-of-hours.' (Observation, call centre, 111)

Another problem that particularly affected the 999 ambulance service was the way in which nursing and care homes used the telephone triage service. The questions in the pathway ask the caller to respond for a patient 'in the room', assuming that the caller is the patient or is with the person who needs assistance. The layout of care homes often meant that the phone call to 999 was made in an office, not from the patient's room or location. There was a suspicion amongst call handler staff that care home staff had learnt that they were less likely to get an ambulance call out if they were able to accurately report on the current status of the patient. This led care home staff to provide accounts of status and symptoms that provoked an ambulance response (e.g. "when I was with them they were unconscious but I am not with them now").

In addition, as the 111 service became embedded and more well-known it appeared that patients were also breaking the rules:

> The clinical adviser says that there a number of patients who are "working the system", bypassing routine general practice and presenting to 111 instead. (Observation, call centre, 111)

Such calls were calls perceived as illegitimate and added to the call handlers' frustrations about their work. Some staff felt that callers often exaggerated symptoms to receive medical attention more quickly, resulting in inappropriate and higher dispositions and care than necessary:

> CallA1 explains sometimes callers will make it sound so bad that 'by the end of the Pathway we have to say 'based on what you've told me I'm going to have to send a blue light ambulance and then the caller is like 'no, no', I'm not that bad''. Sometimes 'they try and play the system'. (Observation, call centre, 111)

Thus patients, or their representatives, were able to thwart the rules by gaming the system.

## Discussion

These studies of the deployment of NHS Pathways for triage in urgent and emergency care services reveal the gap between the theory and practice of networked governance when human and non-human actors are brought into play in standardised digital triage systems. This interpretive break should not be surprising; for example, Nicolini and colleagues (2011) reported a similar disjuncture in their study of the implementation of root cause analysis investigations of adverse safety events in two acute NHS hospitals. In urgent and emergency care triage services the human call handlers work with the (non-human) software and the caller in a socio-technical, human-machine network. This chapter has focussed principally on these three core types of network actors but of course there are others implicated in these networks; clinical advisors, policy stakeholders and other digital technologies and artefacts. The promissory idealised version of the rules for triage that the rational pathways software attempts to incorporate and govern comes apart in situated practice. There are 'work arounds' deviations, deliberate and 'accidental' rule breaking, and the use of experiential and tacit expertise, which the human actors introduce into the network. This too should not surprise: Dowding et al. (2009), Ruston (2006), and Greatbatch et al. (2005) also found that nurses used a CDSS in a range of ways, incorporating and valuing their own expertise, to 'deliver an individualised service' (Greatbatch et al. 2005: 802). Berg, in his now classic examination of clinical guidelines and protocols long since noted that in practice it is often necessary to adapt protocols, which assume a single answer and a clear rational and linear process. He argued, "[P]rotocols are and cannot be anything but a set of rules which, as ethnomethodology has taught us, have to be made relevant to each and every situation at hand (Garfinkel, 1967; Suchman,1987)" (Berg 1997: 1087). Similarly the algorithms of the CDSS operate in a social-technical network that must accommodate and respond to complex contingencies of practice.

This chapter has drawn on ANT to revisit our understanding of network governance, in particular it has responded to its core injunction that scholars should attend to the performance and agentic power of non-humans in networks. As Petrakaki et al. (2018) in their recent study of the role of health apps in the governance of patient conduct noted, "the extant literature on governmentality in healthcare has mostly emphasised the disciplinary effects of health technologies ... but overlooked the agential potential health technologies may also engender". As in their study, the analysis presented in this chapter has highlighted that technology, here the CDSS, performs governance: in the case here, by offering rationalising and standardising rules. Yet at the same time, because of the messy, contingent realities of everyday health care, this technology opens or allows opportunities for humans to develop expertise, adapt pathways and 'break the rules'. The situated practices of call handling and triage are built on interdependency, negotiation, and collaboration between human and non-human actors in the network. Bevir and colleagues (Bevir and Rhodes 2007; Bevir and Richards 2009; Bevir 2011a, b) argue that contemporary governance, is characterised less by hierarchical models and is better understood as networked governance, but hitherto the role of non-human actors in this has not been articulated. In the case presented here 'patterns of rule' were co-created, sustained and adapted by both the CDSS and human actors (call handlers, and also managers, patients and other stakeholders) engaged in triage. The everyday practice of call-handling is thus the outcome of situated interactions between people and software, of humans and machines. When the meaningful practices of these technologies and people interact, they create local dilemmas and affordances that give rise to practices of governance that depart significantly from the assumptions and imperatives of policy makers and ICT developers. Despite the best efforts and intent of techno-optimists who see technology as a mechanism for hierarchical, external governance and control, network governance is effectively retained by those 'on the ground' and decentred.

As noted in the introduction, there are plans afoot to deploy the pathways software in NHS 111 online as a web-based service on computers and smartphone apps, where patients/users will interact directly with the software to 'perform' management and triage in urgent care. This is an attempt to reduce the size of the network, cutting out the call handlers and some associated human stakeholders. But ultimately the model, and the promise, remains that a human and non-human network will act in accordance with the rules. The hubris of the technical solution offered by the CDSS, is that it alone can govern. The reality, on the basis of the evidence presented here, is that the CDSS has to be brought into use, networked with humans who appear unruly and less amenable to the rational, standardisation of the algorithm. We don't know, but perhaps can speculate with some confidence that an online version of NHS 111 will not be immune to the rule adaptation and rule breaking described here.

**Acknowledgements** Thanks are due to the research teams on the series of projects that provided the data used in this chapter. They include Joanne Turnbull, Jane Prichard, Susan Halford, Gemma McKenna, Alison Rowsell, Melania Calestani, Val Latimer, Carl May, Simon Brook, Jeremy Jones, Christine Barrett, Andrew Lennon, and Rob Crouch. The empirical work could not have been completed without them, or the willing participation of the many people involved in the case studies. The good parts of the thinking presented here are due to their input and that of the team involved with this book. Any errors or failings that remain, are mine to own.

The research reported here was funded by the National Institute for Health Research (NIHR) [Research grants SDO 08/1819/217; SDO 10/1008/10; HS&DR 14/19/16]. The views expressed are those of the author and not necessarily those of the NIHR or the Department of Health and Social Care.

## References

Beer, D. (2017). The social power of algorithms. *Information, Communication & Society, 20*(1), 1–13.

Berg, M. (1997). Problems and promises of the protocol. *Social Science and Medicine, 44*(8), 1081–1088.

Bevir, M. (2011a). A decentred theory of governance. In H. Bang (Ed.), *Governance as social and political communication*. Manchester: Manchester University Press.

Bevir, M. (Ed.). (2011b). *The SAGE handbook of governance*. London: Sage.

Bevir, M., & Rhodes, R. A. W. (2007). Decentred theory, change and network governance. In E. Sorensen & J. Torfing (Eds.), *Theories of democratic network governance* (pp. 77–91). New York, NY: Palgrave Macmillan.

Bevir, M., & Richards, D. (2009). Decentring policy networks: A theoretical agenda. *Public Administration, 87*(1), 3–14.

Castells, M. (1996). *The network society*. Oxford: Basil Blackwell.

Castells, M. (2000). Materials for an exploratory theory of the network society. *British Journal of Sociology, 51*(1), 5–24.

Dowding, D., Mitchell, N., Randell, R., Foster, R., Lattimer, V., & Thompson, C. (2009). Nurses' use of computerised clinical decision support systems: A case site analysis. *Journal of Clinical Nursing, 18*, 1159–1167.

Ferlie, E., et al. (2010). *Networks in health care: A comparative study of their management, impact and performance*. Report for the National Institute for Health Research Service Delivery and Organisation Programme SDO Project (08/1518/102). http://www.netscc.ac.uk/hsdr/files/project/SDO_FR_08-1518-102_V01.pdf. Accessed 29 April 2019.

Ferlie, E., Fitzgerald, L., McGivern, G., Dopson, S., & Bennett, C. P. (2011). Public policy networks and 'wicked problems': A nascent solution? *Public Administration, 89*(2), 307–324.

Ferlie, E., Fitzgerald, L., McGivern, G., Dopson, S., & Bennett, C. P. (2013). *Making wicked problems governable*. Oxford: Oxford University Press.

Ferlie, E., & Pettigrew, A. (1996). Managing through networks: Some issues and implications for the NHS. *British Journal of Management, 7*(s1): S81–S99.

Greatbatch, D., Hanlon, G., Goode, J., O'Cathain, A., Strangleman, T., & Luff, D. (2005). Telephone triage, expert systems and clinical expertise. *Sociology of Health & Illness, 27,* 802–830.

Hanlon, G., Strangleman, T., Goode, J., Luff, D., O'Cathain, A., & Greatbatch, D. (2005). Knowledge, technology and nursing: The case of NHS Direct. *Human Relations, 58*(2), 147–171.

Hughes, D. (1989). Paper and people: The work of the casualty reception clerk. *Sociology of Health & Illness, 11*(4), 382–408.

Latour, B. (1987). *Science in action: How to follow scientists and engineers through society.* Milton Keynes: Open University Press.

Latour, B. (2005). *Reassembling the social: An introduction to actor-network-theory.* Oxford: Oxford University Press.

Law, J. (Ed.). (1986). *Power, action and belief: A new sociology of knowledge.* London: Routledge & Kegan Paul.

NHS England. (2016). *NHS 111 Minimum data set 2015–16.* https://www.england.nhs.uk/statistics/statistical-work-areas/nhs-111-minimum-data-set/nhs-111-minimum-data-set-2015-16/. Accessed 29 April 2019.

Nicolini, D., Waring, J., & Mengis, J. (2011). Policy and practice in the use of root cause analysis to investigate clinical adverse events: Mind the gap. *Social Science and Medicine, 73,* 217–225.

Pearson, S. A., Moxey, A., Robertson, J., Hains, I., Williamson, M., Reeve, J., et al. (2009). Do computerised clinical decision support systems for prescribing change practice? A systematic review of the literature (1990–2007). *BMC Health Services Research, 9,* 154. PMID: 19715591.

Petrakaki, D., Hilburg, E., & Waring, J. (2018). Between empowerment and self-discipline: Governing patients' conduct through technological self-care. *Social Science and Medicine, 213,* 146–153.

Pope, C., Halford, S., Turnbull, J., Prichard, J., Calestani, M., & May, C. (2013). Using computer decision support systems in NHS emergency and urgent care: Ethnographic study using Normalisation Process Theory. *BMC Health Services Research, 13,* 111.

Robertson-Steel, I. (2006). Evolution of triage systems. *Emergency Medicine Journal, 23*(2), 154–155.

Ruston, A. (2006). Interpreting and managing risk in a machine bureaucracy: Professional decision-making in NHS Direct. *Health, Risk & Society, 8*, 257–271.

Turner, J., Lattimer, V., & Snooks, H. (2008). *An evaluation of the accuracy and safety of NHS Pathways*. Sheffield: Medical Care Research Unit, University of Sheffield.

# Sharing Stories or Co-Constructing Practice? Challenges to Undertaking and Researching Innovation Using Evidence from the English NHS

Simon Turner and John S. F. Wright

## Introduction

Innovation can be defined as the planning and implementation of new ideas, products, processes or organisational forms (Schumpeter 1934; Van de Ven 2017). While central to improving health care services, innovation is recognised as challenging to say the least in this context. Multiple reasons have been given for this, some of which include: professional power, complexity of 'the product', multiple organisational relationships, and system-wide regulatory processes. We also know that innovation at scale or major system change—where the number of stakeholders involved that need to coordinate their activities is multiplied—generates

S. Turner (✉)
School of Management, University of Los Andes, Bogotá, Colombia
e-mail: s.turner@uniandes.edu.co

J. S. F. Wright
Institute of Public Policy and Governance,
University of Technology Sydney, Ultimo, NSW, Australia


M. Bevir and J. Waring (eds.), *Decentring Health and Care Networks*, Organizational Behaviour in Healthcare,
https://doi.org/10.1007/978-3-030-40889-3_7

particular governance challenges in aligning the various professional groups and organisations involved (Turner et al. 2016a). For example, contemporary policy interest in different forms of 'integrated care' appear ambitious and fraught with difficulty, even in agreeing what is meant by 'integration' (Cameron et al. 2014). One reason for this is that such integrated initiatives, where different agents and organisations need to coordinate their behaviour, are set against decentred forms of governance, under which different organisations act with relative autonomy and in response to localised understandings of policy reforms and initiatives.

Some of the academic thinking on decentred governance offers a possible way forward in referring to the mechanisms, or 'glue', that might hold such networks together. For instance, Bevir and Richards (2009a) highlight the importance of the 'stories', 'traditions', and 'dilemmas' that bind together networks. Such ideas can be linked to social constructivism which rejects the primacy of top-down or hierarchical forms of governance by focussing on 'the social construction of a practice through the ability of individuals to create and act on meanings' (Bevir and Richards 2009a, p. 3). Governance is decentred because ideas about coordinating the planning or delivery of innovations are said to subsist as much in the responses of individuals involved in implementing change, the so-called 'street level bureaucrats' (Lipsky 1971), as the architects of policy or organisational reform that seek to influence change processes top-down by acting from other (often 'higher') parts of the system.

This chapter, while sympathetic to social constructivist approaches to understanding continuity and change in organisational and governance processes, seeks to question the status of the 'individual'—as a key source of agency—in such accounts of policy or innovation processes. In order to do this, we turn to scholarship from within social psychology which takes issue with the idea of attributing 'rationality' or 'cognition' to an individual's mind and, therefore, questions the notion of individuals having agency. Instead, this approach suggests a repositioning of the role of the individual in creating or acting on meanings or the stories in which those meanings are situated. Such thinking suggests that, while agency is similarly decentred or distributed, it can be attributed to shared or 'joint action' rather than individual's cognitions. This move from individual to joint action suggests a greater degree of ambiguity and uncertainty in the negotiation of change, including potential for partial or non-implementation of innovation, than decentred governance theory currently proposes.

This chapter applies Bevir's ideas concerning decentred governance to analyse the innovation processes observed within a specialist provider of eye care services that are organised and delivered through a network of clinics. The chapter then engages critically with the suggested mechanisms of decentred governance proposed by Bevir using the notion of 'dialogical' or shared practice drawn from John Shotter's work. In doing this, the chapter addresses the following research question: what mechanisms influence the planning and implementation of innovations within decentred organisational networks?

In the next section, we outline the conceptual approach of decentred governance, especially the key role of stories, dilemmas, and traditions as mechanisms for holding networks together. We also discuss the status of the 'individual' in network theory and contrast this with scholarship from within social psychology that suggests agency comes from shared or 'joint action' to tease out the implications for conceptualising agency within innovation networks. These ideas are then explored in relation to an example of health care innovation, a decentralised network of outpatient clinics led by a specialist provider of ophthalmology services within the English National Health Service (NHS). The findings are described through vignettes based on observations of the planning and implementation of innovation by this provider; these are then discussed using decentred governance theory in order to identify key mechanisms that shape innovation within networks and, in particular, the conceptualisation of agency within such networks. The chapter concludes with implications for research and for policy and practice.

## Stories, Dilemmas, and Traditions

Bevir and Richards (2009b) describe the theory of decentred governance as offering, "a micro-theory based on individuals acting in accord with beliefs and desires forged against the background of specific traditions and dilemmas" (p. 140). They outline three mechanisms that allow networks of distributed individuals to coordinate their activities: stories, dilemmas, and traditions. Stories, as they are told and retold, are a by-product of social interaction wherein the narratives associated with networks are developed. By telling stories to one another, individuals share information and engage in learning activities (e.g. by comparing stories). Shared understanding is possible because story telling takes place against a common background of traditions and dilemmas. Traditions are a background of relevant interests and conventions associated with a network that help to inform individuals' beliefs. Dilemmas or problems faced by individuals are an organising device as individuals develop responses to them. Failure to respond to dilemmas can cause individuals to reconsider their traditions and shared beliefs. There is interplay between dilemmas and traditions: beliefs help to guide individual's approaches to the problems posed by dilemmas, while individual's responses to dilemmas can lead to change in beliefs and traditions (Bevir and Waring 2018). Ethnography is regarded as a key research method for uncovering how and why 'everyday' activities and practices come to be associated with decentred networks. Ethnographers construct stories about people's stories.

## Interaction as Shared or Dialogical Practice

The mechanisms of interaction within decentred networks offer a useful way of engaging with the 'everyday' practice of interaction. In this chapter, we wish to develop these ideas further, and to critically evaluate their influence on the coordination of innovations, by drawing on John Shotter's work from the field of social psychology. A key area of contention is around the status of the individual, and their cognitions or rationality, as an agent of continuity and change in decentred network theory. Rather than beginning with the individual's cognition (including consciousness, rationality, and beliefs), Shotter focusses on experience and interaction as a shared practice, and holds that this does not belong to any one individual. In particular, Shotter draws attention to the shared context of interaction and the ways in which this shapes practice. In describing such interactions, Shotter refers to a 'third' type of knowledge that does not belong to any one individual, but is emergent in the context of interaction itself. Shotter (1997) argues that, at the moment 'when a second human being responds to the acts of a first' (p. 349), their encounter becomes a spontaneous 'dialogical' practice. Such activity does not emerge from the knowledge that participants have acquired prior to their encounter, but depends instead on a non-cognitive response to the affordances of the encounter itself. Often, in the context of shared practice:

> though we may be loathe to admit it - we all remain deeply ignorant as to what we are doing, or why we are doing it. Not because the 'ideas' or whatever, supposedly in us somewhere informing our actions, are too deeply buried to bring out into the light of day, but because the formative influences shaping our conduct are not wholly there, in our individual heads, to be brought out. Activity of this kind occurs in response to what others have already done, and we act just as much 'into' the opportunities and invitations, or 'against' the barriers and restrictions they offer or afford us, as 'out of' any plans or desires of our own. Thus, the stony looks, the nods of agreement, the failures of interest, the asking of questions, these all go towards what it is one feels one can, or cannot, do or say in such situations. This is joint action; it is spontaneous, unselfconscious, unknowing (although not unknowledgeable) kind of activity. (Shotter 1993, p. 47)

Shotter's rejection of the idea of knowledge being 'deeply buried' could be seen as questioning the idea of individual's subconscious or tacit knowledge informing activity. Instead, Shotter turns to social practice—and specifically social interactions—in order to understand how what we might term 'knowledge' is constructed. Thus, to understand the construction of knowledge in networks we need to inquire into how social interactions are organised. Shotter calls such interactions 'joint action'.

The interpretation of social interaction as 'joint action' allows us to reimagine the key mechanisms of change described in decentred governance theory (dilemmas, stories, traditions). There is still an important role for dilemmas or problems facing actors in joint action. Shotter refers to a task, a difficulty, that is presupposed in joint activity, that such activity is responding to. There is something that needs to be 'understood'; one proposed way of understanding is by 'seeing connections' in relation to one's circumstances that had not been made before

(Shotter 2010, p. 271). With regard to traditions, Shotter (2010) refers to the importance of a 'larger activity' (p. 210) or background in which utterances or gestures can be understood and allow the shared activity at hand to progress or 'go on'. With respect to stories, Shotter (2010) points out the 'unintended and unpredictable outcomes' (p. 271) associated with joint action. Boje (1991) advocates the study of stories 'as performance' whereby they are observed directly in the context in which they take place, including the performance event, audience involved, and how one story is actively related to others. Utterances are shaped by both our past experiences and our immediate surroundings. In the construction of a story, therefore, what we experience is not the essence of a story—put together based on past experience—but something more creative and unpredictable, because it draws on the moment-to-moment sharing of agency available in the immediate situation.

Thus, the concept of joint action encourages us to examine the aspects of the social and material setting which appear to inform the construction of stories. Moreover, it suggests that the outcome of storytelling is unpredictable, meaning that it can direct activity in unexpected ways. In the rest of this chapter, we explore empirically the relevance of the mechanisms proposed in decentred theory for supporting the coordination of behaviour around innovations. Drawing on Shotter's work, we also explore the relevance of seeing interactions as 'joint action' and how this influences the planning and implementation of innovations.

## Methods

This chapter draws on a longitudinal case study of the planning and implementation of innovation by an NHS Foundation Trust in England that provides specialist eye services. This provider runs a network of clinics across multiple locations within a metropolitan area, the surrounding region, and internationally. The innovation related to the provision of outpatient clinics for the diagnosis and treatment of glaucoma, a chronic eye disease. Glaucoma is the second most common cause of irreversible blindness worldwide. Glaucoma affects almost 10%

of England's population over the age of 75, 2% of the population over 40, and accounts for over a million outpatient visits to health services annually. Once diagnosed, this potentially blinding condition requires lifelong and often complex treatment, which is necessary for preventing irreversible visual loss. Referrals to hospital of patients with suspected glaucoma have been increasing each year due to population ageing, and the introduction of national clinical guidelines that lowered the clinical threshold for referral (NICE 2009).

Increasing demand has placed pressure on hospital eye services; delays in glaucoma follow-up appointments have caused patient harm (National Patient safety Agency 2009). For glaucoma, the standard pathway involves the treatment of newly referred and follow-up patients in consultant-run clinics. Standard clinics are staffed by a consultant-led multidisciplinary team composed of nurses, optometrists, orthoptists, trainee ophthalmologists, technicians, clinic clerks, and liaison officers. A range of diagnostic tests is conducted, including eye pressure check, visual fields test, and imaging of the optic nerve. The consultant makes treatment decisions at the clinic, e.g. further monitoring, prescription of medication, laser treatment or discharge.

In order to improve patients' experiences, an improvement programme was established across the Trust, which included a focus on reducing patient journey times through glaucoma clinics. New care pathways involve reorganising patient flow through the system with the aim of improving resource use to alleviate pressure on services caused by increasing demand. For instance, some patients with glaucoma may be allocated to different types of clinic based on their risk of progression of disease. This includes 'virtual' or 'remote review' clinics in which diagnostic tests are conducted face-to-face by ophthalmic technicians or other non-ophthalmologist staff. The consultant ophthalmologist then reviews these data electronically at a later point in time to make treatment decisions and prescribe medications. The wider studies from which this chapter derives involved analysing barriers and facilitators to the planning and implementation of innovations to improve the provision of outpatient services for glaucoma.

In the wider studies, data were collected during two periods of ethnographic fieldwork, one over the period 2013–2014, and the other over the period 2016–2017. In 2013–2014, 28 interviews and 40.5 hours of non-participants observations were conducted; in 2016–2017, there were a further 25 interviews and 9 hours of non-participant observations. The interviews included senior executives, operational managers, clinical academics, and a variety of clinical staff, including consultants, nurses, technicians, and clerks. Observations covered senior management level meetings, including board meetings, planning meetings by those leading innovations, communication and consultation meetings where updates on the improvement programme were shared and discussed, and the delivery of a number of outpatient clinics for glaucoma patients. All interviews were guided by a semi-structured topic guide, audio-recorded and professionally transcribed. Notes from observations were recorded contemporaneously.

Data analysis for this chapter was geared toward existing ideas concerning both network-based governance (e.g. Bevir and Richards 2009a) and the characteristics of social interaction (e.g. Shotter 2010). Specifically, we constructed stylised vignettes based on observations and stakeholders that we felt represented key events in the planning and implementation of innovations. We then applied the three mechanisms of coordination from decentred governance theory (dilemmas, stories, and traditions) to analyse critically the events described through the vignettes, including the potential relevance of individual and joint action in both the empirical observations and theorised mechanisms of coordination. Thus, data analysis was relatively 'deductive' as these concepts were applied to the dataset systematically. However, we also compared and contrasted the fieldwork material with ideas from the literature and were attentive to 'deviant' cases, gaps in existing literature, and pointers for developing the literature further where the empirical work suggested new insights about the coordination of innovation in networks.

The meetings (2013–2014 dataset) were chosen as the basis for the vignettes because they were attended by a range of clinical and managerial staff, with differing degrees of authority, meaning that a variety of stakeholder views were shared, discussed and debated, allowing orientations toward dilemmas, traditions, and stories to be assessed across a multidisciplinary grouping.

# Findings

In this section, we present two stylised vignettes concerning the planning and implementation of innovation respectively, which draw on interviews, non-participant observations, and documentary evidence relating to the innovation. We then apply three key ideas from Bevir's work on network-based governance (dilemmas, traditions, stories) to the vignettes and also explore ideas about 'shared practice' or dialogical practice in explaining the empirical material.

## Vignette 1: Deciding Whether to Roll Out Local Quality Improvement Work More Widely

Results are being shared from quality improvement work at one site within the Trust's network of clinics. The consultant lead for the work at this site is presenting findings with other glaucoma consultants from across the Trust. Both senior and operational managers involved in the work are also sharing their views on the quality improvement work and contributing to the discussion. A representative from an external management consultancy that was employed to support the improvement work is also present. A multi-professional group from the hospital was established to reflect on the purpose and delivery of existing clinics. The improvement work involved mapping patient flows within different outpatient clinics at the site and experimenting with changes to patient flow and staff roles, before, during and after each clinic. The amount of time spent by each patient in the clinic, and what happened in this time, was measured. There was a new nurse 'coordinator' role that was used to allocate patients to different staff members. Rather than being allocated a list of patients, the consultant becomes a 'floating resource' available to advise on any patient's care. This meeting is one in a number of events designed to gather consultants' views that will be used to inform decision-making on rolling out this approach to quality improvement more widely within the Trust.

## Vignette 2: Updating Front-Line Staff on the Quality Improvement Work

Members of the multidisciplinary team leading the improvement work are updating staff on progress at a clinical governance meeting at one of the Trust's sites. The meeting is taking place in a large lecture theatre with rows of tiered seats. A formal presentation, with PowerPoint slides, is being used to give the update. The presentation, which is titled 'transformation progress', begins with an outline of the difficult times facing the NHS—chief among these, as described on the slide, include coping with demographic change, the need for financial savings, and responding to new commissioners and competitors. The presenter, an operational manager, also cites the Trust's chief executive who had reportedly said: "it was time for a new approach".

The presentation shares some of the principles being experimented with during the piloting of the new approach to delivering clinics, including 'systems thinking' (rather than focussing on individuals), minimising 'handovers' of patients among staff, telephoning patients prior to the clinic date to reduce those who 'did not attend' (DNA) appointments, and having a team briefing at the beginning of each clinic. The way that the pilot clinic operated was illustrated in a number of ways, including process maps of patient flow through the clinic, descriptions of how staff roles were performed within the clinics, and viewing each clinic in terms of profit and loss (although this was still being calculated), and the scheduling of patient appointments during the clinic.

Perceptions of how the pilot clinic had performed were then shared with the audience by members of the team. For example, it was noticeable that the lead consultant was being consulted a lot by other members of staff as 'the expert'. Telephoning patients in advance had reduced the average DNA rate from 10–12 per clinic to 1–5. The clinics were also perceived to be 'calmer' in part due to the staff briefing at the beginning. The team did admit that only a small team had been involved in the transformation work and that others could be more involved in decision-making to avoid the current sense of change as a 'process done to them, rather than with them'.

## Interpretation: What's the Dilemma?

Our observations suggested that the dilemma was related to overrunning outpatient clinics (the standard consultant-led clinics could overrun by up to two to three hours). Part of the reason that overrunning clinics had been a long-standing issue was because of the complexity of the problem. The complexity and intractability of the problem was acknowledged in the consultant meeting (vignette 1). In response to the consultant outlining the need for the service improvement work, the management consultant present chipped in by advocating the need for a thorough, deliberative approach because of the risk otherwise of 'squeezing the balloon' whereby one problem is solved and it pops up elsewhere. Another potential option raised at the consultant meeting was to introduce additional clinics. However, this was discounted because there was limited space for new clinics; additional clinics were already being offered on some evenings and on Saturdays.

Further ambiguity concerning the nature of the problem was introduced at the clinical governance meeting (vignette 2). Some frontline staff listening to the update on the improvement work queried the rationale for the changes to clinics. One doctor wanted to know, 'what does success look like?' The doctor argued that the background to the work describing challenges at Trust level was about 'money' rather than patient experience. They went on to suggest that, as a teaching hospital, there was a 'tension between service and training', and implying that the improvement work was having a negative impact on the latter. Were the changes more appropriate for independent sector treatment centres, that specialise in delivering more routine procedures, they posited. One of the management consultants responded by stating that the focus was on 'value time' whereby, he argued, if patients were seen more quickly, then this provided an opportunity to use the time in other ways, which could be seeing more patients or finishing the clinic at what could be considered a normal, reasonable time. The doctor responded by arguing that improvement work should not just be about benefiting patients, but also help to improve the workplace for staff. To underline his point, the doctor posed a rhetorical question to the wider audience, '*when was the last time we had training in the lunch hour*'? The management consultant responded by arguing that 'improving morale' was a benefit for staff and that making the Trust a great place to work also had a financial impact, e.g. reducing staff turnover can improve cost and revenue.

In summary, there was debate among front-line staff concerning the nature of the problem that the improvement was designed to address. However, given the variety of potential solutions, and differing views on the perceived efficacy of these, the challenges with the delivery of clinics can be seen as a 'dilemma'. With regard to maintaining staff commitment to addressing the problem, representatives of the management consultancy played an important role in addressing concerns that front-line staff raised and by illustrating how the improvement work could be seen to address those, e.g. making the discursive link between improved staff morale and reducing cost.

## Interpretation: What's the Tradition?

There were traditions of inter- and intra-professional hierarchy. In the consultant meeting (vignette 1), staff had differing views on the new nurse 'coordinator' role that had been introduced to allocate patients to different members of staff across the clinic. Some nursing staff had taken to the role, others had not. The consultant leading the work suggested that a key issue was assertiveness among those in coordinator roles, that is, 'can they tell doctors what to do, confidently?' Those in the role were perceived to need particular capabilities, both clinical knowledge and a particular personality. It was suggested that it was not easy to find staff with 'bossy nurse' characteristics, and "with a matron's hat", another consultant added. Thus, while there was a suggestion that there was a lack of staff able to carry out the coordinator role, the challenge encountered of allocating patient cases to doctors also suggests underlying challenges associated with the negotiation of inter-professional relations. Hierarchy could also be invoked to support change, as illustrated by the reference to chief executive's report endorsement of new ways of working by the operational manager in the clinical governance meeting (vignette 2).

There were traditions of resistance to change among staff. In the consultant meeting (vignette 1), the consultant leading the work suggested that resistance to changing work practices was not just an issue among doctors, but at all levels within the Trust. Another consultant responded with 'that is normal', seemingly questioning the idea that 'resistance' should be seen as problematic and as something that needed to be overcome. Thus, the two consultants agreed that 'resistance' existed and it could therefore be seen as a tradition within the Trust, but their views diverged on whether this was a 'barrier' to improvement work (first consultant) or that resistance should be seen as rational response to the changes being introduced (the second). In the clinical governance meeting (vignette 2), concerns were raised by staff about whether the changes would address concerns about staff training and the work environment. Resistance was also acknowledged as being understandable by the consultant leading the work because the changes being trialled could be perceived by some staff as a "process done to them", especially where they were not involved in the initial discussions about making changes to the clinics.

There were also traditions of not sustaining change. One consultant stated in the consultant meeting (vignette 1) that, in response to managerial requests, they do make changes: "*we do it, then it goes back to how it was*". This could be about change competing with traditional ways of working. For example, one staff member referred to an alternative approach to treating patients in which the 'old mentality was get them in, get them out very quickly'.

There appeared to be interplay between the dilemma and traditions, in that traditions could be seen as playing a part in the dilemma of tackling overrunning outpatient clinics within the Trust. For example, the consultant leading the work appeared exasperated at times at the engagement of some staff with the improvement work. During the consultant meeting (vignette 1), the consultant stated that those involved "*have to be open minded and go through this*" and "*have to challenge yourself about why changing process*". For example, the consultant argued that doctors should not be disengaging because they think that performing a particular diagnostic test within the clinic—one that measured visual acuity—"is beneath them". Thus, the consultant's statement could be interpreted as suggesting that staff needed to reflect on their own beliefs, on the reasons they had for holding those beliefs, and whether those reasons could be justified with regard to what was in patients' interests.

In summary, we were able to distil through our observation of meetings a number of traditions that appeared to thwart the improvement activity. These point to a variety of professional responses to change, some of which can be linked to the approach to improvement (e.g. not sustaining improvement or involving staff sufficiently), others to inter and intra- professional power and hierarchy.

## What's the Story?

Multiple stories were told in relation to the dilemma of the overrunning clinics. Some stories were told about other settings outside the Trust. In response to concerns from a consultant about the lack of progress with addressing overrunning clinics over many years (vignette 1), a senior manager acknowledged that clinicians' loyalty and commitment had been abused by management, adding that in other places where they have worked: "*clinicians have called up management to tell patients in the waiting room why they can't be seen after 5pm*". The reference to another workplace appeared to be used by the senior manager to underline the commitment of clinicians (i.e. in seeing the full list of patients even when clinics did overrun) in the current workplace. However, the consultant took issue with the sense that front-line staff were being held responsible for leaving work at the appropriate time (even in another workplace) and responded: "*don't blame clerks, it's about the situation they've been put in*". The consultant then added that the problem for large clinics with a long list of patients was "firefighting", with the consequence that it was "hard to make change". The senior manager then responded that, for a period of time, they were interested in forgetting about demand and "deliberately running clinics to profile". The consultant responds that they have "done it before and it works".

Other stories were told to draw out the patient experience. In vignette 1, the consultant leading the work highlighted a quotation from a patient on their slide which summed up their experience of traditional clinics: "*eye front, eye back, never the whole eye*". Another quote from a patient was used to highlight additional problems—in outlining these, the consultant adds that when staff undertaking the improvement work took a step back to reflect it was 'quite shocking'. The quotes were supplemented with quantitative data collected by the management consultancy which suggested that patients spent 67% of their journey queuing. This information concerning the way that clinics had traditionally been run had affected patients was used to help build the case for change. There were then questions from members of the audience. For example, the approach of breaking the time spent by patients in clinics into 'value' versus 'non-value' time was questioned by some of the other staff present. They wanted to know what the two terms meant and, indeed, whether the activities allocated to 'non-value' time could accurately be described as a misuse of time. For instance, time spent by patients in between seeing clinicians could be necessary for eye drops to take effect.

Similarly, in the progress meeting with frontline staff (vignette 2), the purpose of the work was questioned by some staff especially with regard to the problem it was addressing. The management consultant present helped to turn the narrative back to one of 'improvement' in this setting by linking the objective of saving cost around another goal of improving staff working conditions, which a doctor had raised. In this context, it appeared easier for those leading the work to maintain a coherent narrative of improvement, relative to the consultant meeting (vignette 1) in which the approach to the work was fundamentally questioned.

In summary, stories were told through exchanges among the stakeholders present, with some appearing to become more accepted narratives, while others were challenged by alternative points of view or interpretations. There were examples of using evidence to add validity to particular stories (e.g. quotes from patients and time and motion studies to represent the patient experience), while others appeared to draw on authority to question alternative stories or reorient the narrative from their professional standing (e.g. senior doctors).

## Individual Story or Joint Action?

The analysis of the vignettes suggests that stories, as well as traditions and dilemmas, are co-constructed. Stories are distributed across the spaces in which they are told. One utterance prompts other utterances; sometimes these appear to build upon the story being told, but more often than not these additions or qualifications take the story in unexpected directions. These movements both can amplify a story—to give it greater weight or credence in relation to the issue being discussed—or can work against the force of a story so its effect is dissipated or gets lost in the criss-crossing of dialogue. This raises the question of how and why some stories get heard—and appear to become influential—while others do not emerge or have less of an effect.

An important process in shaping the influence of stories appears to be the exercise of power. In the vignette, the tradition of inter- and intra-professional hierarchies within the Trust was noted as a mediator of responses to change or improvement activity. Such hierarchies can also influence the force with which stories are heard. In the meeting observed, it was consultants predominantly who sought to challenge both the other consultant leading the improvement work and the senior manager involved regarding the reasons for the problems with existing clinics and how the experiences with the new approaches to delivering clinics being trialled should be interpreted. Thus, power associated with occupying a senior role in the medical hierarchy was exercised in meetings to steer the stories that prevailed about the improvement work.

# Discussion

How does decentred governance help us to understand innovation networks in health care? What does the concept of 'joint action' add, if anything, to this understanding? Decentred governance is about mechanisms that hold together, or coordinate, action over a distance (e.g. a network of outpatient clinics distributed across a metropolitan area). The empirical case study we used to explore decentred governance did not show strong tendencies toward coordination, that is, in addition to aspects of top-down organisation there were also aspects of autonomy among the organisations and agents involved in the delivery of this network of clinics. The stories, dilemmas, and traditions did not always add up, that is, they did not necessarily act as mechanisms of coordination.

Dilemmas were diffuse; they varied depending on who you spoke to and how they were negotiated in the course of social interaction. The sense of a 'tradition' was built on recognition of divisions within the Trust. There was a tradition of recognising these divisions and coping with them. This type of tradition could also be seen as a 'dilemma' given that they were not easily addressed. Stories were told to engage with the need for the improvement work, the approach being taken to improvement, and to evaluate progress or perceived success. Stories were co-constructed during interactions, suggesting that Shotter's concept of 'joint action' is a useful way of describing how stories influence practice.

If story-telling is of a dialogical nature then this suggests greater ambiguity concerning its relationship to innovation processes. It means that the agency associated with story-telling is distributed beyond the individual story teller. This agency is held by others present who make contributions or interject, and through this, become co-authors of stories. Agency can also be attributed to the material context in which stories are told, including the particular space in which they are shared (which may contribute to a greater or lesser degree to interaction or debate that enables co-authorship) as well as the material resources that story-tellers draw on to lend authority, with examples including the use of audit findings, personal experiences of similar initiatives, and experiences gained in other organisations. Positional power also lends some participants greater authority to have their stories, or their views on others' stories, heard.

The findings underlie the importance of medical professionalism, especially the practices of senior doctors, as a mediator of improvement processes (Best et al. 2012; Turner et al. 2016b). They highlight that an important mechanism through which senior doctors command power in relation to improvement processes is through their influence on the hum of narratives or stories that accompany improvement work. The prevailing stories that come to be associated with improvement work matter because they can influence decision-making concerning adoption or further spread. However, we can also see how other stakeholders such as management consultants attract credibility to their stories by drawing on 'discursive resources' (Bloomfield and Danieli 1995), including concepts that provide solutions to different dilemmas (e.g. 'value time'), and by drawing on evidence from audit or research studies, including evidence of patient experience. This ability to attract discursive power around stories highlights an important facilitation role, whether this be management consultancy or other form of boundary spanner, that is able to counteract the positional power of senior doctors to ensure that other stories, and the voices they represent, are heard.

The approach outlined here also has methodological implications for practising ethnography. Firstly, the concept of stories, and other forms of interaction, being co-constructed rather than unilaterally constructed, should promote reflexivity concerning the collection of research 'data' for ethnography and what informs the analysis and writing up process. For example, the conduct of an interview or observation of a practice by the ethnographer shapes what happens during those interactions, including the 'stories' told. For example, one of the authors was collecting data within a hospital on ward-level responses to a medication safety 'scorecard' over a number of weeks as part of broader university and health care provider collaboration on patient safety. On arriving one week to share the data, a senior doctor said jokingly, 'every time I see you my heart sinks'. This jibe could be interpreted in numerous ways (e.g. as a sign of general resource pressures, as a comment on the appropriateness of the 'scorecard', or as an attempt at humour or conviviality), but we include this example to highlight that the ethnographer is not invisible; their very presence, and research methods, influence practice in the field and should be recognised as a key part of the 'stories' being told.

Moreover, the ways in which those stories are retold by the ethnographer will be influenced by other factors, including their particular research question or hypothesis, reading material, conversations with colleagues, the presence of other corroborating or contradictory data, and the ethnographer's style of writing and how ideas translate into a discursive argument that flows (or not) on the page. The apparatus of writing—and how this is informed by social and material interactions—should be explicit in accounts of ethnography, especially if insights from this approach to research are designed to inform future policy or practice.

Secondly, in attempting to describe the mechanisms underpinning innovations, there can be pressure to develop a coherent story or narrative of both the important events that were associated with the planning and implementation of the innovation and of the critical mechanisms that were influential in the empirical data that was collected. The mechanisms could vary depending on the hypothesis in which one is interested, and what is already known about the role of such mechanisms from previous research (e.g. how powerful stakeholders shape evidence use or how organisational culture might influence receptivity to innovations) and whether this is confirmed or better understood by the data collected. However, if we were to accept that stories are constructed, and such construction varies depending on who is involved, what is observed, and how such observations are rationalised into 'stories', then the story of innovation being told looks more precarious, arbitrary perhaps. It becomes more difficult to argue that the data highlights an empirical reality about innovation and, consequently, says something meaningful about "mechanisms" of innovation processes. The messy, co-construction of stories about practice suggests a need to hold back from mechanistic accounts of innovation and overly rationalised descriptions or interpretations of the accompanying interactions. Ethnographic findings, alone, are likely to be accused of being subjective and reliant on subjectivities. One way of addressing this is to combine ethnography with other methods of research, e.g. quantitative findings that add another layer to the story.

## Conclusion

In conclusion, a decentred conception of governance represents a useful approach for analysing how a range of stakeholders make sense of and can help to shape innovation processes. This approach can complement more top-down perspectives of governance by showing how local actors play an important role in the negotiation of innovation processes. However, our analysis suggested that the decentred mechanisms through which innovations undergo triall and implementation are often not attributable to individuals' stories—instead, such stories are co-constructed through social practice. Due to their co-construction, the information or perspective conveyed through such stories is dependent on the context in which they are told and the influence of the actors present who shape the telling of stories. In order to understand the influence of stories on innovation processes, it is important to admit a role for power in understanding how and why some stories carry influence, while others may be marginalised. The inclusion of power in the analysis also helps to develop Shotter's concept of social practice as 'joint action' by highlighting that, while the formative influences on thought and behaviour are distributed and dependent on the context of interaction, the distribution of power plays an important role in shaping these.

## References

Best, A., Greenhalgh, T., Lewis, S., Saul, J. E., Carroll, S., & Bitz, J. (2012). Large-system transformation in health care: A realist review. *Milbank Quarterly, 90*(3), 421–456.

Bevir, M.,& Richards, D. (2009a). Decentring policy networks: A theoretical agenda. *Public administration, 87*(1), 3–14.

Bevir, M., & Richards, D. (2009b). Decentring policy networks: Lessons and prospects. *Public Administration, 87*(1), 132–141.

Bevir, M., & Waring, J. (Ed.). (2018). *Decentring health policy: Learning from British experiences in healthcare governance*. London: Routledge.

Bloomfield, B. P., & Danieli, A. (1995). The role of management consultants in the development of information technology: The indissoluble nature of socio-political and technical skills. *Journal of Management Studies, 32*(1), 23–46.

Boje, D. M. (1991). The storytelling organization: A study of story performance in an office-supply firm. *Administrative Science Quarterly, 36*(1), 106–126.

Cameron, A., Lart, R., Bostock, L., & Coomber, C. (2014). Factors that promote and hinder joint and integrated working between health and social

care services: A review of research literature. *Health and Social Care in the Community, 22*(3), 225–233.
Lipsky, M. (1971). Street-level bureaucracy and the analysis of urban reform. *Urban Affairs Quarterly, 6*(4), 391–409.
National Institute for Health and Clinical Excellence. (2009, April). *Glaucoma diagnosis and management of chronic open angle glaucoma and ocular hypertension, NICE clinical guideline 85.*
National Patient Safety Agency. (2009). *Rapid response report NPSA/2009/RRR004: Preventing delay to follow up for patients with glaucoma.* Available at https://www.rcophth.ac.uk/wp-content/uploads/2015/01/NPSA_RRR_on_glaucoma_2009_supporting_info.pdf. Accessed 7 April 2019.
Schumpeter, J. A. (1934). *The theory of economic development.* Cambridge, MA: Harvard University Press.
Shotter, J. (1993). *Cultural politics of everyday life: Social constructionism, rhetoric and knowing of the third kind.* Toronto, ON: University of Toronto Press.
Shotter, J. (1997). Dialogical realities: The ordinary, the everyday, and other strange new worlds. *Journal for the Theory of Social Behaviour, 27*(2–3), 345–357.
Shotter, J. (2010). Situated dialogic action research: Disclosing "beginnings" for innovative change in organizations. *Organizational Research Methods, 13*(2), 268–285.
Turner, S., Goulding, L., Denis, J. L., McDonald, R., & Fulop, N. J. (2016a). Major system change: A management and organisational research perspective. In Raine, R., Fitzpatrick, R., Barratt, H., Bevan, G., Black, N., Boaden, R. et al. Challenges, solutions and future directions in the evaluation of service innovations in health care and public health. *Health Services and Delivery Research, 4*(16), 85–104.
Turner, S., Ramsay, A., Perry, C., Boaden, R., McKevitt, C., Morris, S. et al. (2016b). Lessons for major system change: Centralization of stroke services in two metropolitan areas of England. *Journal of health services research & policy, 21*(3), 156–165.
Van de Ven, A. H. (2017). The innovation journey: You can't control it, but you can learn to maneuver it. *Innovation, 19*(1), 39–42.

# Networking for Health, Networking for Wealth: A Study of English Health Innovation Policy in Practice

Jean Ledger

## Introduction and Background

There is an observable trend in English health policy that emphasises the productive potential of the National Health Service (NHS) to generate economic wealth whilst also treating ill health. This has manifested in a 'health and wealth' discourse in policy that has progressed with greater urgency during an austerity period and brings together an economically orientated narrative with a population health narrative. The NHS in this context is understood as playing a critical role in supporting the health and life sciences sector in the UK and attracting investors. Importantly, rather than viewing 'health' and 'wealth' policy objectives as fundamentally at odds, these goals are presented as complimentary.

This 'health and wealth' policy discourse has primarily been delivered through network modes of governance in the UK focused on research and

J. Ledger (✉)
Department of Applied Health Research, University College London, London, UK
e-mail: j.ledger@ulc.ac.uk



M. Bevir and J. Waring (eds.), *Decentring Health and Care Networks*, Organizational Behaviour in Healthcare,
https://doi.org/10.1007/978-3-030-40889-3_8

innovation. This has resulted in new forms of networked collaboration within regional health systems involving the NHS, universities, charities, industry and other stakeholders. Ambiguous policy aims have required those working within these networks to translate policy goals into local and regional strategies for health care improvement which also support national economic goals.

While there is a well-established body of research on the role of publicly financed networks in the health sector, particularly research translation networks or CLAHRCs[1] (Currie et al. 2013; Rycroft-Malone et al. 2011; Evans and Scarbrough 2014), far less has been documented about how 'health and wealth' policy objectives have been enacted at the regional level of Academic Health Science Networks (AHSNs). Collaborations for Leadership in Applied Health Research and Care (CLAHRCs) were evaluated from their first wave of implementation, leading to a body of knowledge about these networks and how they varied across England, whereas AHSNs have not been researched to the same degree despite having complimentary responsibilities. In this chapter, I address this gap, presenting an analysis from an empirical study of the early development of AHSNs involving case studies, policy interviews and a social network analysis (Ferlie et al. 2017). I explore how AHSN leadership teams responded to the dual policy ambition of population health improvement and wealth creation in practice. Rather than perceive 'health and wealth' policy objectives as binary and inherently at odds, I apply decentred network theory (Bevir and Waring 2018) to explore how AHSN leaders brought together these goals and turned them into network strategies. Over time, AHSNs began to position themselves at the forefront of the UK's health innovation landscape and forge new partnerships across highly fragmented health systems, operating as innovation advocates and mediating between institutional actors with varied interests. AHSNs were found to be broking different stakeholder groups and, at the same time, seeking to prioritise innovations that would address local population health needs. I suggest that by analysing local and regional-level responses to governmental 'health and wealth' policy ambitions, we arrive at insights about why innovation adoption across the NHS is challenging and the types of contingencies

[1] Collaboration for Leadership in Applied Health Research and Care. In 2019, these networks were re-launched as Applied Research Collaborations (ARCs).

that have to be negotiated in practice by AHSNs which operate across multiple boundaries.

This chapter draws on an empirical study that aimed to understand the networking, policy and leadership dynamics associated with the creation of AHSNs (Ferlie et al. 2017). Data was collected during the first phase of AHSN licensing (2013–2018) and five out of the 15 networks were studied intensively, leading to the production of detailed regional case studies that included 'tracers' of innovations selected by AHSNs for adoption within their regions. The study involved a large number of interviews with AHSNs teams and stakeholders ($n=133$), and analysis of documents outlining AHSN strategies. Finally, national 'AHSN Network' meetings were observed to understand the strategic coordination taking place across the 15 networks. This chapter focuses predominately on the qualitative, meso-level case studies and interview data. For interested readers, the final report of this study and further details about the methods are available online at the NIHR Journals Library (Ferlie et al. 2017).

The chapter proceeds as follows: I briefly outline the study methods before describing antecedents to the creation of AHSNs. An analytical discussion follows about how a 'health and wealth' policy mandate was enacted in English health policy and interpreted by AHSN leaders locally, drawing on decentred governance theory which "analyzes governance in terms of contingent meanings embedded in activity." (Bevir 2013, p. 15). The evolution of the innovation networks is described as involving a balancing act between managing regional conditions, member relationships, and central policy. This was particularly challenging at the outset of AHSNs given ambiguity in policy and a lack of clear, strategic leadership for health innovation at the national level.

During their early phase, AHSNs were predominately focused on what I term 'network anchoring'. With time, greater inter-network coordination and collaboration across AHSNs become increasingly apparent as they sought to balance health and wealth objectives and prioritise specific innovations for adoption and spread. This later period was characterised by consolidation of the AHSN mandate and "brand". Due to their network form and lack of formal powers, AHSNs operated largely through influencing, communication and networking strategies to achieve their aims.

## The UK Health Policy Context: Financial Austerity and Poor Population Health

Since the global financial crisis in 2007–2008, the UK economy has experienced slow economic growth and a period of sustained austerity. Public services are struggling to keep financially afloat and maintain services following a prolonged period of tight fiscal policy and cuts (Dowling 2017; Ferlie et al. 2018). Local authorities, which have responsibilities for public health planning and social care, have had their contributions from government drastically reduced. A referendum on the UK's EU membership in the summer of 2016 has added an additional layer of complexity and pressures on both public services and private industry and unprecedented political and economic turmoil. The context of health policy has become increasingly "turbulent" and focused on tighter financial control and efficiency, especially within commissioning organisations (Ledger 2014). At the same time, a political discourse has arisen focused on greater national self-governance, regionalism and autonomy from the EU.

Consequently, it is arguable that health policy in the UK has become more decentred and nation-centric than in previous decades, especially with Scotland, England, Wales, and Northern Ireland following their own health policy trajectories since devolution. Yet the demographic and epidemiological challenges confronting national health systems remain unifying. These include the prevalence of non-communicable diseases which are consuming increasing proportions of health care budgets (e.g. cardiovascular disease, cancer, chronic respiratory disease and diabetes), a growing ageing population and increasing numbers of persons living with multi-morbidities, including at a younger age, and epidemic levels of obesity (Peralta et al. 2018; WHO 2018). Health inequalities and disparities within nations and across regions have rightly garnered policy attention, raising important questions about the equity of access to innovative treatments and the social determinants of health (Marmot et al. 2010, 2020). The UK is falling behind other Western countries in tackling premature deaths from chronic diseases, such as cancer, with low income communities and minority ethnic groups most likely to be affected by poor health and the consequences of austerity policies (Public Health England 2017; Buck and Maguire 2015). Even though the NHS remains a high performing health system when compared to other countries internationally, particularly in terms of accessibility and affordability (The Commonwealth Fund 2017; Schneider et al. 2017), population health needs are requiring new forms of service delivery innovation, especially at the boundaries of health and social care. It is against this economic, political and demographic backdrop that contemporary policy narratives around 'wealth and health' have emerged.

## Harnessing the Potential of Health Innovation as a Policy Solution

Three policy problems are frequently articulated in health policy discourse in England: (1) rising health costs and increasing demands on services due to chronic diseases and an ageing population; (2) variation in clinical outcomes and standards of care; specifically, patchy compliance with evidence based practice and standards; (3) a slow pace of innovation adoption across the NHS. The English health sector is viewed as well placed to exploit new knowledge originating in scientific research, although the NHS has historically been understood as less strong at adopting innovations at scale. The Five Year Forward View (NHS England 2014) and Five Year Forward View Update (NHS England 2017) describes these policy problems in terms of 'a health gap, a quality gap, and a financial sustainability gap' (NHS England 2017, p. 9), and suggests that one way to help the NHS meet its challenges is by leveraging innovations and new technologies such as Artificial Intelligence (AI), genomics, digital health and improved diagnostics. There is also close alignment between NHS policy at the macro level and the UK's Industrial Strategy which has among its themes the aim of harnessing 'the power of innovation to help meet the needs of an ageing society' (BEIS 2017).

The Cooksey report of 2006 provided a critical review of the fragmented research and innovation landscape in the UK, the under-utilisation of clinical research by the NHS and poor investment in R&D and innovation. Challenges were diagnosed as being predominately cultural with parts of the NHS lacking '*a research and innovation friendly culture*' and research being '*considered a secondary activity*' (Cooksey 2006, p. 49). Since its publication there has been an evident shift to a more pro-research culture in the NHS and sizeable investment in translational and research architecture in England, such as through the creation of the National Institute for Health Research (NIHR), the CLAHRCs, Academic Health Science Centres (AHSCs) and Biomedical Research Centres (BRCs). These programmes have had a strong focus on 'bench' science, applied health research and implementing research into local clinical settings. NIHR spending has been maintained and the UK is ranked fourth in government expenditure on health R&D when compared internationally, behind the USA, Germany and Spain (OLS 2019).

Yet the innovation adoption "problem" has persisted and with it concerns about patchy uptake and poor commercialisation of research and innovations in the NHS. Furthermore, against a backdrop of economic recession and austerity, pressures have emerged for the NHS to demonstrate that is not only cost effective, research-friendly and evidence based, but that it can contribute to economic growth and fully embrace cutting-edge innovations. This is closely connected to national strategies that aim to ensure the UK has an internationally competitive health and life sciences sector attractive to foreign investors, such as large pharmaceutical companies, with opportunities for streamlined clinical trials and research on large, anonymised patient data sets. The wealth dimension is especially distinctive in contemporary health policy since it brings a variety of actors to the cusp of health policy discussions: industry associations, life sciences experts, and university and business representatives. Even though the major health policy problems have remained consistent over the past decade (an ageing population, rising costs, variation in practice and chronic conditions), the policy narrative has noticeably shifted and started to pay more attention to the *productive capacity* of the NHS and its ability to support economic growth in a post-recession climate.

For example, in March 2011, *Plan for Growth* was published by HM Treasury and the Department for Business, Innovation and Skills

(BIS). This plan restated the value of the health and social care system to the UK economy, adjoining the themes of welfare, health and wealth. Health care innovation was viewed as "a key driver of long-term growth" and there were aims to support the growth of "NHS intellectual property" (HM Treasury and BIS 2011, pp. 91–92). But it was the government paper, '*Innovation, Health and Wealth*' (DH 2011a) that most clearly brought together the themes of 'health and wealth' and outlined its meaning for the NHS:

> the NHS remains a major investor and wealth creator in the UK, and in science, technology and engineering in particular. NHS success in adopting innovation helps support growth in the life sciences industries that in turn enables these industries to invest in developing the technology and other products the NHS needs for its development. (DH 2011a, p. 9)

The report *Innovation, Health and Wealth* (DH 2011a, p. 10) outlined six barriers to innovation adoption and diffusion in the NHS:

1. Poor access to evidence, data and metrics
2. Insufficient recognition and celebration of innovation and innovators
3. Financial levers that do not reward innovators (and may actually function as disincentives)
4. Lack of capability/tools to drive innovation amongst health purchasers (commissioners)
5. Inconsistent leadership culture supporting innovation
6. A lack of an effective and systemic 'innovation architecture'.

The NHS is construed as having considerable influence as a 'macro purchaser' of health care technologies, medical products and innovations. Nevertheless, as a public service, the NHS functions somewhat as an innovation paradox: it is a leading health system by international standards, connected to a strong life sciences sector and with many leading research institutions and firms located in the UK. At the same time, the NHS is conceived as being a slow implementer of innovative solutions that have potential to transform services and improve population health outcomes.

Similar themes were later reiterated in the NHS Five Year Forward View (NHS England 2014) which framed the NHS as a 'test bed' for innovations arising from the UK's life sciences sector:

> The NHS will become one of the best places in the world to test innovations that require staff, technology and funding all to align in a health system, with universal coverage serving a large and diverse population. In practice, our track record has been decidedly mixed. Too often single elements have been 'piloted' without other needed components. Even where 'whole system' innovations have been tested, the design has sometimes been weak, with an absence of control groups plus inadequate and rushed implementation. As a result they have produced limited empirical insight. (NHS England 2014, p. 34)

An update of this strategy continued notions of prestigious, cutting-edge scientific advancement and innovation implementation:

> The UK has a world-leading life sciences industry which is both a magnet for investment and an engine for economic growth - enhancing productivity, driving healthcare innovation and employing over 220,000 people across the regions of the UK. Many important healthcare technologies - from vaccines to MRI scanners - have been nurtured by our strong science base and universities, innovative culture and leading healthcare system. (NHS England 2017, p. 68)

## Antecedents to the Formation of AHSNs

Evolving health policies therefore intended to close the gap between leading research in the life sciences, new technologies and frontline NHS services. However, in recent years there has been greater movement beyond research translation and towards evidence-based innovation, implemented at scale. A 'wealth and health' narrative gained traction in policy, yet left open questions about how transformational change and an 'innovation architecture' would be developed in practice, particularly regionally. In June 2011, the Department of Health put out a call for evidence about the adoption of innovations in the NHS and how the process could be accelerated as part of the NHS Chief Executive's Innovation Review. Recommendations received included the need to 'Improve horizontal knowledge exchange, networks and links' and have clearer innovation pathways (DH 2011b, c). In December 2011, *Innovation, Health and Wealth* was published (DH 2011a) and recommended the formation of regional, cross-boundary networks to enact health and wealth objectives, and support innovation uptake at scale in the NHS. An expression of interest followed from the Department of Health to establish the AHSNs. These would provide:

> A systematic delivery mechanism for the local NHS, universities, public health and social care to work with industry to transform the identification, adoption and spread of proven innovations and best practice. It is a partnership organisation in which the partners are committed to working together to improve the quality and productivity of health care resulting in better patient outcomes and population health. (DH 2012).

On the theme of 'wealth', the same document stated that:

> The AHSN will become the single local mechanism to enable productive partnerships with industry and run transparent procurements. The partnership cannot allow individual commercial companies to have unfair advantage or access but must enable a new and constructive relationship between the NHS, educational institutions and the representatives of industry that reflect the diversity of the health technology, information, biotech and pharmaceutical industries. (DH 2012)

Other key developments arose around this time and are noteworthy: firstly, the publication of the Strategy for UK Life Sciences in 2011 (BIS, OLS 2011) which outlined the need to build a national "life sciences ecosystem". The strategy stated the importance of reducing "regulatory bureaucracy to provide a route for early adoption and diffusion in the NHS" (ibid., p. 7). The presence of the Office of the Life Sciences (OLS) was equally important since it connected the Department of Health and BIS, signifying political support for the health and life sciences sectors and cross-governmental working to meet shared objectives.[2] One interviewee from the OLS described their perception of the health innovation challenge thus:

> There's a whole number of issues about the way the NHS works and the way it's structured which actually makes it very hard to get innovation into the NHS. It works for other parts of the, you know, the localisation in the region, it obviously works for other kind of aspects of the NHS but it doesn't necessarily work for innovation. And I think, you know, those issues will have to be addressed if we really want to, you know, speed up the process and, you know, and ultimately benefit patients. (Policy respondent, OLS)

The 15 regional AHSNs were launched in 2013, this leading on from the earlier formation of AHSCs in England. AHSNs were initially licensed for five years (comparable to CLAHRCs) and were later re-licensed in 2018. The latter decision was supported by the independent Accelerated Access Review which recommended that 'AHSNs, tertiary academic teaching hospitals and clinical leaders across the NHS should drive and support the evaluation and diffusion of innovative products.' (Accelerated Access Review 2016, p. 12).

## 'Networking Anchoring': Tracking the Early Progress of AHSNs

Many academics and researchers have attempted to describe the different features of networks in the health landscape to help avoid confusion between policy networks, health care collaborations and more informal, professional networks (Ferlie et al. 2013). AHSNs can be considered examples of *mandated* policy networks because their origins lie in health policy and the terms of their licenses were overseen by a central health agency. Mandated networks provide an 'implementation structure' for a programme of work that can broaden over time (Sheaff and Schofield

---

[2]The Office of Life Sciences is now part of the renamed Department of Health and Social Care and Department for Business, Energy & Industrial Strategy.

2016, pp. 442–444). This was indeed the case for AHSNs as they gradually took on more functions, such as supporting a national Patient Safety Collaboratives programme, providing evaluation support to the NHS and, in some instances, encouraging quality improvement initiatives.

Mandated networks have a tendency to be formally managed by an external body or sit within a hierarchy. During the period of study (2014–2016), AHSNs reported to NHS England, not the Department of Health, and worked with the NHS to develop AHSN metrics. Overall, the empirical evidence on the early development of the AHSNs suggested that, although these were mandated networks, they did not recreate internal hierarchies and operated in practice as relatively flat, flexible and outward-looking organisations focused on building lateral ties with external organisations and partners (both private and public) within their regions and beyond. Early efforts concentrated on organising teams around clinical and local health priorities—such as diabetes, atrial fibrillation, alcohol dependency, dementia and maternal health. AHSNs began, from the outset, to engage with a diverse pool of actors across organisational boundaries and sectors: public health agencies, NHS providers, NHS commissioners, charities, pharmaceutical companies, SMEs, industry associations (ABHI and ABPI), universities and local authorities. Many AHSNs devised plans to compliment other local networks and their regional health research architecture (e.g. CLAHRCs, CRNs, AHSCs), yet there was a broadening out of AHSN partners and stakeholders beyond the groups traditionally found in clinical or research networks. AHSNs were appointing diverse teams with business experience—such as in commercial director roles—because of their wealth creation objectives. Some located their offices in regional science and business parks as opposed to NHS Trusts or universities, perhaps because this signalled independence from any one institution and offered opportunities to network with local firms.

The early stage of the AHSNs concerned priority setting, building teams, identifying sources of additional funding, achieving a balanced membership and establishing self-governing structures. In terms of their approaches, the AHSNs varied considerably. Some of the networks decided to register as limited companies by guarantee providing distance from NHS organisations. Others chose to be hosted by NHS hospitals where this conferred advantages, such as being linked to a leading teaching and research-intensive institution.

Beyond internal business processes, the broader strategic approaches taken by the AHSNs varied too. Some were more overtly ambitious about wealth creation opportunities, such as job creation, regional economic growth plans or connecting with major international firms, such as big pharma. As one AHSN leader put it:

> Industry and wealth, yes, a big part of what we do is widening out this access to the NHS for industry and entrepreneurs and that the AHSN is indeed providing that brokering, signposting, accessibility service if you like. (AHSN 2)

Other AHSNs tended to lean more toward quality improvement and incremental change in the NHS, as another director observed:

> I think some of the problems are that elsewhere some of the AHSNs… have taken a much more QI health improvement focus and are less focused on the wealth creation in terms of the core work and pulling through innovation from an academic and commercial sources… (AHSN 4)

AHSNs managers and directors described a fine-balancing act between "marketing our value to people", attracting partners to the work of the AHSNs, and bringing about measurable improvements to local health systems and the NHS. Another director described the challenge as follows:

> I think one of the things we found most difficult is, you know, the membership is so enormous, is getting out and getting people involved in the dialogue. So my experience of that is a mixture of really positive and really quite negative. (AHSN 1)

The networks were not statutory bodies with formal powers to expedite the uptake of innovations in the NHS and their remit was broad in scope. AHSNs were therefore required to enact strategic influence locally and coordinate themselves nationally as a collective body. These conditions were conducive to a different mode of leadership and management practice from that traditionally found in large, vertical, managed health care organisations, as one AHSN director explained:

> Chief Execs, have been used to authority that a, you know, a direct command and control leadership brings, and actually to influence people in other ways is quite tricky and some people have got that skill and some people haven't. So it's all about sort of negotiation and influencing in more subtle ways than having direct control over people, some people respond well to that and some people don't... you have a lot of senior people involved, all who have a subtly different view of life and what we're trying to achieve. (AHSN 1)

A commercial lead in the same AHSN commented similarly:

> I think people who are very introverted in an organisational sense probably wouldn't go for those roles in the first place. (AHSN 1)

Another director described their role *as having "a good understanding of what you would call various partners' institutional logic models*" and being able to "*wear a set of clothes that appeals to the different logic models that are operating*". The point was, that to enact the remit of 'health and wealth', AHSN leadership teams had to adapt to the interests of different partners and members and find areas of mutual compatibility and interest with their localities. Indeed, to be captured or financed by only one type of institutional member, business or group of stakeholders would be to de-rail the brokering mission and legitimacy of the AHSN locally:

> So getting wholehearted, you know, honest collaboration between the public and private sector is I think a huge leadership challenge for anybody involved in this whole thing. And I think also just keeping people's enthusiasm and momentum going, because there is, you know, you do go through a period of two or three years where you're setting up groups and they're establishing priorities and, you know, they're making some progress, three steps forward, two steps back.. I think the hardest thing actually, as I think about it, is the [network] is about creating networks or encouraging networks that never existed before, however the NHS is an

> in-crowd really. You know, if you've ever been in a room with doctors or, you know, yes, I worked as a registrar with him and, you know, I worked at that hospital, and it's all very – what's the word I'm looking for? I mean it's a world of its own right? (AHSN 1)

The membership bodies of AHSNs reflected their broad policy mandate, and also the dynamic regional health economies of which they were a part. Engagement with a multitude of stakeholders helped to engender a pluralist outlook, with AHSNs essentially networking-upon-networks. AHSN teams purposively engaged with industry representatives, NHS chief executives, government, university researchers, patient charities, health care education boards, and local enterprise partnerships (LEPSs), building on both pre-existing networks and contacts and brokering new relationships. Internally, AHSNs were varied as well with a mixture of industry boards to provide commercial expertise and clinicians to lead health programmes.

## From Network Anchoring to Network Consolidation

> Inevitably we're starting to think around our response to being two years away from the end of the licence and we are sceptical whether the necessary policy thinking and policy framework is going to be put in place quickly enough by NHS England to, for us to rely on their response to sustain our functions which are adding value to the system…I think there are problems with NHS England funding in the entirety of what we do, you know, which relate to the wealth agenda basically. (AHSN 4)

The networks were managed from the centre by NHS England, although there was a lack of clarity about how network effectiveness could best be measured. The networks came together as a collective group (the 'AHSN Network') to discuss how to monitor and demonstrate their impact internally and communicate this externally. Nevertheless, half way through their license period, there was much uncertainty about the types of performance metrics most beneficial for tracking progress. Consistent with decentered theory, there was evidence that the AHSNs were enacting and interpreting policy in response to specific historical circumstances that were shifting (Bevir 2013). This found those working in AHSNs interpreting and negotiating the meaning of moving policy goals—both independently and as part of a collective. AHSNs were anchoring themselves regionally to support cross-sector working and innovation adoption in the NHS. Their opportunities were, however, contingent on the assets found within their particular regional health systems; for example, the prevalence of life and health sciences businesses and universities, the quality of existing relationships between NHS organisations and also commissioners. A further dilemma for AHSNs was how to carve out a leading innovation role that was additive rather than muddying an already complicated health innovation landscape. Locally, many NHS provider organisations were struggling to adopt existing best practice solutions (e.g. NICE-approved interventions and technologies) and maintain financial stability. Would they afford the time and money to support another iteration of health networks in their region? Another challenge was how to demonstrate wealth creation in tangible terms, over short, medium and long-term timeframes, alongside population health improvement:

> there is this tendency, which is like a bureaucratic tendency in the NHS to, you know, draw up the report card and have us spend a lot of time filling it in. And we're actually not spending much public money, so it's not as if we're spending billions on this and we're going to be accountable to the public accounts committee. We will have wasted quite a few million if this initiative doesn't work, but I think we're almost certain to waste it unless we give the AHSNs some freedom to be entrepreneurial. (AHSN 1)

There was not a clear policy blueprint for these looser, cross-sectoral 'entrepreneurial' networks and numerable AHSN practices evolved. These included: leveraging external funds; institutional brokering; mapping local businesses and assets; membership engagement activities; running events to showcase ideas; supporting NHS clinical entrepreneurs; quality improvement projects; and building up networks pan-regionally, nationally and to a lesser extent, internationally. AHSNs were thrashing out the meaning of 'wealth and health' in practical terms, and cooperating as a 'network of networks'. Inevitably, there was a high level of variation found in both structure and strategy, although towards the end of the study, an "AHSN brand" appeared to be consolidating and a clearer narrative about their contribution was being communicated in annual impact reports produced by the AHSN Network. At a local level, AHSNs continued to perceive themselves as inclusive and membership focused networks, larger than their constituent parts:

> So, you know, so the achievements that we make are the achievements of members and wider partners, so that's a difficult thing to pull off. (AHSN 5)

## Discussion

Policy diagnosis of a 'gap' between clinical research and health care practice is already well established, and an economic narrative has been in ascendency in health policy for at least a decade. What appears more novel, however, is the closer intertwining of innovation, 'wealth creation' and 'population health' themes as policy objectives at the macro level, this leading to the creation of regional networks as a delivery vehicle for innovation scale up across the NHS at the meso level. This has resulted in more representation from the life sciences industry within regional networks and AHSNs acting as brokers across public and private sector boundaries, and public and commercial interests. Whilst 'wealth creation' can bring to mind the dynamics of a competitive market and lofty aspirations for economic growth, neither the market nor bureaucracies alone have proved successful in policy terms at expediting the uptake of innovations (or research) in the NHS. Inter-organisational networks like AHSNs therefore represent an alternative in the health care landscape; a solution to intractable, "wicked policy problems" that require joined up working and the combining of resources from more than one professional group or organisation (Sheaff and Schofied 2016; Popp et al. 2014; Ferlie et al. 2011; Ferlie et al. 2013).

The creation of AHSNs fits with accounts of the 'New Public Governance' which describes a 'pluralist environment where the delivery of public services requires the negotiation of complex inter-organizational relationships and multi-actor policymaking processes' (Osborne 2010, p. 2). Newman (2001) views network governance theory as an 'open systems model' in which governance is heavily influenced by the environment and characterised by fluidity, decentralisation and innovation. The AHSNs in this study certainly had more in common with ideas of "collaborative government" (Hartley and Torfing 2016) and decentred governance than they did with more contractual and performance management approaches, such as the New Public Management (Hood 1991). Yet Hartley and Torfing (2016) suggest that there is a difference in motivations between the public and private sector actors in collaborative modes of governance, arguing that: "*diffusion, or spread, of innovation is particularly salient for public organizations, which are morally if not operationally bound to try to share innovations which improve quality or reach of public services or which contribute to greater social justice.*"

AHSNs appeared to be finding ways to mediate between social and public interests and commercial motivations rather than treating them as inherently opposing forces. This obviously created some tensions. The very creation of AHSN networks speaks to the way in which the delivery of modern public services now typically involves multitudinous networks and interest groups rather than a small number of central planning bodies (Osborne 2010). Whereas the New Network Governance theory views networks as a means to handle the fragmentation found in public service delivery, what became evident in the study of AHSNs is that these networks were not providing services that fitted within a traditional conceptualisation of public sector delivery, and instead were playing a distinct brokering and innovation advocacy function across the wider health system. Central government had set the agenda, but was relatively hands-off, with a health agency (NHS England) and the 15 AHSNs negotiating the 'NHS innovation paradox' described earlier in this chapter. As Bevir writes, "The state sometimes may set limits to network actions, but it has increased its dependence on other actors. State power is dispersed among spatially and functionally distinct networks." (2013, p. 9) A decentred theory of governance suggests that the variation found across the AHSNs is not surprising given that the networks were interpreting a broad policy remit and adapting to the local conditions in which they were situated, operating at the boundaries between different institutions and stakeholder interests (ibid., pp. 66–67). Their outcomes were contingent on the interactions, networking strategies and opportunities pursued by each network and the responses they received. Only later, as the networks began to consolidate their focus and remit, did a collective AHSN narrative begin to transpire.

I characterise the earlier phase of AHSNs—the period during which they built up their teams, set strategic priorities and accessed available networks—as 'network anchoring'. In this phase, it was especially important for AHSNs to avoid capture by any particular interest group and to tailor their search for innovations to the health needs of their local populations. This involved developing trust and partnerships with regional health stakeholders and leveraging the social capital of pre-existing professional networks. There was difficulty for AHSN leaders in terms of monitoring progress along these lines, yet with time, there was increased national coordination to demonstrate impact and value. Interestingly, an evaluation of *Innovation, Health and Wealth* by RAND noted that culture change in the NHS and 'leadership for innovation' was one of most tricky policy ambitions to deliver and measure (Bienkowska-Gibbs et al. 2016, p. 12).

AHSNs, with their pluralist memberships have in some ways come to represent the sheer number of stakeholders and actors now involved in innovation adoption pathways in health care, which are by no means linear or straightforward, nor limited to just one sector. Take, for example, a diabetes monitoring tool traced in this study: the development of this product involved a leading academic team of engineers, university-based researchers, a NHS diabetologist and an industry partner that could build a glucose monitoring device. NHS organisations were persuaded by the local AHSN to pilot and adopt the blood-glucose monitoring device so that patients could use it remotely and clinicians better manage their diabetes. The local AHSN helped to mobilise the innovation into NHS clinical care and coordinate activities between different stakeholders, yet the pathway of the specific innovation—from idea to evidence-based product suitable for use in practice—involved numerous parties, sources of funding and had taken many years to come to fruition, this history pre-dating AHSNs. In fact, given the complexity and research behind many of the health care innovations identified in the study, it was difficult to imagine adoption pathways and processes that did *not* involve a complex, mixed economy of public and private actors, even within a publicly financed health system.

In addition, the rather sweeping observation that the NHS is slow to adopt innovations is, when explored more closely, not a feature of singular institutional dynamics nor the result of poor innovation quality in the market. The picture is far more complex and the creation of AHSNs has rendered apparent issues such as poor coordination of innovation and health policy agendas at the macro and meso levels, strained inter-organisational relations within health systems, and longstanding cultural perceptions about both the NHS *and* industry that influence opportunities for collaboration. Because AHSNs have been deliberately situated *between* sectors, they are well placed to perceive how industry and innovators may develop exciting solutions but fail to attend to the most pressing population health needs and problems. At the same time, parts of the NHS can be inward looking and suspicious of industry, with a more conspicuous wealth creation and commercial agenda being particularly unfamiliar to many stakeholders. In short, AHSNs reveal how inter-dependent and complex the relationships behind modern health care systems actually are.

In their review of the network governance literature in public administration, Lecy et al. (2014) argue that collaborative networks require 'the development of significant levels of trust to effectively address new and particularly complex problems that are beyond the capacity of any single actor' (p. 648). Whilst AHSNs were focused on achieving various objectives, it was in practice difficult to measure what many AHSN leaders considered most valuable: high trust partnerships that would result in tangible benefits to patients.

## Conclusions

Academic Health Science Networks (AHSNs) are a particularly decentred form of coordinating network in the English health care system. They are charged with implementing a policy to accelerate the adoption of innovations into NHS frontline services and practice, improve population health and create wealth. This has required substantial partnership brokering by AHSNs across sectors and negotiation at local, regional and national levels. There is uncertainty and ambiguity within the AHSN movement as a whole: how to measure wealth creation and network effectiveness over time; what population and health care priorities should take precedence; what innovations should be scaled up, and when; how to support culture change in the NHS *and* industry to enable meaningful partnership working across private and public sector boundaries? Network actors report that delivering on this mandate requires a different set of leadership and influencing skills than traditionally found in vertically integrated organisations in the NHS or in clinical networks.

In the early phase, AHSNs were engaging in 'network anchoring' and looking outwards to their regions to ground their activities in local health needs and opportunities for generating wealth. The networks were not ashamed to "piggyback" on previous initiatives or programmes (such as CLAHRCs) and borrow ideas from within their health systems, particularly where pre-existing structures had been lost due to structural health care reforms. AHSNs therefore interfaced and often worked alongside other policy-mandated networks, or the remnants of them. There was a risk that the AHSNs would overlap with other initiatives and not add value (e.g. with CLAHRCs), or become too distracted by other national innovation programmes (for example, innovation tests beds, vanguards or patient safety collaboratives). They might also fail to secure enough membership support and funding to place them on a sustainable footing. To have their licenses renewed, the networks were required to demonstrate a unique role and demonstrate their impact as a system of networks, and articulate the "AHSN brand" and contribution. Whilst central funding from government provided the networks with impartiality, the downside was that delays in funding and a re-licensing decision meant that the future of AHSNs was uncertain and this made longer-term planning difficult with AHSN partners. At the end of the study, many of these issues remained unresolved.

## Afterword

The empirical research study of the early development of AHSN finished in 2016 and the findings were published in a full report in early 2017 (Ferlie et al. 2017). The networks were re-licensed in 2018 after a period of ambiguity about their future. However, due to innovation adoption and technology spread remaining a high priority in health policy, one connected to the UK's Industrial Strategy, the networks have since been viewed in policy as a promising mechanism for supporting health care innovation and better relations at the interface of industry and the NHS. At a national level, the AHSNs have continued to demonstrate collective impact, such as by quantifying metrics on wealth and health outcomes. These include statistics such the 15 AHSNs creating over 500 jobs, leveraging over £330m and over 22 million patients benefiting from 'AHSN input'. Attribution of successes to the AHSNs remains complicated to ascertain however given the numerous stakeholders, co-existing health networks and funding programmes involved in health care innovation pathways and processes.

## References


Accelerated Access Review. (2016). Accelerated Access Review: Final Report—Review of innovative medicines and medical Technologies—An independently chaired report, supported by the Wellcome Trust. London: HM Government.

Bevir, M. (2013). *A theory of governance*. Retrieved from https://escholarship.org/uc/item/2qs2w3rb.

Bevir, M., & Waring, J. (2018). Decentring health policy: Traditions, narratives, dilemmas. In M. Bevir & J. Waring (Eds.), *Decentring health policy: Learning from British experiences in healthcare governance* (pp. 1–16). Abingdon: Routledge.

Bienkowska-Gibbs, T., Exley, J., Saunders, C. L., Marjanovic, S., Chataway, J., MacLure, C., et al. (2016). *Evaluating the role and contribution of innovation to health and wealth in the UK: A review of Innovation, Health and Wealth: Phase 1 Final Report*. Cambridge: RAND Corporation.

BIS, OLS. (2011). *UK life sciences strategy*. Retrieved from https://assets.publishing.service.gov.uk/government/uploads/system/uploads/attachment_data/file/32457/11-1429-strategy-for-uk-life-sciences.pdf.

Buck, D., & Maguire, D. (2015). *Inequalities in life expectancy: Changes over time and implications for policy*. London: The King's Fund.

Cooksey, D. (2006). *A review of UK health funding (Cooksey review)*. London: HM Treasury.

Currie, G., Lockett, A., & Enany, N. E. (2013). From what we know to what we do: Lessons learned from the translational CLAHRC initiative in England. *Journal of Health Services Research & Policy, 18*(3_suppl), 27–39.

Department for Business, Energy & Industrial Strategy (BEIS). (2017). *Industrial Strategy: Building a Britain fit for the future*. London: HM Government.

Department of Health. (2012). *Academic health science networks: Expressions of interest*. London: HM Government.

Department of Health and Social Care. (2011a). *Innovation, health and wealth: Accelerating adoption and diffusion in the NHS*. London: Department of Health.

Department of Health and Social Care. (2011b). *NHS chief executive innovation review: Call for evidence and ideas*. London: HM Government.

Department of Health and Social Care. (2011c). *NHS chief executive's review of innovation in the NHS summary of the responses to the call for evidence and ideas*. London: HM Government.

Dowling, E. (2017). In the wake of austerity: Social impact bonds and the financialisation of the welfare state in Britain. *New Political Economy, 22*(3), 294–310.

Evans, S., & Scarbrough, H. (2014). Supporting knowledge translation through collaborative translational research initiatives: 'Bridging' versus 'blurring' boundary-spanning approaches in the UK CLAHRC initiative. *Social Science and Medicine, 106*, 119–127.

Ferlie, E., Fitzgerald, L., McGivern, G., Dopson, S., & Bennett, C. (2011). Public policy networks and 'wicked problems': A nascent solution? *Public Administration, 89*(2), 307–324.

Ferlie, E., Fitzgerald, L., McGivern, G., Dopson, S., & Bennett, C. (2013). *Making wicked problems governable? The case of managed networks in health care*. Oxford: Oxford University Press.

Ferlie, E., Nicolini, D., Ledger, J., D'Andreta, D., Kravcenko, D., de Pury, J. (2017). NHS top managers, knowledge exchange and leadership: The early development of academic health science networks—A mixed-methods study. *NIHR Health Service Delivery Research, 5*(17). Retrieved from https://www.ncbi.nlm.nih.gov/books/NBK436464/

Ferlie, E., Dopson, S., Bennett, C., Fischer, M., Ledger, J., & McGivern, G. (2018). *The politics of management knowledge in times of austerity*. Oxford: OUP Press. Retrieved from https://global.oup.com/academic/product/the-politics-of-management-knowledge-in-times-of-austerity-9780198777212?cc=gb&lang=en&.

Hartley, J., & Torfing, J. (2016). Chapter 20: Innovation. In C. Ansell & J. Torfing (Eds.), *Handbook on theories of governance*. Edward Elgar Publishing.

HM Treasury and BIS. (2011). *The plan for growth*. Retrieved from https://assets.publishing.service.gov.uk/government/uploads/system/uploads/attachment_data/file/221514/2011budget_growth.pdf.

Hood, C. (1991). A public management for all seasons? *Public Administration, 69*(1), 3–19.

Lecy, J. D., Mergel, I. A., & Schmitz, H. P. (2014). Networks in public administration: Current scholarship in review. *Public Management Review, 16*(5), 643–665.

Ledger, J. (2014). *Competing knowledges in turbulent times: The use of management knowledge in commissioning organisations in the english NHS*. PhD thesis. Retrieved from https://kclpure.kcl.ac.uk/portal/files/67208901/2014_Ledger_Jean_0975118_ethesis.pdf.

Marmot, M., Goldblatt, P., Allen, J., et al. (2010). *Fair society healthy lives (The Marmot Review)*. Retrieved from http://www.instituteofhealthequity.org/resources-reports/fair-society-healthy-lives-the-marmot-review/fair-society-healthy-lives-full-report-pdf.pdf.

Marmot, M., Allen, J., Boyce, T., Goldblatt, P., & Morrison, J. (2020). *Health equity in England: The Marmot Review 10 years on*. London: Institute of Health Equity.

Newman, J. (2001). *Modernizing governance: New labour, policy and society*. London: Sage.

NHS England. (2014). *Five year forward view*. Leeds: NHS England.

NHS England. (2017). *Next steps on the NHS Five year forward view*. Leeds: NHS England.

Office of Life Sciences. (2019). *Life science competitiveness indicators*. OLS.

Osborne, S. P. (2010). Delivering public services: Time for a new theory? *Public Management Review, 12*(1), 1–10.

Peralta, M., Ramos, M., Lipert, A., Martins, J., & Marques, A. (2018). Prevalence and trends of overweight and obesity in older adults from 10 European countries from 2005 to 2013. *Scandinavian Journal of Public Health, 46*, 522–529.

Popp, J., Milward, H. B., MacKean, G., Casebeer, A., & Lindstrom, R. (2014). *Inter-organizational networks: A review of the literature to inform practice*. IBM Center for the Business of Government. Retrieved from http://www.businessofgovernment.org/report/inter-organizational-networks-review-literature-inform-practice.

Public Health England. (2017). *Public health outcomes framework: Health equity report—Focus on ethnicity*. London: Public Health England.

Rycroft-Malone, J., Wilkinson, J. E., Burton, C. R., Andrews, G., Ariss, S., Baker, R., et al. (2011). Implementing health research through academic and clinical partnerships: A realistic evaluation of the collaborations for leadership in applied health research and care (CLAHRC). *Implementation Science, 6*(1), 74.

Schneider, E. C., Sarnak, D. O., Squires, D., Shah, A., & Doty, M. M. (2017). *Mirror, mirror 2017: International comparison reflects flaws and opportunities for better US health care*. The Commonwealth Fund.

Sheaff, R., & Schofield, J. (2016). Inter-organizational networks in health care: Program networks, care networks, and integrated care. In E. Ferlie, K. Montgomery, & A. R. Pedersen (Eds.), *The oxford handbook of health care management* (pp. 434–458). Oxford: Oxford University Press.

The Commonwealth Fund. (2017). *Health care system performance rankings*. Available at https://www.commonwealthfund.org/chart/2017/health-care-system-performance-rankings.

World Health Organisation. (2018). *World health statistics: Monitoring health for the SDGs, sustainable development goals*. Geneva: World Health Organisation.

# Tensions Between Technocracy, Scientific Knowledge and Co-production in Collaborative Health and Care Networks

Robert Vickers, Bridget Roe, and Charlotte Overton

## Introduction

Since the late 1990s, a narrative of evidence-based decision-making or evidence-based practices has increasingly guided the modernisation and improvement of UK health and care services. Rather than decisions being based on the conventions of professional practice or the ideologies of government, the expectation is that decisions from macro policy-making through to micro service delivery should be based on the best available evidence of 'what works'. Although evidence-based policy-making (EBPM) might have come to the fore of UK public policy during the relatively affluent years of the early mid-2000s, it arguably has a much longer history in Western 'technocratic' public

R. Vickers (✉) · C. Overton
University of Nottingham, Nottingham, UK
e-mail: Robert.vickers@nottingham.ac.uk

B. Roe
University of Birmingham, Birmingham, UK


M. Bevir and J. Waring (eds.), *Decentring Health and Care Networks*, Organizational Behaviour in Healthcare,
https://doi.org/10.1007/978-3-030-40889-3_9

administration, and continues to act as a guiding principle in more current austere times, in which fiscal deficit reduction has become the dominant narrative amongst the governing elite in Westminster (Stanley 2016). Unlike other areas of public policy, the principles of 'evidence-based' decision-making or practice have a relatively developed influence on health care organisation and delivery, as found in the growth of evidence-based medicine (EBM) since the late 1960s and resulting in the creation of bodies such as the National Institute for Health and Clinical Excellence (NICE). As above, the guiding principle of this movement is that evidence-based decisions can result in reduced variations in care delivery, improvements in care quality, and more cost-effective resource allocation (Sackett et al. 1996).

However, the quality of this evidence is often judged by its 'scientific' merits with particular prominence given to evidence produced through randomised control trials, and increasingly health economic data. As such, particular epistemological and ideological imperatives seem to determine what counts as rigorous evidence. That is, within the broad principle of evidence-based decision-making there are arguably differing schools of thought about what counts as evidence, how it should be produced, and how it should be use. Add to this, the narrative of co-production has also come to re-shape policy decision-making (Bevir et al. 2019), with the idea that various stakeholder perspectives should be brought together to inform more relevant, legitimate and democratic decision-making, where 'evidence' and 'opinion' are seemingly brought together in an un-easy relationship (Crompton 2019). This means that decisions about the organisation and delivery of health and care services, although ostensibly based upon the ideals of evidence, are often sites for disagreement between varying bodies of technocratic, scientific and co-produced evidence.

Taking a decentred approach (Bevir 2013; Bevir and Waring 2018), our chapter examines how different approaches to 'evidence' and 'evidence-based practice' are manifest and reconciled in the production of applied health service research. For us, this approach foregrounds the meanings and beliefs that guide the situated practices of policy actors. These situated practices are seen, on the one hand, has guided by traditions or habitual ways of acting in the context of shared webs-of-meaning, but on the other hand, these practices are the sites for novel meanings and practices as they encounter new situations which result in dilemmas for establish traditions. When addressing the significant pressures on healthcare, for example, a political contest arises over what constitutes the nature of the failings and what should be done (Bevir and Richards 2009). Dilemmas emerge when new ideas compete with existing beliefs or practices, forcing a reconsideration of existing beliefs and allied traditions. They can also arise from theoretical reflection, such as the merits of the implementation of scientific, technocratic or co-produced approaches to healthcare innovation. Our chapter draws upon these ideas through its analysis the situated experiences of actors conducting applied research in one regional Collaborations for Leadership in Applied Health Research and Care (CLAHRC) context. We first outline the different traditions of evidence-based decision-making and practice and show how, in different and sometimes competing ways, they have informed the formulation and implementation of health policies and changes in service organisation and delivery.

## Technocratic, Scientific and Co-produced Evidence

In many ways, the current focus on evidence-based policy-making (EBPM) came to prominence in the UK in the late 1990s with the New Labour government's commitment to modernise government and improve policymaking (Parsons 2002). The emerging pragmatic narrative was that research-based evidence would inform policy making, thereby removing ideology and promoting systems of governance (Clarence 2002). This emphasised "what works" to produce better policy outcomes in the context of a performance management strategy for the regulation of public services (Sanderson 2003), bringing forth a new era of 'technocratic' governance. The term 'technocracy' was coined in the United States during the first half of the twentieth century, to describe a system of governance in which decision-makers give precedence to technological competence, and where expertise (and evidence) is recognised as the primary basis of authority. Such technocracy has much in common with the logic of bureaucracy, rational planning and administrative science, which since the late 1970s have been steadily surpassed by competitive markets and collaborative networks as models of public governance (Bevir 2013). And yet, technocratic models of evidence-based decision-making are again advocated in the context of network governance (Newman 2001).

In the English health policy context, the technocratic narrative has persisted, albeit with different political intent and changed economic circumstances. The publication of the 2011 report *Innovation Health and Wealth, Accelerating Adoption and Diffusion in the National Health Service* (NHS), brought forth the Quality, Innovation, Productivity and Prevention (QIPP) Programme (Department of Health 2011) as major transformation initiative to improve the quality of care which simultaneously involved making up to £20billion of efficiency savings. The Health and Social Care Act 2012 further underlined the goal of making the NHS more responsive, efficient and accountable through the use of more competitive markets for care, combined with the 'scale-up and spread' of evidence-based innovations. At the same time, bodies such as NICE continue provide evidence-based recommendations and guidelines about cost-effective treatments and clinical services.

Unlike other areas of public policy, it might be argued that healthcare services have a longer history of evidence-based practice through the emergence of EBM from the late 1960s (Sackett et al. 1996). EBM emerged as an international priority to improve health and care quality based upon the best available evidence, typically produced through experimental randomised control trials (Adily and Ward 2005; McGinty and Anderson 2008; Melnyk et al. 2012). Where EBM differs from EBPM is that it more explicitly retains the notion of integrating individual clinical expertise with best-practice evidence, conceptualised as the proficiency and judgment that clinicians acquire through clinical experience practice. This expertise is reflected in effective and efficient diagnosis and is especially evident in the use of more empathetic insight into individual patients' predicaments, rights, and preferences in making decisions about their care (Sackett et al. 1996).

Whilst scientific and technocratic knowledge can sometimes become intertwined in dialogues about EBPM or EBM, they are produced through fundamentally different specialisms and disciplines of evidence or knowledge production. Biomedical scientific knowledge is frequently correlated with clinical expertise or the competency to undertake reliable, replicable research and produce valid evidence, whilst technocratic knowledge is more commonly associated with the managerial and economic aspects of policy implementation. It can be argued that these different types of knowledge pull in different directions. Consider, for example, the rise of gene-therapy treatments, a potentially paradigm-shifting breakthrough that could treat or even cure an array of modern-day health problems from Alzheimer's and diabetes to cancer and heart disease. Clinical data may suggest this exciting new line of research should be developed; yet, breakthroughs are often expensive, making high demands on time and resources, meaning technical expertise might say it is impractical or too technical challenging.

In seeking to resolve inherent tensions between clinical and managerial imperatives, and ensure the relevance and legitimacy of policy decision-making, contemporary public and health policies also advocate the principle of co-production (Bevir et al. 2019). Co-production has its origins the work of Ostrom (1996), who in the 1970s, detailed a process by which contributions from individuals not 'in' the same organization are transformed into goods or services. It became intimately linked with the idea of using combinations of state and non-state actors to produce or inform public service delivery (Osborne 2006; Voorberg et al. 2015; Howlett et al. 2017). Over the past decade co-production has become a prominent topic in policymaking, governance and research (Sorrentino et al. 2018). In health and care, it has come to describe a way of collaborative working to improve processes by creating user-led, people-centred health and care services (Filipe et al. 2017). Thus, the ethos of co-production can be considered at odds with both the technocracy and scientific approaches, which rely exclusively on decision making based solely upon the possession of specific technical or scientific expertise.

Co-production in the design and delivery of healthcare has become an increasingly prominent policy narrative (Bevir et al. 2019), which has informed healthcare decision-making and practice in a number of ways. While not always defined in terms of co-production, the idea that service users should have a more meaningful say in shaping the services they receive has become entrenched in post-war welfare services (Department of Health 2012). Co-production represents an alternate model for knowledge production, which entails ensuring the effective participation of those who use health and care services, carers and communities in equal partnership. Rather than simply transferring knowledge produce by technocrats and scientists to them. It is a way of day-to-day working that is far-reaching, engaging stakeholder groups in all stages of developing innovation, at many levels (Batalden et al. 2016), for instance the co-commissioning, co-design, co-delivery and co-assessment of services. Although the aim of co-production is usually taken to be enabling the diverse meanings of stakeholders to influence decision-making, questions remain as to whether this is meaningful to participants. An appraisal of the meaning of co-production must therefore reflect the cultural value judgments of individual actors (Crompton 2019).

## Converging Traditions in Applied Health Research

One place where these different forms of evidence-based decision-making and practice have played out is in the area of applied and translational health research, which is increasingly organised through inter-organisational networks of the producers and users of evidence. In the UK, the Nation Institute for Health Research (NIHR) has funded a variety of networked infrastructure initiatives that cover the entire research lifecycle, from basic science and discovery through to applied and translational research concerned with the spread and adoption of proven intervention. These include, for example, Biomedical Research Centres (BRCs), CLAHRCs, Academic Health Science Networks (AHSNs) and Patient Safety Translational Research Centres (PSTRC) Med-Tech collaboratives and more recently Applied Research Collaboratives (ARCs). These approaches reflect national priorities for service improvement and reduced cost, whilst simultaneously responding to the needs of local decision-makers, commissioners and service providers (Harvey et al. 2011). The intention of the translational vehicles, in particular, is to ensure research relates to the difficulties faced by care providers and the needs of patients, so that outputs are more suitable for implementation into care settings.

A series of influential reports published in the mid-2000s established a new agenda for applied health research, but in different ways these policies brought together the distinct traditions of technocratic, scientific and co-produced knowledge in sometimes a difficult balance. The Cooksey Review (2006) was one of the most significant documents calling for a new collaborative approach to applied health research, given the shortcoming of disciplinary specific and siloed research communities to address the contemporary challenges facing the NHS. Significantly it, presents a more technocratic narrative asserting that the streamlining of research was essential to the wealth of nations. The review noted the UK risked failing to receive the full economic, health and social benefits that public investment in health research should produce.

Technocracy was not the only important narratives shaping applied health research. The national health research strategy launched in January 2006 (Department of Health 2006) placed emphasis on the application of the scientific method to solving social problems. This was based around an elite of professionals and the desire to use resources more efficiently and effectively. The strategy set out five main goals: firstly, to stablish the NHS as an internationally recognised centre of research excellence. Secondly, to attract, develop and retain the best research professionals to conduct people-based research. Thirdly, the commissioning of research focused on improving health and social care. Fourthly, the better management of knowledge resources, to facilitate the application of research outcomes to improve health and delivery of services. Finally, to act as sound custodians of public money for public good. This trend towards EBP is likely to intensify with the *Health Trends* (Stanford Medicine 2017) and *Future of Health* (Corbett et al. 2017) reports both highlighting the potential of 'big data' to push the bounds of evidence based decision-making and clinical practice further and faster, including new approaches to prevention, diagnosis and treatment. Incorporating big data and next-generation analytics into clinical and population health research and practice necessitates employing such things as machine learning, data mining, and machine-based algorithms (Krumholz 2014).

Alongside these technocratic or scientific narratives, there have also been calls for more inclusive models of evidence co-production This became an important policy narrative within the UK, the NIHR commissioned *Future of Health* report, for example, indicated that a key priority for health research funders is to strengthen patient and public engagement in health research (Corbett et al. 2017). Co-production was also a key policy issue identified in the *Best Research for Best Health* report, which stressed the need to involve patients and the public in research and recommending reforms in the structure of research throughout the NHS. The report contributed towards this by establishing the UK Clinical Research Network (UKCRN). In its Strategic Plan 2006–2008 the UKCRN set out its vision for active patient and public involvement (PPI) to become embedded as part of mainstream clinical research activity, delivery and performance (Miles 2006). While many health and care service users might welcome the opportunity to engage healthcare service professionals, there are, however, potential sources of tension. In particular, the notion of shared accountability for outcomes is contentious (Ewert and Evers 2014). Batalden et al. (2016) suggest it is neither possible nor desirable to share power and responsibility equitably between patients and professionals in all situations. They assert that the burden of responsibility for medical and surgical error, for instance, must fall predominantly on healthcare professionals.

These initiatives value and prioritise different forms of evidence, evidence production, and in turn reinforce particular traditions of evidence-based practice. Firstly, they are typically premised on the utilisation and expansion of clinical research through collaboration with research universities, which tend to prioritise and advance 'scientific' evidence through forms of scientific trials and associated scientific publications. Within this community it is often assumed service impact is made through national guideline development and changes in evidence-based clinical practice; and the pathways to knowledge mobilisation and implementation are a particular issue for translational research collaborations. Secondly, they are also expected to involve collaboration with service commissioners and providers, and also industry, including technology and pharmaceutical firms. Such organisations clearly value the development and relevance of clinical evidence, but they are also more often orientated towards the operational costs and benefits of intervention development and application. As such, different forms of management, operational or technocratic evidence are expected to inform decision-making. Thirdly, it is also recognised that the ultimate beneficiaries of health research are patients and the public, and their involvement in research prioritisation, evidence production and implementation is now expected. From this perspective, evidence needs to be co-produced with service users and stakeholders to ensure its relevance and adoption. While the incorporation of all three forms of evidence into a networked model of health research might seem coherent to policy makers, at a local level they can present the basis for dilemma and anomalies as actors from different communities, following different traditions, seek to produce, translate and implement evidence into practice.

## Collaborations for Leadership in Applied Health Research and Care (CLAHRCs)

We now focus on the development of CLAHRCs as a major publicly-funded initiative to promote applied and translational health research, which represents a prominent case of the tensions described above. The need to reform the existing structure of health research was noted by the aforementioned Cooksey Review (2006). It highlighted that health providers and researchers were often disconnected having major cultural differences in terms of aims, language and incentives (Rowley et al. 2012). Equally, the Tooke report (2007) recognised that a new model of applied and translational health research was required that better acknowledged and reflected the actual needs of care providers. It indicated that this necessitated the re-connection of clinical practice with academic research, stating the need for community-wide academic health research collaborations to streamline the co-production of health research and the translation of evidence into practice.

Reflecting the recommendations of these expert reports, the NIHR sent out a call for proposals to create 'pilot' CLAHRCs in October 2007, to forge links between a University and the surrounding NHS organisations. Nine regional CLAHRCs were established, each receiving up to £10 million in funding between 2008 and 2013. The CLAHRCs have operated as partnerships between local providers of NHS services and NHS commissioners, universities, other relevant local organisations and AHSNs. The collaborations were intended to improve patient outcomes through the conduct and application of applied health research. One of their primary focuses has been contributing towards closing the 'second gap in translation', by reducing the time-lags between the development of proven interventions and the implementation of these into routine practice (Cooksey 2006). Hence, their early goals can be seen as focused towards a more scientific agenda.

In 2013 the NIHR allocated £124 million for 13 new CLAHRCs, these 'second generation' CLAHRCs were commissioned between 1 January 2014 and 30 September 2019. They still had the central aim of supporting applied health research and the translation and implementation of research evidence into practice. There were several changes to the policy narrative for the second generation CLAHRCs with technocracy now more on the agenda. Notably, more prominence was given to the importance of collaboration with industry and the contribution to the economy. There was a clearly stated expectation that they would "contribute to the country's growth by working with the life sciences industry". In addition, importance was attached to achieving economic growth through building 'a critical mass' of people involved in applied health research.

However, the CLAHRCs were also created to develop new organisational models and approaches to co-produce changes to frontline practices (Rowley et al. 2012). As can been seen from Table 1, the principles of collaboration and co-production have been clearly articulated as core aims by all thirteen of the second generation NIHR CLAHRCs. In particular, public involvement has been deemed a key priority area for many of them.

Hence, within the broad context framing the development and implementation of the CLAHRC networks were three narratives

**Table 1** Declarations regarding collaboration and co-production from individual CLAHRCs

| CLAHRC | Specified commitment to collaboration and co-production |
|---|---|
| East Midlands | From its inception, CLAHRC East Midlands has placed patient and public involvement (PPI) at the centre of all its activities, including both the generation of new research evidence, and efforts to translate findings from that research into practice |
| East of England | Service users and carers are at the heart of what we do, in parallel with an ambitious public health research programme. Co-production and collaboration at all stages of the research process are fundamental to making a positive impact through applied health research |
| Greater Manchester | NIHR CLAHRC Greater Manchester's vision is to create true and enduring partnerships that deliver high quality research which improves healthcare and has impact in Greater Manchester and beyond |
| North Thames | The applied health research we undertake with our partners and in response to their needs grouped into broad themes. The individual projects in each theme are designed with the close involvement of clinicians, patients and the public, and academics from across our region. We involve patients and the public in everything that we do |
| North West Coast | The mission of the NIHR CLAHRC NWC is to work collaboratively with Partner organisations and other stakeholders including members of the public to co-produce and conduct high-quality, leadership enhancing, applied research designed to decrease health inequalities and improve the health of the population of the NW Coast through applied health research |
| North West London | We use the skills, knowledge and expertise of researchers, health and social care professionals, managers, commissioners and patients to conduct high quality research projects to find new ways of improving healthcare |
| Oxford | We will continue to work with our existing partners and look to develop new partnerships. We will continue to provide high quality, collaboratively produced, research-based evidence from applied research to inform rapid implementation of new services, research and innovation |

(continued)

**Table 1** (continued)

| CLAHRC | Specified commitment to collaboration and co-production |
|---|---|
| South London | The Collaboration for Leadership in Applied Health Research and Care (CLAHRC) South London is a research organisation. It comprises researchers, health professionals and NHS managers working at universities and NHS organisations |
| South West Peninsula | In our view, the theory of co-production provides useful insights into what it is about the qualities of collaborative working that inspire the requisite mechanisms for generating knowledge that is translated into practice |
| Wessex | PPI engagement is actively encouraged in all CLAHRC Wessex applied health research projects |
| West | It has been shown that where genuine co-production has taken place, it can deliver better outcomes, support better use of scarce resources and improve the well-being of those involved—clearly a win/win situation for patients and the public, as well as health service providers |
| West Midlands | Our co-production model between clinicians, patients and academics has strengthened, and our drive to stay true to this model is crucial to our continued success and deepening engagement |
| Yorkshire & Humber | We will undertake high quality applied research and evidence-based implementation that is responsive to, and in partnership with, our collaborating organisation, patient, carers and the public |

that were not always complementary. Firstly, the tradition of scientific knowledge as embodied by clinicians and researchers focusing on the production of research, trials and evidence. Secondly, technical or technocratic experts with separate jurisdictions, acting as managers and commissioners, allocating resources based on population data and economic outcomes. Thirdly, the idea of co-production, where multiple patient and professional perspectives inform both the production and use of innovation. The way in which these narratives were accommodated and expressed within the case study CLAHRC seem to have helped shape how it has evolved and developed.

## The Example of One CLAHRC

Implementing the case study CLAHRC mandated an array of specialist knowledge. This was provided by agents who could be subdivided into three main categories: scientific experts, including the subcategories of (a) clinicians with specialist medical knowledge and academics with an understanding of conducting research, (b) technocrats, who were decision-makers and administrators tasked with the effective and efficient management of human and financial resources and (c) stakeholders, this subdivision encapsulated a wide array of people, some of whom like the above categories worked within the CLAHRC structure, such as patient and public representatives. While yet others were located in external organisations including Clinical Commissioning Groups (CCGs), research funding bodies or medical facilities. It is also worth acknowledging that these categories could be relatively fluid, with individuals holding hybrid or conjoint positions across different communities. That said, the following considers how these traditions were manifest within the evolution of one CLAHRC, and how situated agents responded to these traditions and tensions manifest between them.

### The Prerequisite for Scientific Knowledge and Technocracy

The second CLAHRC call placed an emphasis on scientific knowledge within research teams, with the application process requiring them to have a proven track record of 'world-class' research (WCR). Thus, there was an expectation within the CLAHRCs that a primary goal was to be the production of high-quality publishable research. The vast majority of those interviewed noted the prominence given to academic research; some suggested this had the potential to create conflict within the network between partner universities and clinical institutions.

> I mean one tension is that for world-class research, well the easiest type of study to publish and if you do it well is always well-regarded and

> always great to put on a university REF return and journals, it would be a well-conducted randomised controlled trial. But the normal Health Service does not ever do a randomised controlled trial, it's not a delivered way. And it uses evidence in different ways. So most of which would be seen as poor in terms of methodology. So there is a tension there. **Research Director**

Other participants suggested that prioritising research could result in the CLAHRC being forced in more of an academic direction, creating a tension with those having with a technocratic focus. One Programme Manager hinted at the frustrations evident at the outset of the case study CLAHRC caused by a lack of dialogue between research and clinical staff, saying '*its academics in their boxes that have decided these things, without reference to the clinical practice areas*'. This clearly represented a threat to the notion of collaboration and was in direct conflict with the intension behind establishing the CLAHRCs.

Even though the stated goal of the CLAHRCs was to develop and conduct applied health research and translate research findings into improved outcomes for patients; the observed governance structures continued to place great importance on academic research. One of the headline performance indicators in their Annual Progress Reports, for instance, was the number of publications they produced; with an emphasis placed on high impact journals such as Nature and The Lancet. For some participants this raised the question of academics being able to influence the agenda in a direction that suited their interests. This could be an obvious source of conflict with the network, as other actors' views or priorities were potentially side-lined. As one member of the CLAHRC, who did not categorise themselves as an academic, noted:

> The academics … I mean again this is a generalisation and by no means true of everybody but there is you know, a predisposition for academics to focus on their interests. And if they're controlling the agenda of what happens in the … without having to engage with external influences, then as I said there's going to be a tendency that those silos, to a greater or lesser extent, will be sustained. **Programme Manager**

## Technocratic Operations

Within the CLAHRC another set of actors believed that historical pressures would inevitably lead the network in more a technocratic direction, both in terms of research management, and in terms of its engagement with NHS commissioning bodies. In terms of research management, for example, a significant area of operational focus was given to prioritising the efficient allocation of research, and measuring research processes and outcomes, such as the number of projects completed, PhD students recruited or website hits. There was a wide-ranging acceptance within the case study CLAHRC that an element of technocratic governance was inevitable. This was based upon an understanding of the policy landscape, in which managerial and commissioning groups would ultimately decide what services to pay for. Hence, addressing their priorities was essential if the network was to be able to make an impact.

> There are ways of measuring performance, there are ways of making sure it's scientifically robust and sound and that everything's value for money. **Research Network Manager**

These views could partly be explained by the national narrative emphasising efficiency, return on investment and demonstrating the CLAHRCs contribution to the country's economic growth. Consequently, there was an expectation that they would have to demonstrate that public funding was being allocated prudently. Hence, from the technocratic perspective the drive for efficiency and cost effectiveness were prevailing concerns, especially if the CLAHRC was to form effective relationships with commissioners. As one senior manager noted:

> fundamentally we've got to be much better in developing our economic argument because whilst the quality is all very nice to have, the bottom line for commissioners is that if we can't demonstrate that we can take costs out of the system they will not be interested. And I still think there isn't enough recognition of that from people in CLAHRC. **Senior Manager**

Within the CLAHRC network actors performed specific technocratic roles, with some specialising in the efficient functioning of its operations, and others focusing on monitoring and compliance.

> And then you've got obviously Karen and Darren at senior levels and Karen's helping more on the operational side, actually making the CLAHRC work. And then you've got Darren who's more making sure our performance is doing what we said it would do in the tender document and reporting back. **Research Lead**

The competing scientific and technocratic tradition led to dilemmas in certain relationships within the network. One the one hand, academics had to focus upon WCR to remain within the network, as one senior academic asserted:

> we know as academics that's what keeps our tenure, that's what we have to do. And I do think that was a tension because I think the ethos behind what NIHR were trying to do with the CLAHRCs was actually to have more impact in the practice areas. **Programme Manager**

On the other hand, the technocrats were under pressure to more rapidly produce tangible results that would create efficiency and cost savings in clinical practice. Thus, a particular source of tension within the network were the differences timescales scientists and technocrats were working towards. While the technocratic aim of the CLAHRCs was to reduce the time taken to get evidence into practice. Producing WCR, however, would it would take several years to conduct and publish, therefore not yield immediate results.

> So there is this drive towards academic excellence and scientific rigor and so on. But what a lot of the purpose of CLAHRCs wanted were more shorter-term evaluative studies. We are thinking of making the change and we have just made the change to see have the improvements that we thought would come have been realised and can you deliver that in six months or 12 months rather than three years to five years? **Programme Manger**

Some participants suggested that the tensions between the scientific and technocratic actors could be found in the way that the operation of some CLAHRC teams played out. An Operations Manager, for instance, commented:

> Yeah, there have been challenges with projects where people are not necessarily in agreement about what they're in it for or they're in it to try and get something for themselves. So that's quite challenging to negotiate your way through that to manage those people's expectations and draw them back to the aims of the project. But I think that's the case with any kind of service implementation, redesign, development work. **Operational Manager**

Hence, situated agents' webs of belief represented a potential source of conflict within the enactment of the case study CLAHRC. If these were the only traditions providing a guidance for future action, there may well have been a strong dynamic tearing the network in different direction. As one faction dominated by technocratic traditions pushed in one direction and another focusing on academic or scientific knowledge pulled in another. However, there also was a third tradition evident within the CLAHRC, suggesting that co-production should be its guiding principle.

## The Desire for Co-production

The CLAHRCs stated aims and mission repeatedly emphasised the importance of undertaking scientifically robust world class research that would importantly be implemented into practice, thereby making a tangible impact on frontline service delivery. For some within the CLAHRC, closing this 'translation gap' was best addressed through co-producing research between service providers and users, commissioners and researchers. However, this brought into stark contrast different viewpoints about the quality and value of different types of evidence. A prominent example was the idea that co-produced, service-facing research should be iteratively developed to meet real-world problems with learning feeding rapidly into how services are organised and delivered. For those more accustomed to scientific methods, however, this type of iterative process compromised the controlled design of conventional research trials. While the need for scientific and technocratic expertise was a prerequisite for enacting and operationalising the CLAHRC, the extent of stakeholder engagement was a dilemma that would have to be resolved as the product of individual agency. As a Research Manager observed: '*All the CLAHRCs are doing different things, there isn't a remit for us to do the same things. So different CLAHRCs have different approaches*'.

The desire for co-production within the case study CLAHRC was clearly articulated by one Research Manager, who stated: "*And the whole idea of co-production and engagement or mode two research, well that's what CLAHRCs are for anyway*". While a Project Manager also asserted the belief that the purpose of the CLAHRC was to be inclusive:

> And spreading it out and networking and collaborating and joining up, which is getting all the relevant people in, not just academics you know, AHPs, nurses, PPI, we've got to get their views constantly about what's needed. **Participant 12, Project Manager**

It could have been the case that this desire for co-production would have been another source of tension within the network, attempting to take it in yet another direction. However, we argue this tradition, rather than being a source of conflict, helped to resolve tensions in the enactment of the CLAHRC.

## Resolving the Tensions

The dominant discourse within the case study CLAHRC network was that collaboration, rather than conflict, was the underlying principle guiding their actions. This narrative was most strongly embodied in belief surrounding the value of co-production and PPI.

> Work with partners, both natural NHS partners, local authorities, the voluntary sector, industry and the HSNs. And generally, be seen … I mean the key vision I think from my point of view both internally and

externally was having impact within our projects and making a difference. **Performance Manager**

Everything must have a proper PPI involvement which is more than trivial, it's got to be more than just reading a patient information sheet and agreeing or changing a couple of words on it. It's got to be a meaningful sort of consultation and really through the whole project. **Research Director**

It appeared that the network was constructed in such a way that the social context in which situated agents thought and acted made cooperation and collaboration a primary concern. This helped to resolve the tension between technocratic, scientific and co-production approaches within the structure of the network, with a new emergent local narrative synthesising the three potentially competing priorities emerging.

In an idealised world, the CLAHRC is a unique vehicle for bringing together a whole range of different people who want to make a difference in making healthcare better through actually researching … doing research on interventions, on practices, on procedures, on anything that can make healthcare better. And it's almost like a hook or a nexus point and it brings all these people together and they should work in this kind of dynamic mode two way of kind of interdisciplinary problem-solving. **Research Lead**

So, it wasn't academics working in their silos, clinicians doing the job, the patients receiving the care all separate. The idea was if you got everybody together, then you'd do things smarter and quicker. So that was what I understood as sort of the main driver to do applied health research in a sort of more pragmatic way that could actually be rolled out rather than just sitting on an academic shelf in some library for years and years and not being picked up. **Research Coordinator**

This, however, had been an evolving process, participants noted the narrative around co-production had been developing since the previous iterations of the CLAHRC. During which time it became viewed as mechanism to ensure that the innovation they developed were appropriate for implementation into health and care settings.

The discourse enforcing collaboration and co-production originated in the responses of individual situated agents within the network. While there were forces pushing predominantly for scientific discovery, technocracy or co-production. The overall result was the construction of a new tradition, which exerted an influence on those being socialised into the CLAHRC. Meaning agents were not operating in a context that explicitly reinforce the potential tensions between within the network. Nevertheless, they would have to resolve this dilemma themselves when their own traditions and paradigms did not coincide with this background.

> People I would say when they come to work for us they either get it or they don't. So people that tend to like working within a CLAHRC study, as opposed to a more traditional study, they're the sort of people who have that already, who have that say for example the idea of making sure that if there is any way of working with the organisations that are going to be implementing the research, that they're the sort of people that want to do that anyway and that they don't have to be told to. And it's not a new thing to them. **Applied Researcher**

## Conclusions

This chapter has drawn upon decentered theory to explore the ways in which collaborative healthcare research networks are made, and remade, through the activities of the individuals who compose them to resolve conflicts. It focused upon the potential tensions between technocracy, scientific knowledge and co-production in the context of the send iteration of a regional CLAHRC programme. The decentered approach provided an effective analytical lens through which to examine the views of situated agents and their perceptions of tensions within the enactment of the network.

While we expected people act on their beliefs, findings indicated these were construct against the background of tradition and discourse.

Hence, the way the tensions between technocracy, scientific knowledge and co-production were addressed within the CLAHRC was not simply a product of agents' roles within the network. However, these exerted an influence as the traditions associated with being an academic, manager or practitioner etc. resulted in dilemmas often manifest through particular network relationships. The relationships between those with having a scientific focus and those with a more technocratic mode of operating could come into conflict due to their priorities and goals. A particular issue arose from the tension between the competing aims of the CLAHRC, with a technocratic focus aiming to get research evidence into practice as soon as possible to produce greater efficiency and cost effectiveness, and the scientific objective of producing WCR. These conflicting priorities could lead to dilemmas as their realisation would occur on fundamentally different timescales.

Nevertheless, t was not the case that academics only prioritised world-class research or that commissioners only had economic concerns at the expense of each other interests. Nor was the desire for co-production sacrificed to prioritise technocratic or scientific objectives. Instead, the dilemma of how to ensure the effective participation of stakeholders in the network resulted in a tradition underlining the desire for collaboration.

The NHS habitually encounters the operational tensions of continually improving quality of care for people using their services while also delivering better-value care. It has been suggested EBP has the potential to address the quadruple aim of: improving the patient experience; improving the health of the population; reducing the per capita cost of healthcare; and improving the work life and conditions of clinicians (Bodenheimer and Sinsky 2014). This creates a powerful narrative suggesting the basic focus should be upon research the efficient translation of research-based advances into practice.

Research evidence indicates that a networked approach can be an effective way of sharing such learning and ideas. Also, that it is an effective means of building community and purpose, influencing new solutions to entrenched problems, tapping into talent and knowledge, and providing a means to innovate and embed change (Provan et al. 2007). It is important that the push for technical expertise in the form of scientific knowledge or technocracy do not come to dominate such networks. As this could be at the cost neglecting co-production as a means of altering essential relationships and ongoing practices (Mitlin and Bartlett 2018). The knowledge derived from the experience of patients and service users and working with health and social care partners to design and disseminate research, can be invaluable in ensuring innovation is suitable for the health and care context. Thus, there is a potential tension between EBM and co-production because they serve different agendas within networks.

Decentred theory changes the conception of networks. It encourages networks to be treated as arising from the ways in which people act on beliefs they adopt against the background of traditions and in response to problems. As situated agents' beliefs and actions constructing the nature of networks, central to collaborative healthcare research networks is the creation of inclusive traditions. Our findings align with the proposition of decentred theory that a networks dimensions and characteristics are not given, rather they are constructed by individuals in the stories they hand down to one another. Within the case study setting the tensions between technocracy, scientific knowledge and co-production were recognised and addressed through the situated meaningful practices of local actors as networked practice was enacted. Change involved the push and pull of the dilemma between actors. The network became a nexus point that brought professional and private stakeholders together, it was able to include clinicians, policy experts, academics, patient, carers and communities as partners. So that they could work in a dynamic mode two way of interdisciplinary collaborative problem-solving. Consequently, the case study CLAHRC became a context in which dilemmas were resolved and new inclusive traditions formed.

## References


Adily, A., & Ward, J. E. (2005). Enhancing evidence-based practice in population health: Staff views, barriers and strategies for change. *Australian Health Review: A Publication of the Australian Hospital Association, 29*(4), 469–477. Available at: http://www.ncbi.nlm.nih.gov/pubmed/16255712. Accessed 2 January 2019.

Batalden, M., Margolis, P., Seid, M., Armstrong, G., Opipari-Arrigan, L., & Hartung, H. (2016). Coproduction of healthcare service. *BMJ Quality & Safety, 25*(7), 509–517. https://doi.org/10.1136/bmjqs-2015-004315.

Bevir, M. (2013). *A theory of governance.* Berkley: University of California Press.

Bevir, M., Needham, C., & Waring, J. (2019). Inside co-production: Ruling, resistance, and practice. *Social Policy & Administration, 53*(2), 197–202. https://doi.org/10.1111/spol.12483.

Bevir, M., & Richards, D. (2009). Decentring policy networks: A theoretical agenda. *Public Administration, 87*(1): 3–14. https://doi.org/10.1111/j.1467-9299.2008.01736.x.

Bevir, M., & Waring, J. (2018). Decentring health policy: Traditions, narratives, dilemmas. In M. Bevir & J. Waring (Eds.), *Decentring health policy: Learning from British experiences in healthcare governance* (pp. 1–16). Routledge.

Bodenheimer, T., & Sinsky, C. (2014). From triple to quadruple aim: Care of the patient requires care of the provider. *The Annals of Family Medicine, 12*(6), 573–576. https://doi.org/10.1370/afm.1713.

Clarence, E. (2002). Technocracy reinvented: The new evidence based policy movement. *Public Policy and Administration, 17*(3), 1–11. https://doi.org/10.1177/095207670201700301.

Cooksey, D. (2006). *A review of UK health research funding.* Available at: https://assets.publishing.service.gov.uk/government/uploads/system/uploads/attachment_data/file/228984/0118404881.pdf. Accessed 25 July 2018.

Corbett, J., Batalden, P., Margolis, P., Seid, M., Armstrong, G., Opipari-Arrigan, L., & Hartung, H. (2017). *Future of health: Findings from a survey of stakeholders on the future of health and healthcare in England.* RAND Corporation. https://doi.org/10.7249/RR2147.

Crompton, A. (2019). Inside co-production: Stakeholder meaning and situated practice. *Social Policy & Administration, 53*(2): 219–232.
Department of Health. (2006). *Best research for best health*. Available at: www.dh.gov.uk/researchstrategy. Accessed 24 February 2019.
Department of Health. (2011). *Health and wealth: Accelerating adoption and diffusion in the NHS*.
Department of Health. (2012). *Liberating the NHS: No decision about me, without me*. London. Available at: https://assets.publishing.service.gov.uk/government/uploads/system/uploads/attachment_data/file/216980/Liberating-the-NHS-No-decision-about-me-without-me-Government-response.pdf.
Ewert, B., & Evers, A. (2014). An ambiguous concept: On the meanings of co-production for health care users and user organizations? *VOLUNTAS: International Journal of Voluntary and Nonprofit Organizations*. https://doi.org/10.1007/s11266-012-9345-2.
Filipe, A., Renedo, A., & Marston, C. (2017). The co-production of what? Knowledge, values, and social relations in health care. *PLOS Biology, 15*(5), e2001403. https://doi.org/10.1371/journal.pbio.2001403.
Harvey, G., Fitzgerald, L., Fielden, S., McBride, A., Heather, W., Bamford, D., et al. (2011). The NIHR Collaborations for Leadership in Applied Health Research and Care (CLAHRC) for greater manchester: Combining empirical, theoretical and experiential evidence to design and evaluate a large-scale implementation strategy. *Implementation Science, 6*, 96. https://doi.org/10.1186/1748-5908-6-96.
Howlett, M., Kekez, A., & Poocharoen, O.-O. (2017). Understanding co-production as a policy tool: Integrating new public governance and comparative policy theory. *Journal of Comparative Policy Analysis: Research and Practice, 19*(5), 487–501. https://doi.org/10.1080/13876988.2017.1287445.
Krumholz, H. M. (2014). Big data and new knowledge in medicine: The thinking, training, and tools needed for a learning health system. *Health Affairs, 33*(7), 1163–1170. https://doi.org/10.1377/hlthaff.2014.0053.
McGinty, J., & Anderson, G. (2008). Predictors of physician compliance with American heart association guidelines for acute myocardial infarction. *Critical Care Nursing Quarterly, 31*(2), 161–172. https://doi.org/10.1097/01.CNQ.0000314476.64377.12.
Melnyk, B. M., Fineout-Overholt, E., Gallagher-Ford, L., & Kaplan, L. (2012). The state of evidence-based practice in US nurses. *The Journal of Nursing Administration, 42*(9), 410–417. https://doi.org/10.1097/NNA.0b013e3182664e0a.

Miles, M. (2006). *UKCRN patient & Public involvement strategic plan: 2006–2008*. Available at: www.ukcrn.org.uk. Accessed 24 February 2019.
Mitlin, D., & Bartlett, S. (2018). Editorial: Co-production—Key ideas. *Environment and Urbanization, 30*(2), 355–366. https://doi.org/10.1177/0956247818791931.
Newman, J. (2001). *Modernising governance: New labour, policy and society*. Sage.
Osborne, S. P. (2006). The new public governance? *Public Management Review, 8*(3), 377–387. https://doi.org/10.1080/14719030600853022.
Ostrom, E. (1996). Crossing the great divide: Coproduction, synergy, and development. *World Development, 24*(6), 1073–1087. https://doi.org/10.1016/0305-750X(96)00023-X.
Parsons, W. (2002). From muddling through to muddling up—Evidence based policy making and the modernisation of british government. *Public Policy and Administration, 17*(3), 43–60. https://doi.org/10.1177/095207670201700304.
Provan, K. G., Fish, A., & Sydow, J. (2007). Interorganizational networks at the network level: A review of the empirical literature on whole networks. *Journal of Management, 33*(3), 479–516. https://doi.org/10.1177/0149206307302554.
Rowley, E., Morriss, R., Currie, G., & Schneider, J. (2012). Research into practice: Collaboration for Leadership in Applied Health Research and Care (CLAHRC) for Nottinghamshire, Derbyshire, Lincolnshire (NDL). *Implementation Science, 7*(1), 40. https://doi.org/10.1186/1748-5908-7-40.
Sackett, D. L., Rosenberg, W. M., Gray, J. A., Haynes, R. B., & Richardson, W. S. (1996). Evidence based medicine: what it is and what it isn't. *BMJ, 312*(7023), 71–72. https://doi.org/10.1136/bmj.312.7023.71.
Sanderson, I. (2003). Is it "what works" that matters? Evaluation and evidence-based policy-making. *Research Papers in Education, 18*(4), 331–345. https://doi.org/10.1080/0267152032000176846.
Sorrentino, M., Sicilia, M., & Howlett, M. (2018). Understanding co-production as a new public governance tool. *Policy and Society, 37*(3), 277–293. https://doi.org/10.1080/14494035.2018.1521676.
Stanley, L. (2016). Legitimacy gaps, taxpayer conflict, and the politics of austerity in the UK. *The British Journal of Politics and International Relations, 18*(2), 389–406. https://doi.org/10.1177/1369148115615031.
Stanford Medicine. (2017). *Harnessing the power of data in health* (Stanford Medicine Health Trends Report). Available at: https://med.stanford.edu/content/dam/sm/sm-news/documents/StanfordMedicineHealthTrendsWhitePaper2017.pdf.

Tooke, J. (2007). *Aspiring to excellence: Findings and recommendations of the independent inquiry into Modernising Medical Careers* (Interim report. MMC Inquiry). Aldridge Press.

Voorberg, W. H., Bekkers, V. J. J. M., & Tummers, L. G. (2015). A systematic review of co-creation and co-production: Embarking on the social innovation journey. *Public Management Review, 17*(9), 1333–1357. https://doi.org/10.1080/14719037.2014.930505.

# Is Co-production Just Really Good PPI? Making Sense of Patient and Public Involvement and Co-production Networks

Oli Williams, Glenn Robert, Graham P. Martin, Esmée Hanna, and Jane O'Hara

## Introduction

The recent special issue 'Inside Co-production' (edited by Bevir et al. 2019) of the journal *Social Policy and Administration* called for a 'decentring of co-production' (p. 199) by focusing attention on elite narratives, local traditions and resistance, and meaningful practices. We


O. Williams (✉) · G. Robert
King's College London, London, UK
e-mail: oli.williams@kcl.ac.uk

O. Williams · G. P. Martin
THIS Institute, Cambridge, UK

E. Hanna
De Montfort University, Leicester, UK

J. O'Hara
University of Leeds, Leeds, UK

Bradford Institute of Health Research, Bradford, UK




M. Bevir and J. Waring (eds.), *Decentring Health and Care Networks*, Organizational Behaviour in Healthcare,
https://doi.org/10.1007/978-3-030-40889-3_10

continue the analysis of these themes in this chapter by highlighting what we view as important distinctions between co-production and Patient and Public Involvement (PPI) in applied health research. In introducing their editorial, Bevir et al. (2019) acknowledge the rich and distinct tradition(s) of co-production around the 'radical goal of challenging dominant interests and emancipating marginalised groups' (p. 197). But they also—in our view problematically—ascribe flaws found in PPI (e.g., widespread tokenism) to co-production. We argue that conflations of this kind arise from an uncritical acceptance of how proponents of the PPI agenda have adopted (at least in rhetoric) key principles distilled from the work of academic researchers and others associated with co-production, while neglecting or failing to comprehend its distinct and radical origins.

In this chapter we briefly outline the emergence of PPI in the English National Health Service (NHS) and explore the rationales for the promotion of PPI—and the more recent adoption of the label 'co-production'—by the National Institute for Health Research (NIHR). We then draw distinctions between PPI and co-production within the English healthcare and research contexts and assess their respective need for a decentred analysis. More specifically we examine whether the discourse of co-production itself requires decentring, or rather whether the co-option/corruption of co-production through a national mandate for PPI has perhaps inadvertently served to translate theory into practices that can only be *mis*labeled as co-production. Central to this analysis is understanding the networks (and associated traditions) through which co-production has become so closely aligned with PPI in English healthcare and research contexts, as well as competing ideas regarding the utility of different forms of involvement as a means to achieving better health(care) outcomes. In short, we suggest that many of the critiques levelled at co-production arise from a misrecognition of its origins, which are rooted less in grand or elite narratives, imposed from the top down, and more in practices that have been developed in multiplicitous locally driven exchanges, and shared through lateral networks. In this light, what is needed is less a decentred understanding of co-production itself, and more a critical analysis of the path by which a policy-driven and quite distinct set of practices (PPI) came to be associated with the term. This implies an approach to analysis that also accounts for structural influences on the practice of PPI—one that we commence in this chapter.

## Bringing the Outsiders in: A Brief History of PPI in England

The frequent and wide-ranging 'redisorganisation' of the NHS has been followed by a well-worn path of academic comment and critique (Hunter 2011; Smith et al. 2001). Different forms of governance with varying (and often competing) logics and aims have reshaped the policies and practices of healthcare provision. Decentred theory has helped to illuminate that the reception, interpretation and implementation of new forms of governance is not universally consistent. Rather the NHS is a collection of fragmented networks upon which the influence of individuals engaging with competing and contingent narratives has a significant bearing, often with unintended consequences as diverse sets of aims and practices are pursued by different people within these networks (Bevir 2013). That attempts to govern the behaviour of public servants with competing frameworks of governance has unintended and regularly counter-productive outcomes is a consistent research finding, and one well documented in healthcare (see, e.g., Martin et al. 2009). However, Martin and Carter (2017: 109) argue that the unpredictability, disruption and resistance that arises as a consequence of discordant governance is 'especially acute' within PPI networks. Therefore, there is a particular need to direct critical attention to the 'various webs of meaning' (Bevir 2013: 25) within which people in these networks act.

While decentred theory 'encourages the researcher to explore the contingent ways in which networks are made and remade through the activities of particular individuals' (Bevir 2013: 95), in this chapter we pay more attention to how networks are formed within, and shaped by, social structures. We use the term 'network' to refer to groups of people joined by formal or informal connections orientated around a common focus. The focus may vary: it could include a common occupation, an interest in civil rights, or participation in a supply chain. In some instances the network is explicit, organised and formal, and people may need to seek membership to join it, e.g., a trade union or sports club. In others the association may be much less formal, with people incidentally connected through common characteristics, interests and/

or circumstances, e.g., use of a local park. The degree of formality may change as a network evolves; indeed, as we shall discuss, the PPI networks on which we focus have increasingly adopted the trappings of formality through time.

Martin and Carter (2017: 110) trace the development of PPI in England from user-led, grassroots movements in the 1960s through to what they describe as a 'turbulent recent history of reform' which amounts to various iterations of bureaucratisation since the turn of the twenty-first Century. In PPI networks, they argue, multiple rationales are invoked for involving members of the public, patients and carers; these rationales can become strange bedfellows at different points in time and within different contexts. As Martin and Carter (2017: 109–110) explain, 'in most areas of governance the aims are broadly agreed but the means may be controversial. In involvement, both the aims and the means are subject to high degrees of contestation, and often irreconcilable difference.' Despite this, PPI has been increasingly recognised and legitimised by the state through time, and is now a requirement in England in both healthcare (e.g. there is a legal duty to consult patients and the public in major service change) and health research (e.g. the NIHR expects projects it funds to include patients and the public as partners as well as participants). But while the mandate for PPI is clear, the differing rationales invoked for it add significant complexity to the formation of PPI networks and the relations between individuals and groups within them, and help to explain the diversity of practice that occurs under the umbrella of PPI. This poses significant challenges for those seeking to understand and develop PPI.

Martin (2008) grouped the rationales for PPI into two overarching categories: democratic and technocratic. Democratic rationales present PPI as normatively desirable and tend to orientate from the outside in e.g., campaigners and groups lobbying for greater influence within healthcare. Their underlying premise is that a national healthcare system with finite resources will inevitably prioritise some needs over others, and thus should be held directly to account by the citizens who support it—through taxation and unpaid caring roles—as well as rely on it as patients. It is an oft-quoted truism that we will all be patients within our lifetimes and that as citizens we make a financial contribution to the

NHS, and thus have a democratic right to, at the very least, a conduit to influence over this public institution. More recently this democratic right has, not unproblematically, been presented as synonymous with consumer rights, as 'users' of public services (in particular healthcare and education) are increasingly framed as 'consumers'. For example, the Department of Health (2010) white paper '*Equity and excellence: Liberating the NHS*' outlined plans for an 'information revolution' that would put patients at the heart of health services and afford them greater choice and control. A central feature of this plan was to establish the mantra 'no decision about me without me' as an organisational norm to embed shared decision-making throughout service design and delivery via the means of PPI. This mantra subtly but significantly differs from the classic political motto that evidently inspired it—'Nothing About Us Without Us!' (originally 'Nihil de nobis, sine nobis!'). Among other causes, this mantra was used prominently within disability activism in the late twentieth century (e.g., Charlton 1998). But this shift from the collective (us) to the individual (me) realigns the sentiment with the consumer model. This individualisation presents interesting dilemmas in terms of representation within PPI which will be explored in further detail later in this chapter. Technocratic rationales on the other hand are premised on the notion that patients and the public can provide insight and inputs that are instrumentally useful and distinct from those offered by professionals and thus tend to orientate from the inside out, e.g., professionals charged with designing/improving services consulting with those who have lived experience of the relevant health conditions and/or associated services.

While democratic and technocratic rationales can be mutually reinforcing, they are not always harmoniously paired—see example of limb disposal in Box 1. Furthermore, differing definitions of and approaches to PPI (including a diversity of practices labelled as 'co-production', sometimes after the fact), and tensions between alternative rationales, have sometimes led to disagreement between patients and healthcare professionals and researchers about what PPI is 'for' and how it should be operationalised (Maguire and Britten 2018). These tensions are well illustrated in contemporary debates about the evaluation of PPI, particularly PPI in health research (Boivin et al. 2018). The differing motives for, and emphases in, these rationales offer possible explanation for a lack of evaluation (Kislov et al. 2018) and thus predictable scarcity of robust evidence of the impact of PPI (Conklin et al. 2015; Mockford et al. 2011). Although some researchers view robust evaluation of PPI impact as the 'holy grail' (Wilson et al. 2018), a democratic rationale does not require a sound evidence-base to justify the normative desirability of PPI. Consequently, calls for evaluation of PPI premised on professional norms of measurement and regulation in pursuit of efficiency and improvement (e.g., Staniszewska et al. 2008) will often meet opposition from those for whom democratic rationales are foremost in their motivations for participation. This opposition is commonly expressed through questioning the plausibility of inferring causality from PPI activities (impact itself is notoriously difficult to measure, and subtle or long-term effects risk being rendered invisible in evaluation), and even mistrust in funders to continue to support PPI if evaluation indicates insignificant technocratic utility. Given trends in reform, and the ebb and flow that defines the history of social activism, it is difficult to argue that this mistrust is unfounded, even if a democratic rationale is not necessarily at odds with technocratic advances in part developed and established through sound evaluation.

**Box 1: A case in point—Limb disposal**

The disposal of limbs after amputation (Hanna 2019) offers a useful case through which to consider the relationship and tensions between the technocratic and democratic rationales of PPI. This is in part due to the unusual nature of the topic but also the aspects of healthcare to which it relates. Currently patients' limbs are disposed of via 'medical waste' within clinical settings. Some patients, however, have particular preferences regarding the disposal of their body parts, e.g., due to religious beliefs.

The recent scandal in the UK regarding the stockpiling of medical waste, including human body parts (Hanna 2018), demonstrates the potential overlap between democratic and technocratic aspects of PPI in considerations of disposal. In autumn 2018 it was discovered that hundreds of tonnes of hospital waste, including body parts, had been stockpiled by the company Healthcare Environmental Services, which was contracted by the NHS to remove, manage and dispose of medical waste from a number of NHS organisations across the country (Carding et al. 2018). This was deemed a 'national incident' and illuminated concerns around contracting of waste disposal within the NHS. Given it is the bodies of patients that are 'in parts' (Sobchack 2010) within such waste, PPI regarding how limb disposal should be approached could serve a useful democratic function—aiming to address failings in the system and preserve people's right to dignity and thus (potentially) prevent future scandals. Such PPI could also serve technocratic aims by improving patient experience as a by-product of the democratic function.

However, there are potential tensions between the democratic and technocratic aims of PPI in this case. We found that patients primarily see choice as a key aspect of how limb disposal should be framed (Hanna and Robert 2019). Patients want opportunities and options regarding their own limbs, with autonomy and self-determination central to their wishes being enacted and their limbs disposed of in a dignified manner. Choice could create multiple pathways for the disposal of the amputated limb. This would however involve greater cost and rely on additional resourcing (such as staff time). Indeed, in a system with finite resources responding to a diverse set of limb disposal preferences would involve opportunity costs, reducing the budget for things that a different public—or even the same public—would value more (e.g., prosthetic services). Outsourcing hospital waste management, as is routine within the NHS, transforms waste into a commodity for which payment is received. Thus the logic of industry becomes part of the healthcare system, but this is often at odds with the logic and motivation of involvement that serves democratic aims (Martin 2008).

Democratic approaches to PPI are often more unwieldy, create diverse outcomes and speak to different agendas. The example of limb disposal illuminates this usefully; technocratic and democratic ends can be achieved together through PPI, but more often there is tension and conflict between them. Moreover, different forms of democratic PPI, involving different publics towards different ends, may themselves give rise to conflicting outcomes. ◀

Policies around PPI often leave space for both democratic and technocratic contributions. This may lead to disputes in practice as individuals within PPI networks (both PPI representatives and professionals) can have conflicting notions of why and how PPI should be done. A decentred analysis highlights the inevitably of such a situation even in less contested arenas, as the 'fate of policies depends on the ways in which civil servants and citizens understand them and respond to them from within all sorts of traditions' (Bevir 2013: 32). In other words, it is not just the ambiguity of PPI itself that gives rise to contestation, but also the different meanings that those involved breathe into the process; these meanings derive from actors' personal and institutional histories.

Given that bringing together a diversity of opinions is a fundamental goal of PPI, these tensions are not in themselves problematic. Indeed, Donetto and Cribb (2011: 910) advocate 'epistemic involvement' ('taking patients' perspectives seriously not as an extra source of data to feed into clinical epistemologies but as a source of epistemically alternative framings and insights'), arguing that 'tidiness can only really be accomplished within the context of untidiness, and that the gains to be garnered from embracing complexity far outweigh any losses'. This creates a situation ripe for diverse local meanings and situated practices to occur throughout the PPI network. However, research often finds that the unequal power relations that tend to characterise PPI networks, comprising patient and public contributors and healthcare professionals and/or researchers, lead to the latter holding sway over what kinds of contributions are considered legitimate and, ultimately, what constitutes 'involvement' (e.g. Hodge 2005; Martin et al. 2018). Correspondingly, Barnes et al. (2007) argue that the 'parallel discursive arenas', in which patients, carers and publics (outsiders) organise themselves, are increasingly accompanied by 'invited spaces of governance' where the purpose and terms of reference are orchestrated by professionals and managers (insiders). The practice of 'outsiders' being invited by 'insiders' to become involved with the design and delivery of health services and applied health research, is akin to fish inviting people to swim. In short, a professional advantage is held no matter how competent or confident a patient, carer or public contributor may be. Even if great efforts are made to neutralise the professional-lay hierarchy and the potential for professional norms to exclude those who are not embedded in them, there are pre- and post-selection issues, chiefly those of representation (who is invited to contribute and why?) and outcome (involvement is no guarantee of influence).

Who is invited to contribute within PPI networks is a major issue and demonstrates the unequal power relations at play. This issue is of particular importance within discussion of a decentred theory of governance as a normative model for informing social action, rather than a descriptive account of empirical reality freed from common structuralist social scientific tropes about the determinants of individual behaviour. Bevir (2013) states that the decentred approach has 'sympathy for' (p. 34) and 'encourages' (p. 101) bottom-up approaches. However, it could be argued that the theory as a whole fails to adequately recognise the relevance and history of unequal power relations and structural exclusion (read injustice) in the formation, organisation and activities of networks. For instance, the notion that to 'decenter networks' is 'to focus on how they are constructed by individuals acting on conscious, subconscious, and unconscious beliefs and desires' (Bevir 2013: 95) displays an atomisation incapable of fully comprehending or adequately analysing why and how individuals come to have conscious, subconscious and unconscious bias, how dominant cultures and power structures create and maintain these biases and, significantly, how this impacts which networks are formed as well as the patterns of inclusion in and exclusion from networks and the activities that subsequently occur in them (cf. Speed 2017). In this way it seems unlikely that a decentred understanding of networks would have highlighted that white, middle-class women of moderate liberal politics might not be the catalyst of or conduit to liberation and justice for many women whose lived experience was, and is, largely defined by their positioning at the intersections of minority and disadvantage (see e.g., hooks 1981). Networks do not just 'aris[e] from people acting on the beliefs they adopt against the background of traditions and in response to dilemmas' (Bevir 2013: 95). Rather, they play a significant and reciprocal (one might even say structural) role in *forming* traditions and *creating* dilemmas through, for example, a history of exclusion. Racism is a case in point. These structural inequalities are important to the analysis of networks, and PPI networks offer an important example why.

## The Structural Underpinnings of Inequitable PPI Practice

Due to the way these societal-level, structural injustices play out within healthcare and health research—as well as through individual (sometimes unconscious) bias—recruitment for and participation in PPI tends be inequitable. There are pressures within healthcare and research to minimise expenditure. Competitive tendering and funding calls implicitly discourage costing for extensive or innovative (but costly) PPI, and this can lead to 'light touch' approaches becoming the norm. Such approaches are particularly problematic, as ensuring inclusivity and diversity relies on the availability of adequate resources and support for the inclusion of those who are typically referred to as 'hard to reach' or 'seldom heard'. It is also an explanation for an overreliance on mobile retirees in PPI networks (as distinct from frail older people, who may by contrast be under-represented—see Beresford 2013). Those who are retired but well off and healthy are convenient PPI contributors for healthcare professionals and researchers who are often time-poor, and restricted by ethical and governance boundaries, and thus may lean towards PPI activities taking place within their places of work, and during office hours. While this population group is not homogeneous and certainly has a valuable contribution to make, this 'convenience sampling'—whether borne of insufficient funding, ill-equipped infrastructure, researcher laziness, individual bias, or misguided logic—is neither equitable nor capable of delivering the diversity of views that would be expected of a fair and democratic process. This practice is particularly problematic when the task is defining core tenets of PPI (e.g., Green 2018) and the need for change is well-documented (Ocloo and Matthews 2016). This is a reminder that if some people are 'hard to reach', it is in part because 'reaching' is a dual dynamic that reveals as much about those reaching (or not)—and the institutional contexts they work within—as about those seemingly beyond reach. It is also a reminder that any democratic rationale for PPI must be accompanied with equitable practice, otherwise inequalities equivalent to those observed in other 'opt in' democratic processes and universal services will be replicated, e.g., voting in elections; cervical screening (Dorling 2016; Marlow et al. 2015).

Even if equitable involvement were achieved, current norms dictate that the influence of PPI contributors is almost entirely dependent on the professionals who invited them. This is of course implicit in the name 'patient and public involvement'—outsiders are invited in, and the degree of their involvement and influence is by and large determined by the priorities, and at the discretion, of those doing the inviting, i.e., funders, healthcare professionals and researchers. While the aspiration signalled by an explicit mandate for PPI is to be applauded, it has given rise to a professional and managerial culture of 'box-ticking' exercises (Martin et al. 2018). Although 'outsiders' may be involved, there are various ways in which their contributions are stunted or omitted due to established professional norms. Having a seat at the meeting table does not guarantee an opportunity or the confidence to speak up, or that contributions made are officially recorded in meeting minutes, let alone give rise to tangible influence on services or research. Needless to say, reporting the presence of PPI contributors at team meetings can provide the façade of involvement required for official documentation, and satisfy compliance with policy irrespective of whether the process allowed and supported meaningful contributions to be made.

These pitfalls in current PPI processes and practice have led to calls for more meaningful involvement. Notably, this can be seen in the definition of PPI in research put forward by NIHR INVOLVE (a body within the wider NIHR network charged with promoting, facilitating and improving the standards of PPI): research that is 'carried out '*with*' or '*by*' members of the public rather than '*to*', '*about*' or '*for*' them' (INVOLVE 2012: 6—emphasis in original). What is apparent in this definition is the delineation of good *and* bad practice. Defining good practice as PPI 'with' or 'by' the public moves away from more conventional and conservative ideas about involvement that are more broadly accepted and operationalised within the PPI network (i.e., inviting outsiders into make a contribution, with insiders delimiting their influence), towards a process that on the face of it may seem more akin to co-production. In essence this has led to the elevation of co-production to a gold standard for those in the PPI network to aspire to, justified in part as a way to stymie the trend for poor PPI practice and tokenism.

However, the contested nature of co-production is highlighted by INVOLVE (2018) themselves who state:

> Some argue that co-production in research is just 'really good PPI'. For others it is very different; a much more deliberative process which requires public members and 'professionals' to be involved on an equal footing throughout every stage of the design and delivery of research.

This highlights the problematic trend towards viewing co-production as merely different in degree—but not in nature—from involvement practices that more commonly occur in, and have come to define, PPI in English healthcare and applied health research. This is where we take issue with understandings of co-production that conflate its principles and practices with those of PPI, such as Bevir et al. (2019).

Bevir et al. (2019: 198) argue that 'critical questions need to be asked when those in power claim to be empowering those without power through forms of co-production'. This is a position with which we unreservedly agree in theory, although it is worth noting that in practice few would claim that patients, carers and members of the public are 'powerless' and consequently such claims might be viewed as hyperbole. The authors justify this stance through examples (Martin 2008; Crompton 2019) taken exclusively from studies of patient and public *involvement* within English healthcare policies and practice—where until relatively recently co-production has played a rather minor role in establishing traditions and influencing practice. Bevir et al. (2019: 197) quite legitimately assert that for advocates, co-production 'is more than a method or tool of better decision-making, rather it reflects a political agenda to rebalance inequalities and promote democracy'—not something that can usually be said to be a defining quality of PPI (as evidenced by the overarching influence of the technocratic rationale). Their critique of the championing of co-production by policymakers, healthcare professionals, citizen groups and services users alike, however, is in part premised on Martin's (2008) identification of the risk that public involvement may be tokenistic. Yet Martin's (2008) paper is concerned with PPI: it does not include a single use of the term co-production. Therefore, this appears tantamount to calling for a more critical approach to apples, because it has previously been found that there are flaws with oranges. This is not to claim that co-production is flawless. However, this apparent conflation of co-production with PPI—reflecting the common perception that co-production is just 'really good PPI'—is problematic. Co-production is called to answer for PPI's failings rather than its own. This is neither a logical intellectual exercise nor practically useful for healthcare improvement. This highlights a need to account for the parallel networks of PPI and co-production, noting their different genealogies and hence traditions, their distinctive characteristics, and their points of convergence. As we have already delineated the origins of PPI in England, we begin to address this need with a short overview of the origins of co-production and how—whilst interest has waxed and waned since—it has very recently come to be promoted as the gold standard in PPI, at least in England.

## Co-production: Gold Standard or Mis-Sold PPI?

In recent years—the era of 'the participatory zeitgeist' (Palmer et al. 2019)—the term 'co-production' has been elevated to 'gold standard' status in PPI. Ongoing work of formally constituted PPI networks seeks to codify associated practices through the development of checklists, guidelines and recommendations, particularly in relation to how to 'co-produce' applied health research (e.g., Hickey et al. 2018). However, we argue that—rather than enhancing citizen involvement—the notion that 'co-production' constitutes 'really good PPI' has increased its risk of becoming a vacuous buzzword used instrumentally by those with disproportionate power in these networks (e.g., researchers) to secure funding and appease ethics committees by providing rhetorical cover in the face of increasing demands to 'embed' PPI in research. That is, it is a semantic rather than a substantive shift, which is predictable given that 'rhetoric about involvement has tended always to be in advance of the reality' (Beresford 2019a: 6). To set such recent developments and critiques in context we now outline the early history and political (democratic) origins of co-production—which preceded the UK mandate for PPI—and highlight how traditional ideas of co-production might be viewed as incongruous with the (largely technocratic) enactment of PPI within applied health research.

Through her innovative studies of police services around Chicago in the early-mid 1970s, the political economist Elinor Ostrom conducted the foundational empirical work relating to the identification and exploration of co-production as a social phenomenon (Ostrom and Whitaker 1973). In the context of observing the variable performance of different police services, Ostrom et al. (1978) highlighted that:

> Citizen activities may affect both the output and outcomes of public agencies. Citizens in some neighborhoods may lock their doors, while those in other areas do not. In this way citizens may affect victimization rates and, thus, objective outcomes. Citizens may also call the police about a victimization in progress or give evidence that leads to the arrest of a felon. In these instances citizen activities supplement police activities in the production of an output, the arrest. Citizens, then, in some instances become coproducers with police through the contribution of their activities.

Ostrom et al. (1978) later noted how '[v]iewing citizens as coproducers of police (and other social) services is a rather novel and important aspect of our approach.' In an appreciative critique of Ostrom's overall contribution, Alford (2014) reflects upon how her early conceptualisation of co-production tended to be overshadowed in subsequent years and that—whilst 'sound in itself' (p. 309)—her original formulation of the concept was 'insufficiently elaborated to deal with multiple facets of co-production' (*ibid.*). Nonetheless practical examples of community-based initiatives drawing on Ostrom's work emerged in the late twentieth century, perhaps the best known being the creation of time-banks which drew on the participation of volunteers who were also service users. Other later commentators sought to distil from Ostrom's early writings the conditions necessary to promote the co-production of contemporary public services (Durose et al. 2017).

Outside of—and largely separate from—PPI networks, community-led (e.g., We Coproduce) and third sector (e.g., the Scottish Co-production Network) organisations have continued to advocate for co-production as a radical approach to citizen and service user engagement with public services, producing reflective tools and values frameworks to help guide participants (e.g., the *Co-production Catalogue from Wales*). Arm's-length government agencies—such as the Social Care Institute for Excellence—have also been active for some time in promoting co-production in their governance, decision-making and programme delivery. The distinction we are drawing here between such examples and PPI in applied health research has recently been touched on by Beresford (2019a: 10) in the context of public participation in mental health and social care. He notes that:

> increasingly tensions have emerged between the consumerist/managerialist aims of such [PPI] in much mainstream psychiatric and other health research under neoliberalism and the emancipatory goals of mental health service users/survivors (Rose et al. 2018). Thus PPI is coming under increasing attack as 'centered on a construction of the abstract, rational, compliant, and self-managing patient' under neoliberalism. (Madden and Speed 2017)

Consistent with Beresford's critique, we highlight an important distinction between what we would term 'state-sponsored PPI' and 'grassroots co-production'. In our view the former (e.g., NIHR-funded research) more commonly leans into technocratically oriented and conservative forms of involvement, and sits in strong contrast to the more radical and democratically-focused work of community-based organisations. Here we see the relevance of a distinction made by Glynos and Speed (2012) between 'transformative' and 'additive' forms of co-production. For them co-production with an 'additive accent' describes instances where service users and/or citizens are seen as helpful in producing change in, for example, a health service, but without necessarily changing the way they or the 'professionals' involved are seen or see themselves or the fundamental structures through which the service is provided. Co-production with a 'transformative accent', in contrast, has more radical potential in terms of altering the statuses and identities of those involved and the possibility for more significant public service reform.

Figure 1 is offered as a heuristic to illustrate how co-production as originally conceptualised by Ostrom in the 1970s—and more recently used to inform debates about how the 'next era' of healthcare quality improvement should focus on 'co-producing health' (Batalden 2018)—might be considered not only in relation to similar but distinct bodies of work (including co-creation and co-design) but also specifically in relation to PPI. Some examples are positioned beyond the boundaries of the transformative/additive co-production circles to represent how

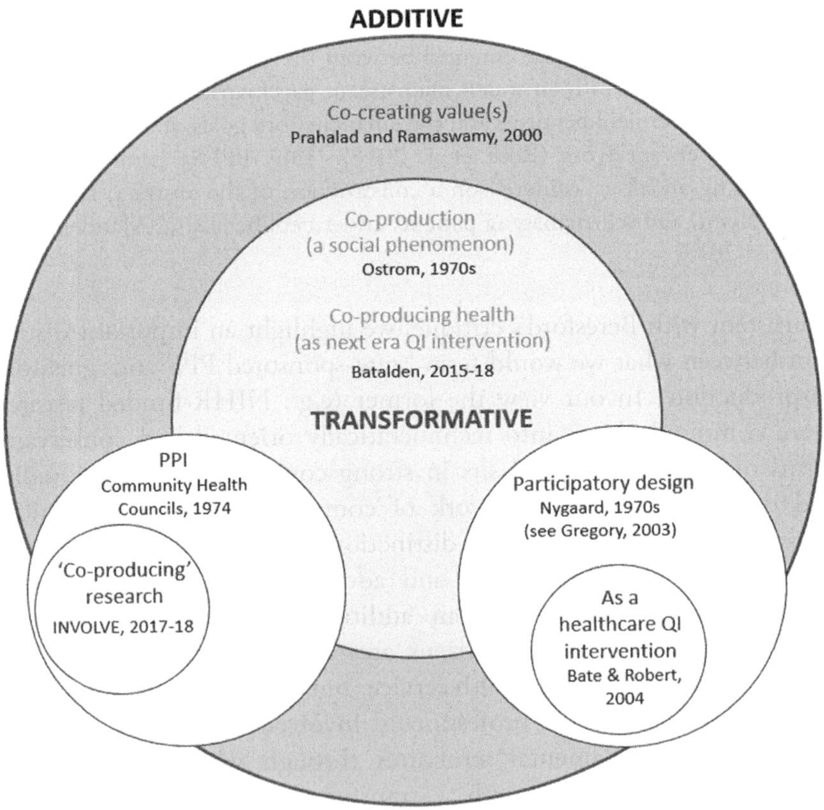


**Fig. 1** Transformative and additive co-production in the healthcare sector

commonplace box-ticking is in different domains and how such tokenism serves to benefit neither transformative nor additive aims.

As Martin and Carter (2017) note, whilst early initiatives to increase PPI in the design and delivery of healthcare services in the UK tended to be based on a democratic rationale (e.g., Community Health Councils), over time successive policies and structural reconfigurations have placed greater emphasis on a technocratic rationale, leading to the current trend towards 'co-producing research'. As we argued earlier, whilst democratic and technocratic rationales are not necessarily mutually exclusive, it is not uncommon for tensions to emerge between the two. Likewise, transformative and additive accents can 'often part company' but they are not necessarily 'antagonistic' (Glynos and Speed 2012: 423).

Our argument is that the NIHR has perhaps inadvertently set the tone so that contemporary PPI rationales and practices encourage the selection of certain citizens as 'co-producers' and then allow them to act within narrowly defined boundaries, rather than enabling more radical, democratic and transformative forms of participation to help reshape public services. We are not arguing that more radical and democratic forms of co-production are intrinsically better than more technocratic forms of PPI, but simply that to conflate the two does a disservice to both and confuses the matter. The relative utility and influence of each approach will be defined by its context and intended outcomes, which is why neither should be considered the standard by which the other is judged.

However, the contemporary UK health and social care context is said to be witnessing a 'crisis' amongst community-led and third-sector organizations within which the more radical, democratic and transformative forms of involvement largely reside. As Beresford (2019b) notes:

> User-led organizations (ULOs) that offer the most direct and effective expression of user voices are being lost at an unprecedented rate… Yet there doesn't seem to be widespread or official recognition of this crisis. Without these organisations, we can have little hope that the pressure for participation will be maintained. User and public involvement commands enormous popular support and its achievements have been

> groundbreaking…Retreat from meaningful involvement impoverishes public provision, undermines accountability and creates a vicious circle of ever-diminishing engagement and support.

This uneven shrinking of involvement networks risks preserving the technocratic norm at the expense of more radical practice that is often the catalyst for setting an agenda for much needed change. Using the term 'co-production' to describe practice which is largely uninformed by the democratic rationale underpinning co-production and—unconcerned by the imperative within this tradition of harnessing the *transformative* (rather than additive) potential of lived experience and collective endeavour—misrepresents more technocratic forms of PPI. This may carry a high long-term cost, i.e., undermining the enterprise of involvement and reverting to the tradition of top-down decision making. It also comes with short-term costs. Mis-selling PPI as co-production dilutes and even perverts a common appreciation for the transformative tradition (and even the additive applications) of co-production, and its potential for utilising the insight of lived experience and redistributing power in decision making. This results in the tokenistic practices common in PPI networks coming to be thought of as failures of co-production—as in Bevir et al.'s (2019) otherwise well-meaning invitation to critically reflect on the meaning and utility of co-production. Consequently, what would otherwise be useful critique focused on the potential 'dark side' of co-production occurring within research contexts will at times neglect the structural and systematic impediments that to a large extent define the problematic PPI practice that passes as 'co-production' within these contexts (e.g., Oliver et al. 2019).

State-sponsored PPI is more generally geared towards achieving technocratic ends, usually within a relatively short time period. This is not in itself a failing, but it does illuminate the potential incongruence of these priorities and those that define the tradition of co-production. That useful co-production often occurs outside the structural restraints that face PPI networks is no accident. Indeed, it is these structural factors that support what critiques of PPI have labelled tokenism but what principal investigators on NIHR grants may view as necessary or even prudent project management. The same principal investigators may ultimately find validation in metrics that do not relate—at least directly—to type or degree of involvement (e.g., number of publications, journal impact factors, REF scores, completing a project on time and within budget). As such, tokenistic practice within this specific context can be overshadowed, or even justified, by success measured through the metrics endorsed by the most powerful actors in the networks. In co-production that occurs outside of this system, these metrics hold less or no sway, and consequently what is considered successful co-production looks rather different. Therefore, it is important to be wary of critiques of involvement that concentrate on the beliefs and practices of individuals operating in networks (as encouraged in a decentring of networks) without giving due attention to how and in what ways the structures within which these networks were formed shape these beliefs and practices.

While our critique seeks to make distinctions between what might be called state-sponsored PPI for research and grassroots co-production—and the practices that tend to be labelled or mislabelled as co-production in these respective networks—we do not seek to set up a false dichotomy of 'good' and 'bad' involvement. It is not an either/or choice but rather a challenge to determine when co-production has most to offer, and ensuring a technocratic rationale cannot legitimise tokenism and inequitable practice. One area in which this debate has been evident recently is the involvement of patients and families in supporting patient safety. For example, O'Hara and Lawton (2016) argue that because patients are differentially able, or willing, to provide their time and emotional, physical, or fiscal resources, ranking more intensive forms of involvement as better than less intensive forms, risks disadvantaging the very people who would stand to gain most from having a voice in creating, managing, or supporting patient safety improvements. Similarly, setting up 'bad' PPI as merely technocratic, and 'good' co-production as democratic, risks side-lining the imperative to foster diversity of participation and equitable practice in both endeavours. Structural constraints and bad practice leave the processes of PPI *and* co-production susceptible to exacerbating inequalities and marginalisation. Co-production does not have a monopoly on inclusive practice; as proponents of decentred theory would no doubt emphasise, we need to critically examine the practices involved in both.

## Conclusion

Our delineation of the distinct but overlapping networks of PPI and co-production highlights the need to dedicate more critical attention to the involvement enterprise. We suggest that the co-optation of the discourse of 'co-production', and the conflation of PPI with co-production, at best fail to challenge the traditional power relations between professional and lay actors, and at worst redefine co-production as a practice largely separated from the transformative tradition. Our intention is not to make a one-sided endorsement of the democratic rationale for involvement. Both democratic and technocratic rationales have merit, as do both transformative and additive practices. If engaged with critically, all can lead to meaningful practice with mutually beneficial outcomes for professional and lay actors alike. But who benefits from framing relatively inexpensive and 'convenient' forms of involvement as 'co-production' and thus blunting the emphasis within co-production on a levelling of power relations and mutual agenda setting? Framing co-production in this way can provide those operating within applied health research, for example, with a façade of inclusivity and shared decision making while maintaining a status quo that preserves the traditions and interests of the more powerful actors in this network.

In terms of PPI we advocate more inclusive and considered recruitment, increased emphasis on ensuring the representation of a diversity of lived experience of patients, carers and publics, and greater accountability for ensuring they are not merely involved but make meaningful and formative contributions to healthcare service design, delivery and research. In order to achieve this, we argue for the need for time and resources dedicated to involvement activities which match the commendably lofty ambitions of the involvement agenda. Without this kind of investment, PPI will do little to challenge elite narratives that have traditionally defined healthcare; rather it runs the risk of disguising traditional power structures with practices that can only be *mis*labelled as co-production. A move to decenter networks may offer some impetus to this cause and will certainly help to illuminate that within PPI networks the same policy will take on different local meanings and consequently lead to a diversity of situated practices, but it will likely prove insufficient in providing structural analysis, and supporting collaboration conducive to securing a more meaningful contribution to healthcare delivery and health research from patients, carers and the public. However, we suggest greater appreciation of where PPI and co-production networks are distinct, but also overlap, is a useful grounding for furthering the involvement endeavour, improving health and social care and promoting health equity.

**Acknowledgements** Graham Martin and Oli Williams were supported during the writing of this chapter by the NIHR Collaboration for Leadership in Applied Health Research and Care East Midlands (NIHR CLAHRC East Midlands). The views expressed are those of the authors and not necessarily those of the NHS, the NIHR, or the Department of Health and Social Care.

Graham Martin and Oli Williams are supported by the Health Foundation's grant to the University of Cambridge for The Healthcare Improvement Studies Institute. The Healthcare Improvement Studies Institute is supported by the Health Foundation—an independent charity committed to bringing about better health and healthcare for people in the United Kingdom.

## References

Alford, J. (2014). The multiple facets of co-production: Building on the work of Elinor Ostrom. *Public Management Review, 16*(3), 299–316.

Barnes, M., Newman, J., & Sullivan, H. (2007). *Power, participation and political renewal: Case studies in public participation*. Bristol: Policy Press.

Batalden, P. (2018). Getting more health from healthcare: Quality improvement must acknowledge patient coproduction—An essay by Paul Batalden. *BMJ, 362,* k3617.

Bate, P., & Robert, G. (2006). Experience-based design: From redesigning the system around the patient to co-designing services with the patient. *BMJ Quality & Safety, 15*(5), 307–310.

Beresford, P. (2013). *Beyond the usual suspects: Towards inclusive user involvement—Findings*. London: Shaping Our Lives.

Beresford, P. (2019a). Public participation in health and social care: Exploring the co-production of knowledge. *Frontiers in Sociology, 3*, 41.

Beresford, P. (2019b, January 14). Austerity is denying patients and care service users a voice. *The Guardian*. Viewed 29 April 2019. https://www.theguardian.com/society/2019/jan/14/austerity-denying-patients-care-service-users-voice.

Bevir, M. (2013). *A theory of governance*. London: University of California Press.

Bevir, M., Needham, C., & Waring, J. (2019). Inside co-production: Ruling, resistance, and practice. *Social Policy & Administration*. https://doi.org/10.1111/spol.12483.

Boivin, A., Richards, T., Forsythe, L., Grégoire, A., L'Espérance, A., Abelson, J., et al. (2018). Evaluating patient and public involvement in research. *BMJ, 363*, k5147.

Carding, N., Lintern, S., Clover, B., & Illman, J. (2018). Exclusive: Trusts alerted as firm stockpiles clinical waste and body parts. *Health Service Journal* [Online]. Available at: https://www.hsj.co.uk/policy-and-regulation/exclusive-trusts-alerted-as-firm-stockpiles-clinical-waste-and-body-parts/7023511.article. Accessed 12 April 2019.

Charlton, J. (1998). *Nothing about us without us: Disability oppression and empowerment*. London: University of California Press.

Conklin, A., Morris, Z., & Nolte, E. (2015). What is the evidence base for public involvement in healthcare policy? Results of a systematic scoping review. *Health Expectations, 18*(2), 153–165.

Crompton, A. (2019). Inside co-production: Stakeholder meaning and situated practice. *Social Policy & Administration, 53*(2), 219–232.

Department of Health. (2010). *Equity and excellence: Liberating the NHS*. London, UK: The Stationery Office Limited.

Donetto, S., & Cribb, A. (2011). Researching involvement in health care practices: Interrupting or reproducing medicalization? *Journal of Evaluation in Clinical Practice, 17*(5), 907–912.

Dorling, D. (2016). Brexit: The decision of a divided country. *BMJ, 354*, i3697.

Durose, C., Needham, C., Mangan, C., et al. (2017). Generating 'good enough' evidence for co-production. *Evidence & Policy: A Journal of Research, Debate and Practice, 13*(1), 135–151.

Glynos, J., & Speed, E. (2012). Varieties of co-production in public services: Time banks in a UK health policy context. *Critical Policy Studies, 6*(4), 402–433.

Green, D. (2018, November 15–16). *UK PPI perspective on evaluation*. Paper presented at the International Perspectives on Evaluation of Patient & Public Involvement in Research, Newcastle, UK.

Gregory, J. (2003). Scandinavian approaches to participatory design. *International Journal of Engineering Education, 19*(1), 62–74.

Hanna, E. (2018). Patient dignity must be central to appropriate disposal of body parts. *BMJ Opinion* [Online]. https://blogs.bmj.com/bmj/2018/10/19/esmee-hanna-patient-dignity-central-appropriate-disposal-body-parts/.

Hanna, E. (2019). "What do you want to do with the leg?" A critical narrative review of the understandings and implications of disposal in the context of limb amputations. *SAGE Open, 9*(2), 2158244019859953.

Hanna, E., & Robert, G. (2019, July 29). Ethics of limb disposal: Dignity and the medical waste stockpiling scandal. *Journal of Medical Ethics*. https://doi.org/10.1136/medethics-2019-105554.

Hickey, G., Brearley, S., Coldham, T., Denegri, S., Green, G., Staniszewska, S., et al. (2018). *Guidance on co-producing a research project*. Southampton: INVOLVE.

Hodge, S. (2005). Participation, discourse and power: A case study in service user involvement. *Critical Social Policy, 25*, 164–179.

hooks, b. (1981). *Ain't I a woman?: Black women and Feminism*. Boston: South End Press.

Hunter, D. J. (2011). Change of government: One more big bang health care reform in England's national health service. *International Journal of Health Services, 41*(1), 159–174.

INVOLVE. (2012). *Briefing notes for researchers: Involving the public in NHS, public health and social care research*. Eastleigh: INVOLVE.

INVOLVE. (2018). *Examples of co-producing research: Expression of interest form*. INVOLVE. Viewed 4 April 2018. https://www.invo.org.uk/current-work/co-production/#.

Kislov, R., Wilson, P. M., Knowles, S., & Boaden, R. (2018). Learning from the emergence of NIHR Collaborations for Leadership in Applied Health Research and Care (CLAHRCs): A systematic review of evaluations. *Implementation Science, 13*(1), 111.

Madden, M., & Speed, E. (2017). Beware zombies and unicorns: Toward critical patient and public involvement in health research in a neoliberal context. *Frontiers in Sociology, 2*, 7.

Maguire, K., & Britten, N. (2018). 'You're there because you are unprofessional': Patient and public involvement as liminal knowledge spaces. *Sociology of Health & Illness, 40*(3), 463–477.

Marlow, L. A. V., Wardle, J., & Waller, J. (2015). Understanding cervical screening non-attendance among ethnic minority women in England. *British Journal of Cancer, 113*(5), 833–839.

Martin, G. P. (2008). 'Ordinary people only': Knowledge, representativeness, and the publics of public participation in healthcare. *Sociology of Health & Illness, 30*(1), 35–54.

Martin, G. P., & Carter, P. (2017). Patient and public involvement in the new NHS: Choice, voice, and the pursuit of legitimacy. In M. Bevir & J. Waring (Eds.), *Decentring Health Policy* (pp. 121–139). London: Routledge.

Martin, G. P., Carter, P., & Dent, M. (2018). Major health service transformation and the public voice: Conflict, challenge or complicity? *Journal of Health Services Research & Policy, 23*(1), 28–35.

Martin, G. P., Currie, G., & Finn, R. (2009). Reconfiguring or reproducing intraprofessional boundaries? Specialist expertise, generalist knowledge and the 'modernization' of the medical workforce. *Social Science and Medicine, 68*(5), 1191–1198.

Mockford, C., Staniszewska, S., Griffiths, F., & Herron-Marx, S. (2011). The impact of patient and public involvement on UK NHS health care: A systematic review. *International Journal for Quality in Health Care, 24*(1), 28–38.

Ocloo, J., & Matthews, R. (2016). From tokenism to empowerment: Progressing patient and public involvement in healthcare improvement. *BMJ Quality & Safety, 25*, 626–632.

O'Hara, J. K., & Lawton, R. J. (2016). At a crossroads? Key challenges and future opportunities for patient involvement in patient safety. *BMJ Quality & Safe, 25*, 565–568.

Oliver, K., Kothari, A., & Mays, N. (2019). The dark side of coproduction: Do the costs outweigh the benefits for health research? *Health Research Policy and Systems, 17*(1), 33.

Ostrom, E., Park, R. B., Whitaker, G. P., & Percy, S. L. (1978). The public service production process: A framework for analyzing police services. *Policy Studies Journal 7*(2), 381.

Ostrom, E., & Whitaker, G. (1973). Does local community control of police make a difference? Some preliminary findings. *American Journal of Political Science, 17*(1), 48–76.

Palmer, V. J., Weavell, W., Callander, R., Piper, D., Richard, L., Maher, L., Boyd, H., et al. (2019). The participatory zeitgeist: An explanatory theoretical model of change in an era of coproduction and codesign in healthcare improvement. *Medical Humanities, 45*(3), 247–257.

Prahalad, C. K., & Ramaswamy, V. (2004). Co-creation experiences: The next practice in value creation. *Journal of Interactive Marketing, 18*(3), 5–14.

Rose, D., Carr, S., & Beresford, P. (2018). Widening cross-disciplinary research for mental health: What is missing from the Research Councils' UK mental health agenda? *Current Issues Disability & Society, 33,* 476–481. https://doi.org/10.1080/09687599.2018.1423907.

Smith, J., Walshe, K., & Hunter, D. J. (2001). The 'redisorganisation' of the NHS. *BMJ, 323*(7324), 1262–1263.

Sobchack, V. (2010). Living a 'phantom limb': On the phenomenology of bodily integrity. *Body & Society, 16*(3), 51–67.

Speed, E. (2017). Transforming a public good into a private bad: Political legitimacy, wilful deceit and the reform of the NHS in England. In M. Bevir & J. Waring (Eds.), *Decentring health policy*. London: Routledge.

Staniszewska, S., Herron-Marx, S., & Mockford, C. (2008). Measuring the impact of patient and public involvement: The need for an evidence base. *International Journal for Quality in Health Care, 20*(6), 373–374.

Wilson, P., Mathie, E., Poland, F., et al. (2018). How embedded is public involvement in mainstream health research in England a decade after policy implementation? A realist evaluation. *Journal of Health Services Research & Policy, 23*(2), 98–106.

# Professional Pastoral Work in a Kenyan Clinical Network: Transposing Transnational Evidence-Based Governmentality

Gerry McGivern, Jacinta Nzinga, Mehdi Boussebaa, and Mike English

## Introduction

Health care management research has recently drawn on the Foucauldian (2007) concept of *governmentality* to examine and explain the way health professionals have internalised evidence-based medicine (EBM) (Ferguson and Gupta 2002; Bejerot and Hasselbladh 2011; Ferlie et al. 2012, 2013; Ferlie and McGivern 2014; Martin et al. 2013; Martin and Waring 2018; Waring and Martin 2016; van Rensburg et al. 2016).

G. McGivern (✉)
Warwick Business School, University of Warwick, Coventry, UK
e-mail: Gerry.mcgivern@wbs.ac.uk

J. Nzinga
KEMRI Wellcome Trust, Nairobi, Kenya

M. Boussebaa
Adam Smith Business School, University of Glasgow, Glasgow, UK

M. English
Nuffield Department of Medicine, University of Oxford, Oxford, UK


M. Bevir and J. Waring (eds.), *Decentring Health and Care Networks*, Organizational Behaviour in Healthcare,
https://doi.org/10.1007/978-3-030-40889-3_11

EBM is defined as 'the conscientious, explicit, and judicious use of current best evidence in making decisions about the care of individual patients… integrating individual clinical expertise with the best available external clinical evidence from systematic research' (Sackett et al. 1996: 71). EBM was developed and has become institutionalised in Western health care systems as the 'gold standard' of health care provision (Timmermans and Berg 2003). Consequently, most Western health professionals, and many professionals globally, now draw on its governing principles when they think about and enact clinical work.

However, research on the rise of this 'evidence-based governmentality' in health care (Ferlie et al. 2013; Ferlie and McGivern 2014) has given limited attention to the micro-level work entailed in the construction and promotion of, or resistance to, the internalisation of EBM. We also know little about the historical context in which governmentality unfolds. Significantly, most literature on governmentality in health care is based on studies conducted in Western high-income countries, neglecting low- and middle-income counties (LMICs) where *transnational* evidence-based governmentality regimes, originating in the West, shape health care systems (Ferguson and Gupta 2002; Lemke 2011). So, how is EBM developed, internalised and used by health professionals working in LMIC health systems?

Network organisations provide a key mechanism through which government policy, EBM, evidence-based practices and standards have been developed and implemented into health care practice at local level, with professional leaders responsible for and also adapting this process in local contexts (Ferlie et al. 2012, 2013). In LMICs networks are also often more transnational, diffusing evidence between Western countries and LMICs (Ferguson and Gupta 2002), although most research on health care networks has been conducted in the former, again neglecting LMICs.

Addressing this oversight, in this chapter we examine the development and implementation of an evidence-based governmentality in Kenyan paediatric care nationally and, more specifically, in a 'Clinical Information Network' (CIN) spanning paediatric departments in 14 Kenyan district hospitals. We trace the roots of this evidence-based governmentality in Western transnational organisations and its development and implementation in Kenya, examine how CIN made visible and transformed local clinical practices and professional identities, and highlight the central role and work of key medical professional network leaders ('pastors') within this process.

Our chapter highlights the importance of a 'decentred' (Bevir 2013) approach to analysing health care networks, showing in particular how the dynamics of power need to be situated within particular contexts, traditions, practices and norms. As explained in the introduction to this collection, this approach seeks to look beyond the grand narratives or discourses of policy, to look instead the situated and enacted meanings and beliefs of local actors, albeit in the context of prevailing traditions and in the face of new circumstances or dilemmas. Without understanding the different practices and norms of Western EBM and philanthropic organisations and Kenyan health care, CIN's leaders would have been unable to transpose transnational evidence-based governmentality into Kenya paediatric practice. Using a decentred approach, we explain the pastoral work of these network leaders', and the situated dilemmas, with implications for personal and professional identity, which they faced about how to engage with divergent local circumstances and governmental practices.

## Evidence-Based Governmentality and 'Pastoral' Professionals in Health Care

Michel Foucault developed the concept of 'governmentality', defined as 'the ensemble formed by institutions, procedures, analyses and reflections, calculations and tactics… that has the population as its target, political economy as its major form of knowledge and apparatuses of security as its essential technical element' (Foucault 2007: 108), to explain government in neoliberal states. For Foucault, and subsequent theorists of governmentality (Rose 1999; Dean 1999; Lemke 2011), this ensemble leads subjects to internalise the mentality of government, interpret their identities and behaviours as part of a (national) population, and so freely act in its collective interest. Thus, neoliberal states could govern 'at a distance' by inciting, seducing and making actions easier or harder, negating the need for direct control. Theorists later explained how a governmentality could be actively constructed and managed to control citizens (Rose and Miller 1992; Dean 1999) and organizational employees (Miller and O'Leary 1994; McKinlay and Taylor 2014; McKinlay and Pezet 2010) from afar. Similarly, in health care contexts, governmentality and the mundane 'grey sciences' of 'enumeration, calculation, monitoring, evaluation' (Miller and Rose 2008: 212) quietly reshaped professional work (Ferlie and McGivern 2014).

Foucault's (2007) related concept of 'pastoral power' explains how individuals internalise external (governmental) discourses; by externalising ('confessing') inner thoughts and hidden behaviours to 'pastors' who then help them internalise external discourses reconceptualising their thoughts and behaviours. Using the analogy of Christian priests leading their 'flock' to 'salvation', Foucault showed pastors' key roles as intermediaries in governmentality (Martin and Waring 2018). Pastoral power thus operates at the intersection between disciplinary discourses, pastors' and other individuals' agentic attempts to cultivate their own identities in ways that align with (but also depart from) such discourses (Martin et al. 2013; McKinlay and Pezet 2010). Today, pastoral power can be understood as about cultivating ethical behaviour benefitting collective social welfare. Contemporary pastors include experts and therapists, promoting and inculcating socially desirable behaviour among their patients, clients and the public and medical professionals (Dean 1999; Rose 1999). Foucault (2007: 199) notes: 'in its modern forms, the pastorate is deployed to great extent though medical knowledge, institutions and practices… medicine has been one of the great powers that have been the heirs to the pastorate'.

The concepts of governmentality and pastoral power have been usefully deployed to explore and explain governance and leadership in Western health care and clinical networks, where evidence-based medicine (EBM) has been institutionalised (Ferlie and McGivern 2014). Ferlie and colleagues (2013) describe an 'evidence-based governmentality', which underpinned effective service reconfiguration and quality improvement in health care networks. This evidence-based governmentality contained four elements: an evidence-based clinical *episteme*; clinical audit making local practices *visible*; local *technical* processes enacting evidence and audit into practice and ways in which they shape professionals' *identities*. Clinical professionals internalised, constructed and regulated their professional identities and behaviours in relation to the governing principles of EBM as a consequence of network leaders' work assembling these four elements (Ferlie et al. 2013).

We suggest that understanding of the work involved in constructing evidence-based governmentality can be furthered through engagement with Foucault's notion of pastoral power. In their study of EBM and health care networks, Ferlie and McGivern (2014) show how pastoral power operates during collective professional discussions of clinical outcomes, which reinforce evidence- and audit-based professional identities and behaviours. The authors explain how, in making clinical practices and outcomes visible against national standards and targets, and sharing these data among clinicians, network leaders (pastors) exerted peer pressure on underperforming professionals to adopt best practice and improve their clinical performance. Furthermore, by encouraging their colleagues to think about and disclose thoughts and practices in relation to EBM-based standards, these network leaders cultivated EBM-based subjectivities among their professional peers more generally.

Similarly, Martin and Waring (2018) discuss the operation of pastoral power within the process of translating and embedding governmental discourses into individual subjectivities and collective routines within medical professional communities. They also describe pastoral medical professionals focusing attention on individuals' statistical performances compared with populations of similar professionals, then creating spaces in which clinicians interacted, expressed and developed collective notions of professionalism and identity drawing on audit, evidence and quality improvement. Again, this then became inherent in the way doctors constructed their individual and collective responsibilities as professionals.

In related work, Waring and Martin (2016) described leadership in health care networks involving four 'pastoral practices': (1) *Constructive practices* re-coding rationalities and translating evidence in a way relevant and comprehensible to local communities; (2) *Inscription practices* communicating and framing the re-coded discourses in ways encouraging network members to internalise them; (3) *Collective practices* in which pastors shape and reframe collective professional subjectivities and social identity through socialising as a professional community; and (4) *Inspection practices* in which pastors provide ongoing guidance to the community, identifying practices and subjectivities conforming with or deviating from acceptable behaviours, and, in doing so, create, maintain or disrupt social order.

McGivern et al. (2017) developed Waring and Martin's (2016) concept of pastoral practices to explain how the Kenyan clinical network discussed in this chapter introduced evidence-based governmentality. They described: Constructive practices developing local *evidence-based guidelines* and *audit practices* making local health care provision and outcomes visible; Inscription practices of *championing* use of guidelines and audit, *demonstrating* how they improved care, and *supporting/mentoring* professionals to use them; Collective practices of *meeting and sharing as a professional community* and *collectively championing and demonstrating evidence-based professionalism*; and inspection practices in which network participants *disciplined* themselves and colleagues to use guidelines and audit to improve health care quality and their professional status. Crucially, these pastoral practices relied upon the work of medical professionals in 'pastoral' leadership roles, influencing their colleagues to adopt evidence-based governmentality (McGivern et al. 2017).

The concept of 'knowledge leadership' (Fischer et al. 2016) may also be useful in explaining leadership in networks. Also drawing on Foucauldian theory, Fischer and colleagues explain how individual knowledge leaders mobilised management research and evidence into health care practice by 'becoming the knowledge object'. By personifying and role-modelling this knowledge as identity projects they were deeply vested in, knowledge leaders *transposed* it into new organizational contexts, *appropriating* salient aspects of knowledge and evidence, using them to *contend* established practice and bring about changes.

Taken together, the Foucauldian literature has been useful in advancing understanding of the way professionals internalise evidence-based discourses in health care, while a number of its limitations have been identified, which we discuss next.

## Criticisms of the Governmentality Literature

The governmentality literature has been subject to several criticisms. First, its relative inattention to agency and work promoting or resisting internalisation of external governmental discourses (Caldwell 2007; Power 2011), perhaps due to neglect of Foucault's later work. As McKinlay and Pezet (2010: 494) note: 'Studying governmentalisation requires us to attend not just to the programmes of the powerful but to their operation and the manifold ways that individuals, groups and populations absorb, comply with and resist these projects'. Likewise, Bevir argues that governance is realised both through the top-down imposition of governance frameworks and also actors implementing them within local circumstances, traditions and beliefs and wider social, economic and political contexts. Understanding governmentality from this 'decentred perspective' therefore requires examples and explanations of how 'agents apply norms in creative ways that transform power relations' (Bevir 2013: 38). Similarly, Martin and Waring (2018) argue that an appreciation of governance in health care also requires attention to both dominant discourses and their agentic use by individuals in local practices.

Second, and relatedly, Bevir (2010) calls for more examination of the *genealogy* of governmentality; examining the historical context in which governmentality arose, the contingent appropriations and modifications to historical traditions in responses to novel circumstances and dilemmas, and the processes of social construction of practices through which individuals construct meaning. He suggests that such analyses focus on specific individuals' micro-level actions and the way they are influenced by specific contexts, narratives and traditions.

Third, most literature on governmentality in health care draws on empirical examples taken from Western high income countries, which represent a type of neo-liberal governmentality that Foucault was talking about, neglecting LMICs (Ferguson and Gupta 2002; Lemke 2011). We thus know little about evidence-based governmentality in LMICs, where governmental regimes may be different to those in the West (cf Bevir 2010, 2013). Moreover, this also leads to ignoring the significance of 'transnational governmentality' (Ferguson and Gupta 2002) in shaping LMIC health care. Medical research in African countries is often conducted in collaborations with Western government institutions and international organisations such as the World Health Organization (WHO), Non-Governmental Organisations (NGOs), and internationally-operating Western philanthropy organisations (e.g., Wellcome Trust or Gates Foundation). These transnational collaborations require surveillance and governance transcending national boundaries, shaping health systems in many African countries that, in the absence of sufficient government funding, rely on such collaborations as a means of providing sufficient health care for their populations (Greissler 2015; Ferguson and Gupta 2002). This transnational context raises a number of important questions, not least the question of (neo)colonialism and its effects on transnational governmentality (see e.g. Boussebaa 2015, 2017, 2020).

In the African context, research suggests that health care professionals continue to follow local 'practical norms', i.e. ways of working which deviate from the professional and official norms as well as standards typically found in the West (de Sardan 2015). For example, Brown's (2016: 595) anthropological study of governmentality in Kenyan hospitals describes 'monitoring and the management of systems as insufficient for managing the conduct of others' and how 'Formal disciplinary procedures were also rarely undertaken. Even in quite serious cases of professional misconduct' (ibid.: 600). Nzinga et al. (2019a) describe clinical-managers navigating between professional, official and practical norms in the challenging Kenyan health care contexts, in ways providing scope for agency and maintenance of professional legitimacy.

In this chapter, we are interested in the question of micro-level implementation and its limits. While the introduction of EBM, transparency and clinical audit have improved health care in many Western countries, there is less evidence of their use and effectiveness in LMIC health systems (Cleary et al. 2013; Nxumalo et al. 2018). Moreover, as in Western health care (McGivern and Fischer 2012), there is evidence of transparency having perverse unintended consequences in LMICs (Cleary et al. 2013). For example, Litorpa et al. (2015), in a Tanzanian study, showed transparency raising fear of blame for poor obstetric care, resulting in an increase in more unnecessary caesarean sections being carried out. Thus, different norms and traditions in LMICs may produce a different form of governmentality to that in developed countries in the West.

Accordingly, we need to understand how and why transnational evidence-based governmentality, commonly originating in Western countries, is enacted into practice and internalised by professionals in LMIC health care contexts. We aim to address limitations in prior research by examining professional work to construct, implement and use a Western evidence-based governmentality as a means of improving paediatric health care in a Kenyan clinical network. We discuss our methodology next.

## Methods

This chapter is written by an international and interdisciplinary team of network insiders and outsiders to CIN, with a diverse range of perspectives on the CIN case study. Mike English, a Kenya-based but UK trained paediatrician centrally involved in CIN with insider experience of the Kenyan health system, commissioned Gerry McGivern, a UK-based organisational theorist conducting qualitative research in health care, to conduct a formative qualitative evaluation of the CIN. Gerry McGivern collected and analysed data on CIN with Jacinta Nzinga, a Kenyan qualitative social scientist, with Mike English supporting data analysis by providing an interpretation of emergent findings based upon his insider experience and expertise. Mehdi Boussebaa, a UK-based international management and organisation scholar, contributed understanding of the importance of the transnational context and postcolonial theory.

We conducted the CIN case study in 2015–2016, drawing on observation and interviews (for more detail about data collection, see McGivern et al. (2017)). Gerry McGivern and Jacinta Nzinga attended three bi-annual CIN meetings as non-participant observers, examining training, discussion of evidence-based guidelines and data collection, network leadership and participants' reactions. Informal conversations with meeting participants also informed understanding of CIN.

Gerry McGivern and Jacinta Nzinga also interviewed 34 Kenyan health professionals (33 Kenyans) involved with CIN, individually and in mono-professional groups, asking them about their careers, professional identities, experiences of Kenyan health care and of CIN, including its impact on them, colleagues, patients and the hospitals involved. Interviewees included: two CIN directors (interviewed individually); 12 consultant paediatricians (ten interviewed individually; two together); Nine nurses 'in-charge' of paediatric departments (interviewed in three groups); a medical officer (junior doctor—interviewed individually); seven Health Records Information Officers (HRIOs; interviewed in two groups of three and one individually); a medical epidemiologist and representatives of the Kenyan Paediatric Association and the Kenyan Ministry of Health (all interviewed individually).

Interviews (22–90 minutes in duration) were then audio-recorded and transcribed, thematically coded and analysed drawing on theory relating to evidence-based governmentality and pastoral power as outlined above.

## Empirical Findings

### Development of a Transnational Evidence-Based Governmentality in Kenyan Paediatric Care

First, we examine the development (genealogy in Foucauldian terms) of the broader evidence-based governmentality underpinning CIN, particularly drawing on the interview narratives of CIN's network director (ND) and clinical director (CD).

CIN's ND is a British paediatrician, who trained at elite medical schools in the UK, where EBM and clinical audit were core elements in the curricula. He worked in Kenya early in his career, experiencing at first hand problems facing its resource constrained public health care system. ND noted: "*Working as a medical officer in the government hospital, which is very… short of resources… I was very well aware of how difficult it can be.*" Indeed, one in five basic resource items necessary for the provision of care to seriously ill children and new-borns were typically not available (English et al. 2014). ND started writing guidelines for clinicians and medical students in a Kenyan district hospital paediatric department he oversaw, as an attempt to improve the quality of care it provided in its resource-constrained context. During this time, he made contact with experts from and visited the World Health Organisation (WHO), an international organisation constructing and promoting evidence-based guidelines in health care globally.

ND then started working at the national policy level in Kenya. ND described: "*Looking at what care was actually provided, whether people were aware of existing technical guidance, whether they had the resources to follow any of that guidance, what the practical challenges were of providing care… [which] suggested major challenges*". This led the ND to question the value of developing clinical guidelines "*in a technical bubble*", which would not be implemented, leading him to refocus his career and research on implementing evidence into practice.

CIN's CD is a Kenyan paediatrician, who initially trained in medicine in Kenya and then did postgraduate medical training in the USA. She was inspired by the senior doctors who taught her in the USA, who always consulted the latest evidence and guidelines, rather than "*what I have always done*" as she had experienced among senior Kenyan doctors. This overseas training stirred the CD's "*passion*" for developing and implementing evidence-based health care, which she brought back to Kenya and enacted in roles teaching in a Kenyan medical school and CIN.

Training in Western countries provided CD and ND evidence-based expertise and an elite medical professional identity, which they enacted in their pastoral roles. In theoretical terms, they personally transposed (Fischer et al. 2016) evidence-based governmentality by personifying and role-modelling it as identity projects they were deeply embedded in. They also experienced professional 'identity violations' (Pratt et al. 2006); ND realising that research and guidelines he had been developing were not being used to improve health care in Kenya in practice; CD realised that the senior clinicians who taught and inspired her in the USA consulted evidence and guidelines rather than just with advocating what they had always done, as she had experienced among senior doctors in Kenya. These identity violations lead them to question their pre-existing professional identities and roles, and engage in professional 'identity work' reorienting their careers mid-career (McGivern et al. 2015) towards implementing EBM into practice.

In 2005, CD and ND then became involved in developing national paediatric guidelines, drawing on existing WHO recommendations, conducting systematic reviews of evidence and meeting stakeholders, including from the Ministry of Health, Medical Schools and Kenyan Paediatric Association to discuss them. These were first published as Kenyan Ministry of Health guidelines in 2006, although only distributed in small numbers initially. 10,000 copies of the guidelines were distributed in 2008. The guidelines were subsequently updated in 2010, 2013 and 2015, with 12,000 copies distributed on each occasion. CD and ND were also involved in developing a training course (an extended version of the WHO's Emergency Triage Assessment and Treatment (ETAT+) training programme) on how to use the paediatric guidelines and practise evidence-based medicine (for more detail see English et al. [2014, 2017a, b]). CD recalled: "*When WHO came up with the [paediatric] guidelines… I was actually chosen to help in adopting… [and] adapting the guidelines to the Kenyan needs and… local context.*"

ND struggling to mobilise financial resources to support the implementation of evidence-based standards in Kenya, noting: "*It took a while to get that funding, because it wasn't very mainstream at that stage*" but eventually "*got funding*" from a Western-based global philanthropic organisation, "*following the sort of biomedical model to develop an intervention and test it*" which "*resulted in developing a set of tools… national guidelines*", adding: "*We used this approach 'GRADE', and I think we were the first country in Africa to do it at country level*". ND convened a meeting of "*various parts of the paediatric community… the Ministry [of Health]… university medical schools*" at which they agreed to adopt the evidence-based paediatric guidelines that the ND had previously developed.

Here we see the ND and CD engaging in pastoral work and related constructive practices (Waring and Martin 2016); identifying and translating evidence in a way relevant and comprehensible and relevant to local communities and health contexts. However, in this transnational context, we also see their work bridging between the WHO, an international organisation with an established set of evidence-based guidelines, and the local Kenyan health system and medical profession. ND also describes mobilising funding by constructing the development and implementation of Kenyan guidelines as a biomedical intervention, tested in a LMIC national context, in which results could be fed back to the transnational funder based in the UK, reflecting the transnational governmentality described elsewhere (Greissler 2015; Ferguson and Gupta 2002).

In 2008, ND and CD both began teaching a postgraduate course in paediatrics at the University of Nairobi Medical School, which then trained over 70% of medical students in Kenya, using the paediatric guidelines and ETAT+ course. This introduced over 1000 undergraduate medical students and trainee specialist paediatricians to the principles of evidence-based paediatrics. CD complained that Kenyan medical schools were "*not using WHO guidelines, we were using textbooks from abroad*" which were focused on the needs of patients in Western countries rather those of Kenyans. ND noted:

> "*I began... teaching at the post-graduate level... helping to push this training into the post-graduate and under-graduate curriculum... the majority of paediatricians in training had been produced through the University... it meant that I knew quite a lot of the younger paediatricians... what we had been up to was more widely known because of our engagements with the university and disseminating these guidelines... We benefitted from trying to present things to them as a new way of doing business. And they were... receptive to that because... there has been a dissatisfaction with the sort of old professor stands in the corner and tells you. Younger clinicians... appreciate that knowledge is changing. So I think we fitted into a... generational issue... people seeing that there is more than just doing what you were told fifteen years ago.*"

Here again we see ND and CD adapting Western evidence-governmentality to the Kenyan health care context and inscribing, communicating and framing the discourse of EBM in a way that resonated with trainee paediatricians' agendas and norms. Indeed, most paediatricians involved in the CIN that we interviewed said they subsequently became involved in CIN because they had been taught and inspired by the network leaders during postgraduate paediatric training. As one paediatrician (4) noted: "*Blame Professor [ND]. Blame Professor [CD]. They were my teachers in University... they're really good mentors.*" We see here knowledge leadership (Fischer et al. 2016); ND and CD personally *transposing* evidence-based paediatrics into Kenyan healthcare by "*becoming known*" to trainee Kenyan paediatricians, fulfilling roles as pastoral role models and mentors, improving the status of professionals they mentored. This created a wider 'pastoral constellation' (McGivern et al. 2017) of professionals committed to promoting and implementing EBM-based practices into Kenyan health care.

This foundational work (developing paediatric guidelines, a paediatric medical curriculum and professional pastoral constellation), involving eight years of sustained 'whole systems' working with political, social and political complexity (for more detail see English et al. 2011, 2014, 2017b; Nzinga et al. 2009a, b), provided the foundation for CIN's establishment, which we discuss next.

## Formation of the Clinical Information Network

We next explore the link between the development of evidence-based guidelines and governmentality and the development of a clinical network focused on implementing them.

ND applied for funding from a UK-based global philanthropic organisation, to develop what he described as "*a network of places to work together to improve what they were doing and demonstrate that improvement, in the hope of spread*". ND commented that he initially proposed "*a kind of 'N of 1' study*", which the funder "*couldn't fathom*", questioning "*where are your controls? How do you know that whatever changes you observe aren't going to be happening naturally? So, I wasn't able to provide a convincing argument, so they rejected the proposal.*" However, he was invited to develop a new proposal, which he submitted a year later, that was "*framed as a randomized control trial... the network was then a vehicle for testing alternative forms of intervention, that... would result in more rapid implementation or adoption of better practices, and thereby improve quality. Trying to steer away from having it labelled as a more quality improvement initiative*". The new proposal was funded.

So here again we see a Western philanthropic organisation and a Western governmentality discourse disciplining local activities through its allocation of funding. ND noted: "*The bottom line is to run these things takes funding. And the funding will have to come from somewhere. And that ... it won't come from government*". We also see the work of ND, whose understanding of the Western medical scientific discourse and experience working in Kenyan health care, enabled him to bridge between transnational governmentality and the Kenyan health system. While CIN's purpose was ostensibly implementing evidence-based quality improvement, we see ND redesigning the CIN proposal to discursively frame it in Western medical scientific discourse to secure funding. Indeed, we also see the Western evidence-based governmentality vested in ND personally as a professional pastor, who noted, "*I am kind of the proxy for... the money*".

## Implementation of an Evidence-Based Governmentality Within the Clinical Information Network

In 2013, CIN was established as a clinical network spanning 14 Kenyan public district hospitals, aiming to improve paediatric health care, including by conducting discrete related RCTs. CIN focused on promoting the adoption of recommended evidence-based best-practices, using clinical audit to highlight poor practice as well as improve quality, and training participants in quality improvement techniques and leadership. CIN also holds regular network meetings, enabling participants to share experience and learning, and providing a form of support network for doctors and nurses working and trying to improve clinical care in challenging circumstances (English 2013; English et al. 2017a).

Developing evidence-based guidelines does not mean that they will be implemented; this depends on the 'inscription practices' (Waring and Martin 2016) of network leaders; *championing* use of evidence-based guidelines, audit and quality improvement techniques, highlighting poor practices in local contexts and *demonstrating* how evidence and audit could improve them, and *supporting/mentoring* local clinicians and nurses in their attempts to make improvements (McGivern et al., 2017). ND and CD initially conducted much of this work. ND noted:

"*Supervision and mentorship was supplied by myself and [CD]… we would go back with the survey results and we would discuss those with them, trying to get them to both acknowledge the problems – which they did quite readily – and then kind of come up with action plans to deal with them.*"

As CIN became more established, this inscription work also involved a wider pastoral constellation (McGivern et al. 2017) of paediatricians, whom ND and CD had first met and inspired during postgraduate training as we noted earlier. For example, Paediatrician 2 commented on the importance of championing, role modelling and checking on interns: "*checking in a guideline … now when they realize that even the consultant refers to it, then it's not a weakness. So that I think mind-set has changed*" and that "*improving the system… should also improve your career.*" Paediatrician 4 commented: "*I mentor a lot of the doctors and tell them why I love paediatrics… [and] leading quality improvements… It's kind of catching… Do it with passion… you can make a difference… You catch more flies with honey than with vinegar*" (Paediatrician 4).

Indeed, CIN's "*passionate*" and positive approach was inherent to its success, which was very different from the practical norm of senior Kenyan doctors intimidating junior clinical staff (cf Nzinga et al. 2019a, b). Paediatrician 11 described many senior Kenyan doctors as:

> "*dictators not really wanting to listen to people and just want to give the solution to problems [but] they don't want to know what your problems are… they just tell you there is no money, they do not help you come up with the solutions…The traditional way of teaching [is] where you are basically want to intimidate everybody and scare everyone… to the point that even trying to consult them [senior doctors] you need to think twice.*" (Paediatrician 11)

By contrast, CIN's modus operandi involved: "*positivity… [CIN] teach you how to not admonish people… you are always told off like there is no tomorrow… during a ward round, in front of your juniors, that has been the trend but they [CIN] have changed things*" (Paediatrician 13) and "*Getting to the bottom of things and sorting them out… not in a harsh way, just finding out where the problem is and not putting the blame on anyone*" (Paediatrician 8). Here we see the affective component of pastoral work implementing the evidence-based governmentality; it was not solely the discourse of EBM that interns bought into but the individual promoting it and their positive approach. We note that in the Kenyan health care context there is usually only one highly trained paediatrician in Kenyan district hospitals, so these individuals have a particularly important pastoral role.

In Foucauldian terms, network leaders were supporting their 'flock' of patients and junior professionals in a way enhancing the identity and status of Kenyan evidence-based paediatrics. Pediatrician 10 commented: "*We [CIN] move together to improve the quality of care for our children [patients], individually and then collectively.*" Paediatrician (11) noted:

> "*The most satisfying [aspect of her involvement in CIN]... has been basically to improve the quality of life for our patients... Not just the child but even the family and the community... [and] teaching younger colleagues, to see the transformation... from a doctor who had just learnt the theoretical knowledge to actually being able to apply it in the bedside.*"

Indeed, CIN attempted to build the Kenyan paediatric community. As English et al. (2017b: 850) note: 'creating social and professional norms among both decision makers and practitioners to use evidence has been an effective strategy for awareness raising at scale and has helped reshape professional identity towards acceptance of common practice standard'. ND commented:

> "*We have worked very much through the paediatricians as professionals... conscious of not trying to tell them what to do... recognising ... fundamental challenges and trying to approach people with possible solutions obviously helps. Particularly when they are very under-resourced themselves and don't have much recourse to developing their own solutions, or implementing their own solutions. So, being seen as somebody who can support an agenda that is meaningful to them... [give] voice to the profession, because they can unite across counties.*"

CIN participants also reported that during CIN meetings there were, "*sharing experiences... meeting as colleagues... from different places facing actual challenges on the ground... being part of this community of people involved to similar work*" (Paediatrician 2). They used CIN meetings as what can be thought of as semi-private 'relational spaces' (Kellogg 2009) in which to build an evidence and audit based collective professional identity, discuss, develop and test ways of contending outdated clinical practices. They then returned to local district hospital sites and began presenting clinical audit data about health care delivery and clinical outcomes in professional meetings and comparing these to local evidence-based guidelines and deliver and outcomes in other hospitals. These district hospital meetings, exposed and undermined the legitimacy of poor practices, bringing in the new evidence-based professional norms. Like Foucauldian pastors, we see that these local pastoral professionals' work purpose and identity was deeply embedded in the evidence-based 'salvation' of their 'flock' of patients and professional community.

## Disciplining and Normalisation of Evidence-Based Governmentality in Kenyan Paediatric Care

Having developed a shared evidence-based professional identity, professionals in CIN engaged in pastoral work and practices *disciplining* (Waring and Martin 2016) peers and junior colleagues in their ongoing use of the evidence-based guidelines. Interviewees described:

> "*Medical Officer interns, often they are not listening to experienced nurses who have done the job a lot, who are, you are able to discipline them and put themstraight when they are doing wrong things... [because] we, I give out the standards of the wards, [as] expectations from them.*" (Nurse 6)

> "*Keep checking [interns] in the [ward] rounds, then they know that it is checked. Unfortunately, that is what it takes to get some people to use guidelines.*" (Paediatrician 2)

Reflecting research in Western health care we discussed earlier (Ferlie and McGivern 2014; Martin and Waring 2018), we see professionals in CIN making clinical outcomes visible and holding colleagues accountable in ways making poor performance professionally untenable. Medical Officer 9 described feeding back results to colleagues in their paediatric department: "I *gave them the feedback. When they saw it for themselves some of them were embarrassed by some of the bad work that had been doing but they were very motivated [to improve]*." So, here again the professional pastoral work that disciplined health care delivery to conform to evidence-based best practice. Accordingly, at least initially, the evidence-based discourse alone did not discipline medical interns and trainee nurses but also the work of their professional colleagues.

Yet, over time, a combination of Panopticon (Foucault 1977) and lateral relational transparency (Nxumalo et al. 2018; Cleary et al. 2013) led to the normalisation of an evidence-based governmentality among professionals within CIN. Nurse 15 commented: "*somewhere somebody watching on you how do to do things you become better and more conscious*". Paediatrician 11 described CIN members: "*all holding each other accountable*". Nurse 7 described working within CIN as, "*a kind of competition when you get feedback and look at the graphs; how you are performing, look at the other hospital... healthy competition*". Knowing clinical provision and outcomes were being monitored against guidelines and observed by peers, professionals disciplined themselves to provide evidence-based care and constructed their identities in relation to clinical outcomes compared with the wider population of hospitals within the network. Like members of a pastoral congregation, professionals within CIN came to accept, normalise and even welcome evidence-based governmentality.

## Discussion

We contribute towards the literature on governmentality in clinical networks and health care by explaining work, practices and process through which a Western transnational evidence-based governmentality was transposed into a LMIC health system. In doing so, we provide new insights addressing previous limitations in this literature (cf Bevir 2010, 2013; Lemke 2011; Ferguson and Gupta 2002). We show the micro-level work involved in developing and implementing a transnational evidence-based governmentality, explore its genealogy in novel circumstances and traditions in the Kenyan context, and thus extend analysis of evidence-based governmentality beyond Western countries into a LMIC.

Our study highlights two particularly novel features of this evidence-based governmentality. First, the *transnational* nature of evidence-based governmentality in LMICs, emanating from Western-based global philanthropic organisations (cf Ferguson and Gupta 2002; Greissler 2015). Second, addressing interest in the work conducted in organisations (Barley and Kunda 2001), professional identity work (Pratt et al. 2006; McGivern et al. 2015), identity management (Boussebaa 2020) and pastoral practices (Waring and Martin 2016), we show the importance of what we describe as '*pastoral work*' by senior medical professionals and highlight the personal nature of transposing (Fischer et al. 2016) governmentality.

We show how a Western philanthropic organisation disciplined the development of CIN and evidence-based paediatrics in Kenya through its allocation of funding essential for these activities. While ostensibly focused on improving the quality in Kenyan health care, CIN's British director (ND) secured funding only after framing his proposal in experimental biomedical terms, reflecting a Western-dominated transnational governmentality. However, allocation of funding can also be seen as a 'practice of freedom' (Rose 1999); ND was not forced to adopt the philanthropic funder's transnational governmentality. Yet after an initial funding proposal for quality improvement work reflecting the needs of local Kenyan paediatrics was rejected, ND would not otherwise had funds to improve the care he knew was so needed. Hence ND chose to adopt transnational governmentality in response to a situated professional dilemma (Bevir 2013) of how to fund improvement work in clinical care.

Funding, along with responsibility for CIN's activities, was then invested in ND (describing himself as a "*proxy for the money*"), again reflecting the personal nature of knowledge transposition, with ND 'becoming the knowledge object' (Fischer et al. 2016). Echoing health care management research drawing on the notion of pastoral power (Ferlie and McGivern 2014; Waring and Martin 2016; Martin and

Waring 2018), we explain network leaders as 'pastors' inculcating the discourse of transnational evidence-based governmentality among their professional 'flock'. This pastoral work was essential for the development of CIN and an evidence-based governmentality in Kenyan paediatrics.

The importance of network leaders and their work reflects the broader literature showing the role of professionals implementing new knowledge and evidence in health care (Mitton et al. 2007; Currie and White 2012; Fischer et al. 2016; Ferlie et al. 2018). The transnational nature of the process and its LMIC context highlight something new. Both ND and CD had training in evidence-based paediatrics in Western medical schools and first-hand experience of the challenges of delivering health care in the resource-constrained Kenyan context. Without experience and understanding of Western evidence-based practice they would not have had the credibility to secure global philanthropic funding to develop evidence-based paediatrics in Kenya. Without long-term experience and understanding of Kenyan health care they would have been unable to implement evidence-based care in it. Thus, CIN's network leaders needed knowledge and experience of both in order to bridge between them, adapt and implement Western evidence-based governmentality into this LMIC context.

However, knowledge and experience alone were not sufficient to transpose this evidence-based governmentality into practice. Significantly, CD and ND were also personally and professionally invested in improving clinical practices in Kenya by transposing evidence-based practice. Both had worked in the Kenyan system long term and experienced mid-career professional identity violations (cf Pratt et al. 2006; McGivern et al. 2015) leading them to question the value of their pre-existing professional work (e.g. ND realising the futility of developing evidence-based guidelines "in a technical bubble" that were not used in practice) and reoriented towards implementation of evidence based practice. Thus, both were motivated to personally develop evidence-based Kenyan paediatric guidelines and medical school curricula, which they taught, championed, mentored and role-modelled as identity work maintaining their status as professionals doing their best for patients.

As a result of these network leaders' affective identity-enhancing pastoral work, challenging pre-existing norms and introducing a new "*positive*" and "*passionate*" approach to paediatric care, a pastoral constellation of professionals developed around them. Trainee paediatricians enthusiastically adopted this new approach, creating a professional network committed to implementing evidence-based paediatrics. CIN formed the basis of Kenyan paediatricians' work to collectively enhance their shared evidence-based professional practice and identity. Professionals governed themselves, their peers and the wider profession using evidence and audit because, in doing so, they demonstrated quality improvement and professionalism, enhancing their identity, legitimacy, and status as a form of individual and collective 'cultivation of self' (Foucault 1990). While top-down transparency and governance is often ineffective, even undermining professionals' ability to improve health care (de Sardan 2015; Cleary et al. 2013; Brown 2016; English 2013; Litorpa et al. 2015), *lateral* relational transparency (Nxumalo et al. 2018; Cleary et al. 2013; Barker 1993) and *synopticon* transparency, involving watching and seeking to emulate an admired few (Mathiesen 1997), normalised evidence-based practice as good professionalism.

Our chapter speaks to the importance of a 'decentred' (Bevir 2013) approach to analysing EBM and networks in their particular contextual circumstances. Without understanding of the traditions, practices and norms of Western EBM, transnational philanthropic organisations and Kenyan health care, network leaders would have been unable to transpose evidence-based governmentality, and we would have been unable to explain their pastoral work. From a 'decentred' perspective, we show that the genealogy of governmentality is inherently personal; it involves situated dilemmas, with implications for personal and professional identity, about how to engage with divergent local circumstances and governmental 'practices of freedom' (Rose 1999) (e.g. ND framing a proposal in biomedical terms to secure funding for activities aimed at quality improvement). Moreover, our case illustrates that people do not simply adopt an impersonal governmentality; people internalise a governmentality promoted by individuals (pastors) whom they know, understand, trust, like and seek to emulate, and a governmentality they can draw upon to maintain and enhance their local circumstances and status.

Our analysis also reveals how LMICs, such as Kenya, occupy a subordinate position vis-à-vis their Western counterparts and one in which the latter play a critical role in constructing the former in line with practices considered 'normal' in the West. In other words, LMIC health care discourses and professional identities are disciplined in line with Western norms and expectations. Yet the process may not go smoothly, as LMIC professionals not only conform but also modify and, in some cases, pay lip service to Western discourses and practices (cf Boussebaa 2015, 2017; Boussebaa et al. 2014). Furthermore, as we noted above, the question of governmentality in African countries and indeed in LMICs more generally needs locating in the wider uneven geography of the global political economy. That is, it requires appreciating that transnational governmentality occurs across 'societies that have been intertwined in a complex and shifting hierarchy of nations' (Boussebaa et al. 2012: 470) and is thus produced in a wider context of power asymmetry rooted in long-term processes of (neo)colonial domination (Boussebaa 2020).

Finally, in closing, it is important to acknowledge that our analysis is based on the experience of professionals in one African country only: Kenya. Based on this analysis, we have tended to generalise to Africa as a whole but this would be to portray Africa in unitary terms; research is therefore required in other African settings. Future research might also examine transnational evidence-based governmentality on a wider basis, examining similarities and differences not only in Africa but also in other LMICs such as those in Asia and Latin America.

## References

Barker, J. R. (1993). Tightening the iron cage: Coercive controlling self-managing teams. *Administrative Science Quarterly, 38,* 408–437.

Barley, S., & Kunda, G. (2001). Bringing work back in. *Organization Science, 12,* 76–95.

Bejerot, E., & Hasselbladh, H. (2011). Professional autonomy and pastoral power: The transformation of quality registers in Swedish health care. *Public Administration, 89,* 1604–1621.

Bevir, M. (2010). Rethinking governmentality: Towards genealogies of governance. *European Journal of Social Theory, 13,* 423.

Bevir, M. (2013). *A theory of governance.* Berkeley, CA: University of California Press.

Boussebaa, M. (2015). Professional service firms, globalization and the new imperialism. *Accounting, Auditing & Accountability Journal, 28,* 1217–1233.

Boussebaa, M. (2017). Global professional service firms, transnational organizing and core/periphery network. In L. Seabrooke & L. Henriksen (Eds.), *Professional networks in transnational governance.* Cambridge: Cambridge University Press.

Boussebaa, M. (2020). Identity regulation and globalization. In A. D. Brown (Ed.), *Oxford handbook of identities in organizations.* Oxford: Oxford University Press.

Boussebaa, M., Morgan, G., & Sturdy, A. (2012). Constructing global firms? National, transnational and neocolonial effects in international management consultancies. *Organization Studies, 33,* 465–486.

Boussebaa, M., Sinha, S., & Gabriel, Y. (2014). Englishization in offshore call centers: A postcolonial perspective. *Journal of International Business Studies, 45,* 1152–1169.

Brown, H. (2016). Managerial relations in Kenyan health care: Empathy and the limits of governmentality. *Journal of the Royal Anthropological Institute, 22,* 591–609.

Caldwell, R. (2007). Agency and change: Re-evaluating Foucault's legacy. *Organization, 14,* 769–791.

Cleary, S., Molyneux, C., & Gilson, L. (2013). Resources, attitudes and culture: an understanding of the factors that influence the functioning of accountability mechanisms in primary health care settings. *BMC Health Services Research, 13*(1), 320.

Currie, G., & White, L. (2012). Inter-professional barriers and knowledge brokering in an organizational context: The case of healthcare. *Organization Studies, 33,* 1333–1361.

de Sardan, J.-P. (2015). Practical norms: Informal regulations within public bureaucracies (in Africa and beyond). In T. de Herdt & J.-P. de Sardan (Eds.), *Real governance and practical norms in Sub-Saharan Africa: The game of the rules.* Abingdon: Routledge.

Dean, M. (1999). *Governmentality: Power and rule in modern society*. London: Sage.

English, M. (2013). Designing a theory-informed, contextually appropriate intervention strategy to improve delivery of paediatric services in Kenyan hospitals. *Implementation Science, 8,* 1–13.

English, M., Gathara, D., Mwinga, S., Ayieko, P., Opondo, C., Aluvaala, J., et al. (2014). Adoption of recommended practices and basic technologies in a low-income setting. *Archives of Disease in Childhood, 99,* 452–456.

English, M., Ayieko, p., Nyamai, R., Were, F., Githanga, D., & Irimu, G. (2017a). What do we think we are doing? How might a clinical information network be promoting implementation of recommended paediatric care practices in Kenyan hospitals? *Health Research Policy and Systems, 15*(1), 4.

English, M., Irimu, G., Nyamai, R., Were, F., Garner, P., & Opiyo, N. (2017b). *Developing guidelines in low-income and middle-income countries: lessons from Kenya. Archives of disease in childhood, 102,* 846–851.

English, M., Wamae, A., Nyamai, R., Bevins, B., & Irimu, G. (2011). Implementing locally appropriate guidelines and training to improve care of serious illness in Kenyan hospitals: A story of scaling-up (and down and left and right). *Archives of Disease in Childhood, 96,* 285–290.

Ferguson, J., & Gupta, A. (2002). Spacializing states: Towards an ethnography of neoliberal governmentality. *American Ethnologist, 29,* 981–2002.

Ferlie, E., Dopson, S., Bennett, C., Fischer, M., Ledger, J., & McGivern, G. (2018). *The politics of management knowledge in times of austerity*. Oxford: Oxford University Press.

Ferlie, E., Fitzgerald, L., Mcgivern, G., Dopson, S., & Bennett, C. (2013). Making wicked problems governable? The case of managed health care networks. Oxford: Oxford University Press.

Ferlie, E., & McGivern, G. (2014). Bringing Anglo-governmentality into public management scholarship: The case of evidence-based medicine in UK health care. *Journal of Public Administration Research and Theory, 24,* 59–83.

Ferlie, E., McGivern, G., & Fitzgerald, L. (2012). A new mode of organising in health care?: Governmentality and networked cancer services in the UK. *Social Science and Medicine, 74,* 340–347.

Fischer, M., Dopson, S., Fitzgerald, L., Bennett, C., Ferlie, E., Ledger, J., et al. (2016). Knowledge leadership: Mobilising management research by becoming the knowledge object. *Human Relations, 69,* 1563–1585.

Foucault, M. (1977). *Discipline and punish: The birth of the prison*. London: Penguin.

Foucault, M. (1990). The history of sexuality, Vol. 3: The care of the self. London: Penguin.
Foucault, M. (2007). *Security, territory, population: Lectures at the college de France 1977–1978*. New York: Picador.
Greissler, P. W. (2015). Introduction: A life science in its African para-state. In P. W. Greissler (Ed.), Para-states and medical science: Making African global health. Durham: Duke University Press.
Kellogg, K. (2009). Operating room: Relational spaces and microinstitutional change in surgery. *Americal Journal of Sociology, 115,* 657–671.
Lemke, T. (2011). *Foucault, governmentality and critique*. Paradigm: Boulder, CO.
Litorpa, H., Mgayaa, A., Mbekengaa, C., Kidantoa, H., Johnsdotterc, S., & Esséna, B. (2015). Fear, blame and transparency: Obstetric caregivers' rationales for high caesarean section rates in a low-resource setting. *Social Science and Medicine, 143,* 232–240.
Martin, G., Leslie, M., Minion, J., Willars, J., & Dixon-Woods, M. (2013). Between surveillence and subjectification: Professionals and the governance of quality and patient safety in English hospitals. *Social Science and Medicine, 99,* 80–88.
Martin, G., & Waring, J. (2018). Realising governmentality: Pastoral power, governmental discourse and the (re) constitution of subjectivities. *The Sociological Review, 66,* 1292–1308.
Mathiesen, T. (1997). The viewer society: Michel Foucault's Panopticon'revisited. *Theoretical Criminology, 1,* 215–234.
McGivern, G., Currie, G., Ferlie, E., Fitzgerald, L., & Waring, J. (2015). Hybrid manager-professionals' identity work, the maintenance and hybridization of medical professionalism in managerial contexts. *Public Administration, 93,* 412–432.
McGivern, G., & Fischer, M. D. (2012). Reactivity and reactions to regulatory transparency in medicine, psychotherapy and counselling. *Social Science and Medicine, 74,* 286–296.
McGivern, G., Nzinga, J., & English, M. (2017). Pastoral practices' for quality improvement in a Kenyan clinical network. *Social Science and Medicine, 195,* 115–122.
McKinlay, A., & Pezet, E. (2010). Accounting for Foucault. *Critical Perspectives on Accounting, 6,* 486–495.
McKinlay, A., & Taylor, P. (2014). *Foucault, governmentality and organization: Inside the factory of the future*. New York: Routledge.

Miller, P., & O'Leary, T. (1994). The factory as laboratory. *Science in Contex, 7,* 469–496.

Miller, P., & Rose, N. (2008). *Governing the present.* Cambridge: Polity Press.

Mitton, C., Adair, C. E., McKenzie, E., Patten, S. B., & Perry, B. W. (2007). Knowledge transfer and exchange: Review and synthesis of the literature. *The Milbank Quarterly, 85,* 729–768.

Nxumalo, N., Gilson, L., Goudge, J., Tsofa, B., Cleary, S., Barasa, E., et al. (2018). Accountability mechanisms and the value of relationships: Experiences of front-line managers at subnational level in Kenya and South Africa. *BMJ Global Health, 3,* e000842.

Nzinga, J., Mbindyo, P., Mbaabu, L., Warira, A., & English, E. (2009a). Documenting the experiences of health workers expected to implement guidelines during an intervention study in Kenyan hospitals. *Implementation Science, 4,* 44.

Nzinga, J., McGivern, G., & English, M. (2019a). Hybrid clinical-managers in Kenyan hospitals: Navigating between professional, official and practical norms. *Journal of Health Organization & Management, 33,* 173–187.

Nzinga, J., McKnight, J., Jepkosgei, J., & English, M. (2019b). Exploring the space for task shifting to support nursing on neonatal wards in Kenyan public hospitals. *Human Resources for Health, 17,* 18.

Nzinga, J., Ntoburi, S., Wagai, J., Mbindyo, P., Mbaabu, L., Migiro, S., et al. (2009b). Implementation experience during an eighteen month intervention to improve paediatric and newborn care in Kenyan district hospitals. *Implementation Science, 4.* https://doi.org/10.1186/1748-5908-4-45.

Power, M. (2011). Foucault and sociology. *Annual Review of Sociology, 37,* 35–56.

Pratt, M. G., Rockmann, K. W., & Kaufmann, J. B. (2006). Constructing professional identity: The role of work and identity learning cycles in the customization of identity among medical residents. *Academy of Management Journal, 49,* 235–262.

Rose, N. (1999). Powers of freedom: Reframing political thought. Cambridge: Cambridge University Press.

Rose, N., & Miller, P. (1992). Political power beyond the State: Problematics of government. *The British Journal of Sociology, 43,* 172–205.

Sackett, D. L., Rosenberg, W. M., Gray, J. M., Haynes, R. B., & Richardson, W. S. (1996). Evidence based medicine: What it is and what it isn't. *British Medical Journal, 312,* 71.

Timmermans, S., & Berg, M. (2003). *The gold standard: The challenges of evidence-based medicine and standardization in healthcare*. Philadelphia: Temple University Press.

van Rensburg, A. J., Rau, A., Fourie, P., & Bracke, P. (2016). Power and integrated health care: Shifting from governance to governmentality. *International Journal of Integrated Care, 16*, 1–11.

Waring, J., & Martin, G. (2016). Network leadership as pastoral power: The governance of quality improvement communities in the English NHS. In M. BEVIR (Ed.), *Governmentality after neo-liberalism*. London: Palgrave.

# Index




M. Bevir and J. Waring (eds.), *Decentring Health and Care Networks*, Organizational Behaviour in Healthcare,
https://doi.org/10.1007/978-3-030-40889-3

The manufacturer's authorised representative in the EU is Springer Nature Customer Service Centre GmbH, Europaplatz 3, 69115 Heidelberg, Germany. If you have any concerns regarding our products, please contact ProductSafety@springernature.com

Printed and bound by CPI Group (UK) Ltd, Croydon, CR0 4YY

22/09/2026

02221064-0004